CRITERIA
FOR THE LIFE HISTORY

WITH ANALYSES OF SIX
NOTABLE DOCUMENTS

BY

JOHN DOLLARD

INSTITUTE OF HUMAN RELATIONS
YALE UNIVERSITY

HM
24
D6

PUBLISHED FOR
THE INSTITUTE OF HUMAN RELATIONS
BY
YALE UNIVERSITY PRESS · NEW HAVEN
1935

PREFACE

So elusive and casual are the sources from which one acquires one's culture that precise acknowledgments of indebtedness are impossible. Usually we accept only the most immediate and significant surrogates of a massive tradition and let them stand for all the rest. One does best, perhaps, if he points at the beautiful pattern of scientific thought in our society and avows humbly that he stands in some relation to it.

Before presenting acknowledgments an important statement must be made about this book. It developed initially at the suggestion of Professors Mark A. May, Gardner Murphy, and Gordon W. Allport who were functioning as a sub-committee of the committee on culture and personality of the Social Science Research Council. They asked the writer to canvass the life-history literature to see what in it was of relevance to the concepts "Competition" and "Cooperation." After the report to their committee was finished and the material assembled, they allowed a portion of the work to be elaborated and to appear under the title of this book. Appreciation is expressed to them and to the Social Science Research Council whom they represented. I am particularly indebted to my chief, Dr. Mark A. May, for many personal and scientific favors and to the Institute which he directs for its support of my work.

He who finds life livable must be indebted to his parents, and I am; both James E. Dollard and Ellen Brady Dollard lived the self-denying lives which made my education possible. My present life is very much an expression of the ambitious and faithful interest of my mother who is now living in Madison, Wisconsin. Particularly warm among relatives is my appreciation of my mother's brother, Attorney Charles E. Brady, for his sterling support.

Appreciation is expressed to Dr. Max Mason who in-

Criteria for the Life History

ducted me into University life and showed me for the first time a scientific mind in action; to Professor William F. Ogburn who was solid as a thesis master and rich in his scientific sympathies; to Mr. Sewell L. Avery who silently provided a fellowship during the period of my graduate work; to Professor Harold D. Lasswell, pioneer in a social science conscious of the individual life; to Dr. Harry Stack Sullivan who first made real to me the possibility of a psychiatrist aware of culture; to Dr. Hanns Sachs, a good friend and my portal to the work of his teacher, Freud; to Professor Edward Sapir, my former chief here at Yale, for a great intellectual debt.

In addition to the above many current friends have helped me form my thought; they include my wife, Victorine Day Dollard, Dr. Erich Fromm, Professor W. Lloyd Warner, Mr. Harald H. Lund, Dr. Margaret Mead, Mr. Earl F. Zinn, Dr. A. Kardiner, Dr. E. VanNorman Emery, Dr. Raymond Bowers, Mr. Willard Z. Park, and Miss Helen L. Watson.

To the following publishers and authors special thanks are due for the privilege of reprinting from their books: *International Journal of Individual Psychology*, Chicago, "The Case of Miss R," by Alfred Adler; Hogarth Press, London, *Collected Papers*, by Sigmund Freud; The Macmillan Company, New York, *The Dynamics of Therapy*, by Jessie Taft; Alfred A. Knopf, New York, *The Polish Peasant in Europe and America*, by William I. Thomas and Florian Znaniecki; and The University of Chicago Press, Chicago, *The Jack-Roller*, by Clifford R. Shaw. Mr. H. G. Wells has considerately given permission to quote from his *Experiment in Autobiography*, published by The Macmillan Company, New York.

CONTENTS

CRITERIA FOR THE LIFE HISTORY

CHAPTER I

INTRODUCTION TO THE CRITERIA

EVERY scientific worker has felt the anxiety associated with an insecure grasp on his object of research. Many of us, too, know the feeling of fumbling while trying to find the right way to think about a given problem. Very often the worker will proceed for his whole scientific life with a gnawing sense, appearing perhaps only at intervals, that he has never gripped his material in a satisfying way. Usually defenses are erected against such anxieties either in the form of indifference to scientific objectives or in the form of compulsive stress on method in disregard of the demand for logical simplicity and novelty which scientific effort puts on the worker.

It is believed that this state of affairs exists in current social science. The element for which we are perennially seeking is a significant concept of the person to set off against our valuable formal descriptions of social life. This lack has served as an irritant leading to the elaboration of many schemes of social psychology and of much speculative thought about the individual. A more realistic effort emerging in many social science branches at about the same time has been the use of the life-history document as a method of filling the gap. In recent years increasing attention has been paid to life-history methods and many claimants for the attention of the scientific public have come forward. The value of the attempts so far has been to center attention on the life of the individual as an event worth the attention of social scientists; many useful though partial views have been developed.

Despite the effort expended so far, the life history remains a much suspected tool of research and no comfortable certainty exists as to what an adequate life history document will eventually look like. Teachers handling life-history materials can only make gestures in the direction of existing systems and allow the student to choose for himself. Since the student rarely has enough experience to choose anything, he usually adopts the bias of his professor and passes on to methods of social science study which are better accredited.

This does not end the problem because in a number of fields the scientific worker is brought up against the necessity of making some kind of sense of material on the individual life. The life history is in reality a common task of a considerable number of fields. At the present time it plays a role in the teaching and research of sociology, psychology and psychiatry. It seems bound to become increasingly important in the development of these fields. The biography is used in both history and literature and not merely for its recreational value but as a scientific tool defining historical and literary movements and personalities. Certainly it cannot be used with too great discrimination. A number of students of anthropology have already turned to the autobiographies of primitive persons as a method of shedding light on alien cultures and this trend seems to be one that will increase. For them also the skillful use of the life history seems a necessity. By no means least of all, the social worker is concerned with the technique of taking and analyzing life-history materials, for she has pressed upon her every day the empirical necessities which make good judgment imperative. It is hoped that the criteria will be useful to all of these groups of workers.

This book is intended to reduce confusion in the life-history field and to offer a blend structure of principles from the fields of cultural studies and clinical psychology. No innovations are attempted except those involved in re-thinking the problem of the life history from both of these standpoints.

Life history defined. We will propose an initial common sense definition of the life history as a deliberate attempt to define the growth of a person in a cultural milieu and to make theoretical sense of it. It might include both biographical and autobiographical documents. It is not just an account of a life with events separately identified like beads on a string, although this is the form in which naïve attempts to present a life history usually meet us; if this were true, every man would be a psychologist, because every person can give us data of this type. The material must, in addition, be worked up and mastered from some systematic viewpoint. The written life history is preferable to oral statement, for obvious reasons.

The life history seen culturally. It is important to notice that the life history is not merely a gadget of psychologists, social workers or clinicians; it can also be viewed from the standpoint of the systematic student of culture. From this standpoint the life history is an account of how a new person is added to the group and becomes an adult capable of meeting the traditional expectations of his society for a person of his sex and age. Students of culture have been curiously blind to this aspect of the life history; it may well be argued that without the life history the transmission of culture forms from one generation to the next cannot be adequately defined. Surely the knowledge of how culture is transmitted, as well as the schematic definition of what it is, once transmitted, is part of the task of the sociologist and ethnologist. If such a definition of the problem tends to shift the plane of vision of the sociologist from the group to the individual, this will prove to be an insight resisted by many; we must point out, however, that the scientist must follow his problems wherever they lead and must unbind himself from traditional points of view (in science) as they prove to be a block to the solution of problems for which he has made himself scientifically responsible. It is remarked that a scientific tradition may at times prove a barrier as well as an aid to investigation, if the scientist does not remain strenuously in contact with his material.

Life history, the long-section view of culture. The taking of a life history is here viewed as a problem of the student of culture; it can, of course, be done by persons who do not formally acknowledge that they are students of social life, but this does not change the essence of the matter; they are students of culture by definition if they attempt to deal with acculturated individuals. What particular "ist" they wear at the end of their field designation is merely traditionally determined and unimportant. It is worth while to distinguish the life-history view of the individual from the conventional cultural view of the individual. In the long-section or life history view the individual remains organically present as an object of study; he must be accounted for in his full, immediate, personal reality. The eye remains on the details of his behavior and these we must research on, and explain. Here culture is bedded down in a specific organic locus. The culture forms a continuous and connected wrap for the organic life. From the standpoint of the life history the person is viewed as an organic center of feeling moving through a culture and drawing magnetically to him the main strands of the culture. In the end the individual appears as a person, as a microcosm of the group features of his culture. It is possible that detailed studies of the lives of individuals will reveal new perspectives on the culture as a whole which are not accessible when one remains on the formal cross-sectional plane of observation. In pure cultural studies, on the other hand, the organic man has disappeared and only that abstracted portion of him remains that is isolated and identified by the culture pattern. If, in the "pure" cultural study, the organic reality of the person is lost, then we should expect that cultural studies would tell us little about individual experience and meanings. This, it is suggested, is the case.

Since students of "culture" do not make our distinctions clearly and since they feel a pressure somehow to deal with the person, they will often accept uncritically the concepts of motivation nearest at hand or, in other cases, go into business as social psychologists for themselves and invent them, without taking the trouble to study minutely the individual life. Such attempts will in most cases give inadequate results. Certainly we are only in a primitive phase of culture-personality study at the present time. The formal view of culture provides an indispensable backdrop for individual studies but via it we do not arrive at theories of meaningful action. As soon as we take the post of observer on the cultural level the individual is lost in a crowd and our concepts never lead us back to him. After we have "gone cultural" we experience the person as a fragment of a (derived) culture pattern, as a marionette dancing on the strings of (reified) culture forms. A culture-personality problem can be identified in every case by observing whether the person is "there" in full emotional reality; if he is not there, then we are dealing with a straight cultural or institutional study. If he is there and we can ask how he feels, then we have a culture-personality problem. It is stressed emphatically that there are no personality problems alone. Personality problems are always culture-personality problems.

For whom this is written. This is written to and for social scientists, that is, for all those who study events related to human beings' action above the level of the mechanistic biological. Biologists, *as scientists*, will naturally not be interested since our concept level is a different one from theirs. It is important in defining the life-history field to be sure that you are "touching bottom" in defining the field of relevance. "Bottom" is here viewed as the preëxisting culture on the one hand, and on the other, those organic aspects of man which are specifically elaborated by culture influence. This point will be discussed later. Many social scientists have stated their expectations of great value from the development of the life history. The aim here is to explore the use of the life history as a tool in social science study, to indicate its present state, to define what we may expect from its use and development. We will proceed in this task without regard to the formal definition of the source of the technique and try to press the point that the life-history view of social facts is a fundamental perspective for the student of culture.

Science and the life history. In the field of the life history we find a confusing array of reports by experienced observers. Any person unwilling or unable to take the risks of a personal exploration of the field can still maintain a skeptical position toward it. We assume here that the life history is still an infant field from the standpoint of its development as a science. Science begins with the problems naïvely offered by the existing culture in its effort to "control" the environment for human ends; it consists at the outset of a refinement on culturally given perception. Later the stream of special scientific perception becomes itself transmitted with authoritative vigor and functions much as any other cultural segment in revealing or concealing what is really going on "out there." Science is advanced in any field by those who recognize problems despite the interference of traditional methods of thought.

Why improve life-history methods. Some writers have referred to the life history as a happy hunting ground for hypotheses which could then be "scientifically" verified. That is not the view of this discussion. It is not that objection is offered to using the best methods on the life-history material, but no contradiction is seen between the life-history view and a beautiful and satisfying "science" which stands off against it. The life history is seen as an event subject to scientific formulation and not referable to scientific canons exterior to its methods and problems. It seems highly important to try out this view since so much of our comparative material from other cultures is likely to come in in the form of life histories, and since only the life history seems able to solve some of the difficulties which arise in pursuing the cultural approach, such as the problems of culture transmission and change. We are led, therefore, to the great desirability of improving life history technique and setting up standards for the evaluation of life-history materials. It may well be that some of the confusion involved in such field definitions as "ethnology," "psychology," and "sociology" can be resolved if we have a firm conceptual grip on the life and growth of the individual.

Need for criteria for the adequate life history. Most social scientists look upon the life history as a way-station to knowledge through which one may or must pass in the search for valuable hypotheses which can then be verified "scientifically." Some regard it as a kind of fairy story which is built out of the imagination of the observer rather than a rigorously constructed map of a series of social events. Most social scientists observe the confusion in the attempts to describe the life of individuals and take the position that they do not *have* to believe anything in this field. Some appear to allege that no systematic sense can be made of the growth of a person in culture. Refuge is often taken by such persons in consoling methodologies which give a sense of security even if they must be used on materials that are not always important. This latter attitude, by the way, needs to be explained rather than accepted, perhaps just by life-history methods themselves.

No realistic observer in the field can take any consolation, however, in the present state of the art. Instead of abandoning the field of the life history as hopeless, we will attempt to suggest some standards for an adequate life-history technique. It is hoped that these criteria will be useful to practitioners of the "art" of life-history taking as well as to theoretical workers who must judge such materials and define needed directions of effort. So far as is known no systematic effort has been made to define the issues which a life-history technique adequate for social science ends must face.

The criteria proposed. Here follows a list of the criteria viewed as indispensable for judging a life history technique:

I. The subject must be viewed as a specimen in a cultural series.

II. The organic motors of action ascribed must be socially relevant.

III. The peculiar role of the family group in transmitting the culture must be recognized.

IV. The specific method of elaboration of organic materials into social behavior must be shown.

V. The continuous related character of experience from childhood through adulthood must be stressed.

VI. The "social situation" must be carefully and continuously specified as a factor.

VII. The life-history material itself must be organized and conceptualized.

It is not assumed that the reader will be able to grasp the relevance of the above definitions simply by reading them. There will follow shortly a detailed discussion of each criterion and the attempt will be made to show why it is indispensable in judging life-history methods. We need only remember how difficult it is to grasp and utilize axioms in a geometrical demonstration to see how necessary this discussion will be. In the course of our consideration of specific life history materials we will need to refer constantly to these criteria; it is very desirable, if possible, that the reader will be able to get them so firmly in mind that they can be handled eventually by reference, say, to criterion I or criterion VI.

Examination of documents. The formulation of our criteria is not, however, just an exercise in conceptualization. We expect to use them on specific materials and to view and review these materials in the light of our demands for a useful life-history method. We have our criteria and we must put them to work. It is proposed to select documents from a series of fields which purport to give a theoretical account of the individual life in culture. We plan to select one document from each of three fields of clinical psychology, two from the sociological field and one autobiography. We will try to see that the materials discussed are representative in each case of the particular school and will confine ourselves to a discussion of the life-history theory as it is manifested in the specific materials. This differentiates our attempt from a comparison of theories in social psychology. It may be that this practice will be unfair to some schools, but we shall have to abide by the material that is concretely set down. The documents will in each case be studied to discover the degree to which they fulfil the standards proposed above and positive as well as negative correspondences indicated. The analysis of specific materials seems to be the only way in which a concrete character can be given to this effort; by using specific materials and citations from them, for example, disagreements with the views here expressed can be indicated with some hope of advancing the discussion of a point.

Can the review be fair? The writer has the highest opinion of the difficulties of this task. It is easy to be unfair to authors who are not present and cannot directly answer back. It would also be easy to use this opportunity as a chance to grind private axes. Perhaps it had best be said that the writer has some familiarity with the literature of culture and is inclined to weigh heavily the importance of understanding the background mass of tradition which is handed on to any individual; he has also some direct experience in the field of clinical psychology, both theoretical and practical, and has striven independently of this report to find the master concepts turned up by clinical students of the individual life. He has long been familiar with the efforts to develop life-history methods in the sociological field and has crawled on conceptual hands and knees through the analyses of such materials.

In this field we shall be forced to an eclectic position with regard to many points. In this we will take no satisfaction, if by eclecticism we derive only a series of unrelated propositions and insights. Scientific thought is not "fair" to erroneous notions; it is rather organized realism. A man cannot indulge his passion for keeping the peace, if he has one, or for staying in good with the right people, and be a scientist. Science is after the "best way to say it," completest, briefest, directest. We shall organize the material as best we can, point out errors and inadequacies wherever necessary and strive to formulate the material in the most useful way for social science ends.

Other possible assumptions. The writer feels that some criteria might be added to the above, though he does not feel that any of those given above can be omitted. It seemed very important not to complicate the task by including any criterion which was not of crucial relevance and so only the seven listed above are given. There might, for instance, be added as a desirable condition that the life-history technique in question should have a method for securing its facts. This is not included for the reason that we are stressing here the document and not the technique of getting it; in other societies techniques developed in our own may not fit. Note well that it is assumed here that a life-history technique must develop its own warrants of reliability; these cannot be gained by reference to any other type of fact, as, for example, correspondence with neurological or physico-chemical theories. (To be sure, organic inadequacy may occasionally be a limiting factor to a life in culture; such a factor would be the presence of a basic brain defect, as in the case of certain types of idiots. Such a factor, however, does not touch the concept level of the life history because this assumes normal organic capability and function, at least until complicating social factors can be cleared away. In the case of a brain defect the problem immediately drops from a social to a mechanistic biological level of description.)

Documents are types. The materials taken for discussion and survey represent, so far as the author can select them, *types* characteristic of a field of life-history technique and practice. In every case the attempt has been to select the best rather than the poorest exhibit and specialists have been consulted for this purpose. The *fields* from which life history documents have been selected were identified by the writer's general knowledge and by an additional survey of current literature. It is obvious that a single document will not present all the complexities and refinements with which a particular school may treat its life-history materials, but we must expect that the main structure of data and logical arrangement will be represented in the best documents from each field. In this first and crude attempt to set up life-history standards we will have to be reconciled to many inadequacies of detail, if in return we secure a valid general perspective.

How criteria were arrived at. The writer hopes and expects that the most intensive thought will be given to the criteria presented. They are naturally the crux of the matter and disagreements about them would immediately invalidate the rest of the research. The seven criteria listed above are developed initially from direct experience in the life-history field, deriving as it does from both cultural and psychological sources. The criteria are only as good as the sources from which they are drawn and, as a second factor, the writer's control of these sources. The standards suggested are an attempt to formulate *where we are* at the present time in our ability to judge the adequacy and scientific usefulness of documents in the life-history field. The writer expects to be able to do a better job than this a few years hence, with the help of sympathetic critics of this attempt.

The "normal" life history. We shall assume that it is a matter of irrelevance to the nature of the life history whether it be a history of a normal or of an abnormal person. Normality and abnormality have reference to specific norms of behavior and not to the life-history criteria proposed. It may well be, indeed, that a psychotic or neurotic person offers just the needed break in the convention of privacy which cloaks the normal person and which makes study of the latter difficult. The study of psychotics and neurotics can be a preferred entry to our problem without which we might not have access to it at all. We shall not shrink, therefore, from using the history of an abnormal person for discussion as a life history type.

CHAPTER II

DISCUSSION OF THE CRITERIA

IN this chapter we shall discuss each proposed criterion for the life history and try to show in what way it is essential for an adequate view of the individual life. The discussion will portray to some degree the pulling and tugging of different views in the mind of the author out of which the necessity of the criterion has seemed to emerge. The root notion of developing criteria at all was followed by a period of reflection and some exciting moments of discovery as different views and materials were canvassed and the outline finally emerged and seemed to hang together. A second stage was that of trying them out on specific life history documents, a feature of the research which is recorded in the following chapters. At times it seemed that one or the other could comfortably be omitted, but experience with a later document brought back the necessity of retaining it. It must be obvious that no one of the criteria can be taken by itself and that their usefulness as a kind of measuring rod for the life history depends on employing them all at the same time on the same document. It may be noted too that the criteria are stated in such a form that they are not limited in application to materials from our own society only; they are intended to serve as well for the analysis of life histories from other cultures, as soon as such materials are available.

Criterion I. The subject must be viewed as a specimen in a cultural series. It is common in studies which refer to the growth of the person to indicate that he grows somehow in a "milieu," or perhaps the word "surroundings" is used, or sometimes "environment." Scholars who use such terms can only have a preliminary glimmer of the idea of culture.[1] The terms above cited seem to imply that the "milieu" of the person is passive and negative in its value for him; the person does not grow up alone but he does have contacts with other people and this fact is indicated by some such term. Or it may be that a term like "environment" calls up a specifically physical image and seems to attribute potency in the shaping of character to the *things* surrounding the individual. The criterion we have suggested above diverges emphatically from such an inadequate view; it suggests that the "environment" has a character, an historical, traditional character, that it is not a mere accidental aggregate of persons and things but that it is an ordered, configurated set of conditions into which the new member of the group comes.

The importance of the criterion given above is best seen if we accept two units for our consideration: first, the group which exists before the individual; and second, a new organism envisioned as approaching this functioning collectivity. The organism is seen at this moment as clean of cultural influence and the group is seen as functioning without the aid of the organism in question. We will suppose that the organism is nearing the group through its intra-uterine development and that it is finally precipitated into group life by the act of birth. Let us ask ourselves at this point what we can say systematically about what this organism will be like when it comes of age, sex granted. All of the facts we can predict about it, granted the continuity of the group, will define the culture into which it comes. Such facts can include the kind

1. It is difficult to overstate the indebtedness I feel to my teacher and colleague, Professor Edward Sapir, for every perception I have of the fact and nature of culture. Each of his students can testify to the clarity and vitality of his views. It was especially during the seminar on the Impact of Culture on Personality, of which he was director and which was held at Yale University during the academic year, 1932–1933, that I became familiar with his position. I much fear that I have not succeeded in acknowledging in this book all of the valuable turns of phrase and ways of thinking that he has given me.

of clothes it will wear, the language it will speak, its theological ideas, its characteristic occupation, in some cases who its husband or wife is bound to be, how it can be insulted, what it will regard as wealth, what its theory of personality growth will be, etc. These and hundreds of other items are or may be standardized before the birth of the individual and be transmitted to the organism with mechanical certainty.

In order to make this idea clear to themselves some persons like to think of the society itself as the "living" thing; at one end, the new organic material is funneled in by birth, and at the other end of old age, the used up organic material is buried out of the society. If you reify a society in this way you can view it as an entity with an organismic stream flowing in and out of it. What is seen to persist are sets of folkways and *mores* which are only slightly altered from generation to generation in the normal course of things.[2] In order to get this point of view you have to close your eyes slightly so that the individuals disappear but the connected sense of their habitual life remains. This point of view can show how the rough but powerful outline of the new individual life is forecast by the traditional life of the group itself.

A life historian, sophisticated in the above sense, can see his life history subject as a link in a chain of social transmission; there were links before him from which he acquired his present culture; other links will follow him to which he will pass on the current of tradition. The life history attempts to describe a unit in that process; it is a study of one of the strands of a complicated collective life which has historical continuity. The fact that an individual believes his culture to be "his" in some powerful personal sense, as though he had thought out for himself how to do the things which he actually does by traditional prescription, will not impress the observer who has the cultural view. He will re-

2. Sumner, William Graham, *Folkways,* Boston and New York, Ginn and Company, 1906, p. 30.

gard this conviction as unimportant and will stress the point of uniformity of the subject's behavior with that of persons who have lived before him and who now live in the same group. In such a "march" of a culture through time the individual is seen as less than a phantom; in point of fact, the individual only appears in times of crisis when the *mores* are not adequate to meet some real life situation which the group faces.

We are stressing at this point the fact that the scientific student of a human life must adequately acknowledge the enormous background mass of the culture; and not as a mere mass either, but rather as a configurated whole. Before any individual appears his society has had a specific social life organized and systematized, and the existence of this life will exercise a tyrannical compulsion on him. Seen from this point of view the problem of the life history is a statement of how the new organism becomes the victim or the resultant of this firm structure of the culture. Each life history that is gathered will be a record of how a new person is added to the group. It will be a case of seeing "the group *plus* a person." To state the point in an extreme manner we can think of the organic man as the mere toy of culture, providing it with a standardized base, investing its forms with affect but creating very little that is new alone or at any one time.

At this point we do not have to beat the devil of the instinct theory around the stump; that theory is now largely discredited. It has been discredited by the evidence which has enabled us to formulate the above postulate for an adequate life history, namely the scientific reports from other cultures which have shown the extreme variability of human action and the great importance of a vested tradition in determining the action of any new member. Organic motive power for a society there certainly is, but it does not directly determine the form of the social life. We do not need to assume that culture is transmitted via the gene structure of man when we can perfectly well see how the new organism is laboriously indoctrinated with the traditional views. The individual does not generate himself in a colorless environment; rather he "gets generated" by the surrogates of a potent cultural order.

If our life historian is not equipped with the above criterion he will certainly fall into error by referring to accident, whims of individuals, or organic propulsion, much that is properly seen only as a part of the society into which the individual comes. These errors seem so chronic and immortal in social science thinking that it is hard to overdo the necessity of a very schematic statement of the cultural view. Many individuals who are quite able to state the point, after one fashion or another, are persistently unable to work it through into their manner of dealing with problems. One of the marks of an effective grasping of this point is the stated or implied "in our culture" whenever one makes any point in connection with individual behavior; it is a good thing to get into the habit, for example, of saying "men are more able than women to exhibit aggressive behavior in *our* culture." One might venture that to the social psychologist the three most indispensable letters in the alphabet are I. O. C. (in our culture). Students readily learn to think this way in referring to any matter of socialized motivation. In the examination of specific life histories which is to follow we will find many sins committed against the above criterion. It implies that the life history worker must have a good conscious as well as unconscious control of the culture in which he expects to take life histories.

Criterion II. The organic motors of action ascribed must be socially relevant. This criterion sounds rather difficult to understand, but this is not the case; it is really very simple. It means merely that in order to have a theory of motivation we must make some statements about the body and what it can and will do; the organic properties which we assume as

the basis of the life of the individual in the group must be of
such a kind that they will submit to social elaboration. The
organic activities of the body must come to meet the social
influences that we have just described.

Let us take a case where this criterion is not met. If we
begin by postulating a set of instincts which begin to function at birth, or later, which will carry the life of the person
on its spiral curve to adulthood, then we do not need the
culture to explain the behavior of an individual. The instincts, given in the package, will work themselves out
naturally in social behavior, warfare, mating, and the like.
We have indicated, however, that we cannot make such instinct assumptions because we know of the great variability
of behavior from group to group and we would be forced
then to postulate a new set of instincts for each such group.

Nor can we begin with the endocrine actions of the individual. Culture patterns cannot tie onto endocrine behavior
directly; they can deal with endocrine functions only in-
directly, that is, through influencing the craving life of the
individual. This is not to deny that the "cravings" of the
individual cannot be effectively seen in some instances from
the endocrinological level of sight. The endocrine glands
must deliver into the theater of perception, directed inward,
impulses which can be affected by social influence before we
have the "*socially relevant* biological factors." Those aspects
of the body which are seen as functioning on a mechanistic
biological level are, by definition, least accessible to social
influence.

Let us take the case of the conventional "stimulus" of psychology and examine this point. The meaningful social act has
to be reduced to a "stimulus" at some nerve end of the body
before it comes into the mechanistic biological universe of
discourse. When this reduction is made the stimulus is no
longer social but has been redefined in neurological terms.
There is no question that such a redefinition is sometimes use-

ful, but it gets us off the "social" level of perception to a mechanistic level.

The key to the matter is that the organic activity must come within the possibility of "perception directed inward," must be an urge which the person *can* consciously attempt to carry out. For example, the hunger reaction is not "socially relevant" if defined as the interaction of certain chemicals in the stomach; it is relevant if defined as a pressure toward overt total behavior which can motivate conscious action. Culture cannot affect chemicals in the stomach directly; it can only deal with the body cravings and through them with the sensory equipment which serves to mediate and release these cravings with the aid of the surrounding (acculturated) persons. The physiological definition of hunger, serviceable for certain purposes, does not usefully interlock with the idea of culture. The erroneous notion that it does is held by large numbers of workers who expect to come to solutions of problems pitched on the cultural level by ever finer analyses on the physico-chemical level.

Another way to think about the matter is to say that culture must begin with the body itself and with what it can plainly be observed to do. To have this ground plan of the body in mind is more important for the student of the life history than to have sophisticated definitions of the body functions in mind. Culture would be quite different if men peaceably accepted losses of pleasure or property, if they had eyes in the back of their heads, or if they walked with the aid of their hands; it would also be different if the food eaten were totally consumed and part of it were not excreted, or if procreative activities were possible in some other way. The body's stipulations for conducting these major activities are the "organic" facts with which culture must deal and with which the life history must begin.

It is, therefore, understandable that concepts of motivation which are "socially relevant" are likely to be more plastic, modifiable and ductile than the instinct theory used to offer us; they will also deal, not with mechanistic definitions of body function, but with the plain-to-be-seen cravings and needs of the organism. The idea of "drive" or "tension" has been invented to indicate the modifiability and social relevance of the organic potentialities; these drives are not rigid entities which work themselves out despite social influence, they are rather a kind of motive power, blind but powerful, offered to society.

These types of motivation will not appear as isolated activities of the organism but will rather be seen only in social interaction, that is, as humans deal with the new organism. Nor will they disappear once they are touched and influenced by the habits of others, but will rather persist as an organic thrust through the cultural cloak of the individual during his whole life. They will offer us a description from the organic side that will deal with the pressure toward action in the individual; they will be, in fact, the horse power for social action. Our organic theory must explain the craving nature of man and the projectile character of his behavior and not show him merely as the passive recipient and the executant of stimuli and responses.

The life history can begin with the body structures and functions as they can be roughly made out even by the layman. It is important to resist the tendency to skid down to definitions of the body which cannot be reached (conceptually) by our cultural world of discourse. What the research future may bring in the way of better knowledge of the organic life we do not know; we suggest, however, that the place to begin is the one indicated. We must say whatever we have to say about the organic basis of behavior in terms that can hook on to our cultural superstructure.

Criterion III. The peculiar role of the family group in transmitting the culture must be recognized. The reader will have noticed that our criteria have a kind of sequence of their own, beginning with the group existing before the individual and carrying through to a series of specific social situations existing during his whole life. Why, it may be asked, should we jump from the organic nature of man to the family? The answer is not difficult. The "group" into which the child comes is not the group in general; the child is not born into the church or the army; rather he is born into a very definite specification of the larger group, namely the family. We should remark, too, the fact that the family into which the child comes has a cultural lineage; it is not formed just previously to the birth of the child for the purpose of taking care of him. In the case of the "family," the patriarchal family form can be traced through twenty-five hundred years of European history, and it is certainly much older than that. It has been modified in recent days, to be sure, but it is a very solid institution even yet.

The above criterion is stated in the given form to stress the fact that it is useful not only in our own culture but in any culture, because some kind of family form exists in every known society. In discussing this criterion we will deal mainly with our own family form because most life history materials have been gathered within the boundaries of our own culture and this form is well known to all of us, in practice at least if not in theory. Our present modern family brings only a few persons in contact with the child during its early life. We note that originally the patriarchal family also included a group of kinsmen who might be important in the child's life; now it frequently happens that the child has very little contact even with its own grandparents. In our "small" family the parents must take more varied roles; it is more difficult for the child to divide its affection and rebellious tendencies between various personages in the family group. The mother, for example, must be the helpful one as well as the "bad" denying person who is "bad" because she must impose the elementary restrictions of the culture on the

organic life of the child. It is more difficult for the child to
"escape" from such a family and we see the child held to his
sociological parents. These facts are recited in order to indicate, *a priori*, the special importance of the family in the life
of the child in our society; it is a question of "more" or "less"
importance because there will be no society in which the
parents are not important and in which the family form must
not be specifically noted in the life of the individual. However, differences in the form of family, such as the equal
rather than inferior role of the mother in some societies, may
be very important for the character formation of the growing individual.

Another way of stressing the significance of the family is
to note that the early transmission of opportunities and
limitations characteristic of the wider culture is done by the
family, or rather by the father, mother, and siblings; for the
maturing child these persons *are* the culture. Most of the
culture appears to the young child as something mother
wants the child to do or will not allow or that father insists on
or disapproves. It is no accident that during the rest of the
life of the child the culture forms will carry plus and minus
signs of specific parental character. This may be illustrated
by the way in which the "policeman" takes over the emotional
tone of the parents in their prohibitory roles and probably
passes it on to the "law" in general.

An adequate life history technique must count with this
powerful role of the family as the matrix of early life; the
traditional roles of father and mother will be seen as important in respect of discipline as well as giving gratification to the child and facilitating culturally approved activities. It cannot be overstressed that the parents are not
merely progenitors or ancestors giving biological life alone
to the child, but also that they are culture surrogates, themselves organized and constellated in family situations of their
own; the parents no less than the child have histories in cul-

ture. It is into such a "social situation" that the new organism comes and that is why we stress the idea of the family at this point.

We will expect from the adequate life history technique a specific statement of the interaction between the parents and the new organism; in particular we will want a discussion of the parents as targets of the emotional life of the child. We will be prepared to state in advance that a life history which gives us a blank in the space where this account ought to be can hardly be sufficiently realistic for use in the social sciences. Our argument is made largely from the evidence of culture and the highly fixed character of the family form rather than from specific life history evidence itself, though it could also be made from the latter. We shall expect that the mark of the specific family form would be on an individual so long as he lives and that experience in the family would necessarily be integrated closely with the later, wider social participation of the child. For instance, we would expect a relationship between the roles of the parents in the family and the expanded field of socially symbolic persons which appear in later life, that is, with persons in such roles as those of teacher, policeman, minister, "boss," social service worker, wife, life history taker, and others. As a practical example the life historian would suspect, *a priori*, that he could easily be fitted into one of the family roles by his subject.

The family is, of course, one type of answer to the helplessness of the child. During this long period of helplessness and in his very first social contacts he is in a particular type of family milieu. We must note, for instance, that the wide prevalence of the patriarchal family form through the Western European culture area has made understanding between individuals easy throughout this area, whatever the language they speak and whatever be the minor differences in culture and costume which they exhibit. It may well be that the patriarchal family in turn is related to the wider economic structure of our society, but this is not the province of our analysis at the moment. It will suffice if the reader agrees that a useful life history will invariably give a detailed account of relationships between the child and its parents.

Criterion IV. The specific method of elaboration of organic materials into social behavior must be shown. In the life history the body is what we have to go on; it is the primary unit of naïve perception. The life history must begin with it and stay close to it during the whole of its course. We have seen the body and its organic tensions in criterion II as clearly set off from the environing (parental) culture. We must now stress the juncture between the organic urges and the culture itself. The completed person, able to act with reference to his group standards, is the resultant of these urges and the culture impacting on them.

The useful life history of the future will begin (theoretically) at the bottom, that is, with the organism; and it will show in detail how this organism slowly becomes capable of social life in its particular group. We have noticed already that the group is represented at the outset by the parents who exercise its molding pressures and permissive tendencies on the growing person. This translation from the sheer "socially relevant biological" to socialized motivational forces must be carefully delineated and formulated theoretically because it is of utmost importance to get this straight. Otherwise we will have our person fitted out as a mature individual with a set of attitudes corresponding to a culture but we will have no idea how he got this way and we are likely to miss altogether the initial and continuing importance of the biological substratum of the social life of the person.

A chronic sin against this principle is manifested in the "instinct" theories; they begin by postulating a set of instincts as initial motors of the individual's life and then jump in theory to the adult behavior of the person. In between is a long and arid area, theoretically seen, in which little of importance is shown to happen to the person. Those who begin without any biological assumptions at all make a comparable mistake but of another type; in this case we first see the person as mature and we are not advised as to what has happened during his earlier life. He has been somehow "socialized" but it is taken for granted that this is a process which everyone ought naturally to understand. Very likely the latter group is deterred from the task of studying the life of the individual by its difficult nature and by the lack of appreciation of its necessity. We must stress again that in a useful theory of the life history the social influences must hook directly onto the initial biological factors and the elaboration of these initial potentialities in social life must be seen as a series of connected events, without any missing links.

Nor will it do to postulate wishes and instincts that appear up along the genetic tree of development, say at four or five years, and treat them as primary. Many persons have invented out of their own heads "wishes" and "instincts" which emerge at some defined time point and which are not related specifically to the organic nature of the person. Such notions cannot be adequate. Our "motors of behavior" must appear in the first instance as unembellished by social influences and their gradual merging into motivational elements with social content should be specifically described. This does not need to mean that the biological components will appear during the whole life of the person as they show themselves at its outset; they will, of course, be molded and modified under specific social pressures.

The "social pressures" referred to will be mediated, as we have said, by specific persons with traditionally determined roles, namely the parents and siblings. The course of elaboration of the impulse life within this family unit will be described realistically and in detail. In the adequate life history we may never take our theoretical eye off the fact that we are dealing with an organism, an animal, which views its culture as a method of impulse expression. The culture, on its side, has another view; it is not concerned with the impulse expression of the organism except in so far as this can be led into socially valuable channels, channels which serve to maintain the collective life of the group. As practitioners of a life history method we must keep both points in mind. We stress the organic side at this point because it is apparently the more easily disregarded and undervalued.

Criterion V. The continuous related character of experience from childhood through adulthood must be stressed. It is sometimes easier to understand the force and relevance of the criterion when we call up before our minds a mistaken theory. Some writers treat life history material as if it were a series of incoördinated, unrelated events without sequence or necessary relationship. If they wish to study the religious behavior of adolescents, for instance, they will simply drop a statistical bucket into the well of adolescent experience and draw it out; they will view their bucketful of data as self-explanatory and not as a part of an individual unified life. If our criterion is accepted this procedure would be found invalid. The religious behavior of adolescents could not be seen except as part of the continuous experience of the individual adolescent and the "religious events" would have to be set in series with the rest of the life of the person. It might well be that we would miss the whole sense of adolescent religious experience unless we understand the organic problems of adolescents and the particular character form which adolescents *in our culture* bring forward at this age level.

Our criterion as above stated emphasizes rather that "life begins at zero" and not at seven or fourteen or forty or otherwise, at the option of the theorist. We state that the theorist has no option but to begin it where it begins and this seems the reasonable initial assumption. It may well be that experience of significance is acquired during intra-uterine life as well, but we will be content with emphasizing the time of birth as a beginning point of the life history.

From our point of view the life of the individual is a single connected whole and may be viewed as a unit event itself; if we accept the fifth criterion, it is such a unit from the standpoint of the life history. Our life historian will then study perforce the events of this interwoven character of individual experience; in studying any given event he will peer down the long avenue of the individual life to see how the present-day event matured. Very likely he will have to stress the unity of the experience of the individual and the connected character of the residues of experience which become the character pattern.

In this manner of seeing the life history every act has a representative character and is a summative response to inner as well as outer "stimuli"; in no case will we find isolated segments of character operating independently of the total self. In the perfect life history a complete purchase on the life of the person would be required to explain totally any given act, and by "explain" here we mean to set the act into its proper context and sequence. Such a standard for the life history would regard as quite naïve the explanation of a suicide by such a factor as business reverses; it would be plain that the "business reverse" in question comes at the end of a long life history and that it can function only as a cue which sets off a process already there. To be sure, the severity of the "cue" shock may set off a suicidal response in a person immune to lesser trials. This view would also give another perspective on the "nervous breakdown"; such breakdowns now are viewed with appalling unconcern and lack of scientific curiosity by thinkers in the social science field. As social scientists they do not feel required to do anything about such a fact; it will be handled, they negligently explain, by the psychiatrist. Quite possibly; but it may be handled in such a way as to negate the very premises under which social scientists work and thus become a challenge to our whole network of understanding. If, on the other hand, a "nervous breakdown" is seen as the end of a life history pattern and the stimulus which sets it off a weak one, this event may well assume significance in social science thinking. The nervous breakdown is indeed one of the pressing situations which ought to arouse keenly the curiosity of the social scientist and serve as a stimulus for investigation, using our premises and insights. In the scientifically valuable life history any act performed in adulthood will have a network of references to character sets, external situations and drive impulses along the whole length of the life sequence. Apparently the only way of avoiding the necessity of this premise is to refuse to delve into life history materials. Another way of saying it is to stress the fact that the life history document is a *Gestalt*, paralleling point by point the configurated experience of the individual; in a functional sense there are no isolated parts.

We cannot come by this view through analogy with the behavior of rats or dogs; it would be very remarkable if such a concept occurred to the student of other animal groups. We can approach the importance of this criterion only by studying the person, and his aid is essential in developing a life history document; we will make out the pattern primarily through his reports on his actions, inner and outer, and by such observation of his social relationships as our technique permits; but we must not suppose that he will be able to give us a *theory* of his life that is accurate, for in fact he can only give us by his speech and show us by his actual and reported action the material on which we may build the theory. It is our purpose in this discussion to point out that we will hardly come out with anything valuable unless the above criterion is firmly stressed.

We do not affirm here that all events in an individual life are of equal significance; such a possibility would make the life history valueless since the number and character of such events would be beyond accurate determination. The patterned character of culture and family life into which the individual comes and the limited number of his main organic pressures make it seem extremely likely that some experiences will be more important for the determination of character than others, and some few will be of central crucial character. Such events will leave the individual with a formed character and a central feeling core which will be of highest relevance for any later behavior which we attempt to explain. The useful life history will likewise give great emphasis not only to the longitudinal roots of behavior but to the chronology of events; a useful sub-postulate would be that the earlier the defining social situation works on the maturing organism the better its chance for adding a lasting element to the character of the individual.

This is not an acultural view; it is, however, set off against the cross-cultural institutional view of behavior. It shows, so to speak, the culture in long-section, the culture as coagulated around a center of feeling. From this point of view the life history record shows a center of feeling and positive motivation moving through a culture, over time. The culture offers to this moving center of feeling its preferred barriers and permitted exits, much as in the psychologist's maze. An important difference is that the cultural "maze" is not experimentally thought out in advance, nor is the moving organism a rat.

Criterion VI. The "social situation" must be carefully and continuously specified as a factor. To make this point clear I want to suggest an image that we frequently encounter in the moving pictures. In describing, let us say, the route of a caravan across an unknown country we see before our eyes a moving black line which proceeds across the map with many bends and detours. We will assume that this line represents the movement of a life through a social situation. At the temporary end of a line at any moment in its course we have a "situation"; in the geographic example a natural physical situation, in our field, a social situation. The organism is presented with a series of such situations in its course; in fact, life is just one such after another. Like most analogies ours falls down at a certain point; the caravan moving through African forests may come to its destination the same caravan which began the journey; this is never true of the individual moving through a culture, unless he be mechanically insusceptible to culture (an idiot). We wish rather to stress that out of the situation which he faces he steadily acquires his "present" culture, he changes by virtue of growing up to and through these situations. The "culture" waiting for him in the future is always presented to him as a series of such concrete situations. At the beginning of the individual's life he brings only his organic needs to the new situation, but very rapidly thereafter he begins to "accumulate experience," to grow his character, and this character he brings as it accumulates into each new situation. The constant "situation" of early life is the family situation and its presentation of particular demands and opportunities.

The "situation" is, however, more complicated than has been indicated so far and we will point out two ways of viewing it; there is an objective view or a sort of average of what others would recognize in it; and there is also an extremely private or personal view of the situation to which the subject actually reacts. We mean here the first or "average" view of it when we speak of the "situation." If we mean to indicate the private version, we shall in every case say so.

We need a good clear example at this point to show the state of affairs and we will take the case of a six-year-old boy who is asked to go frog spearing by other boys. The average (or cultural) definition of this situation would be something like this: the boy is free and able to go; frog spearing is a culturally permitted activity in his community and is even

specifically encouraged by his parents since they would welcome the edible frog legs; he has a spear; he has the encouragement and example of the other boys; there are frogs
accessible; he has the necessary arm-eye coördination to
throw a spear; as a normal boy he ought to respond posi-
tively to the excitement of the proposed hunt. We could go
on specifying these elements in the "average" view of the
situation but it is hoped that the point is clear.

However, he cannot hunt; he goes along with the other
boys, takes his spear, intends to hunt but when he actually
sees a frog his arm is somehow "held" and he cannot throw
the spear. He feels humiliated that he does not bring anything home from his hunting and the other boys josh him
about being a sissy. Even this pressure does not enable him
to conform to the behavior expectation in the situation. Our
only remaining assumption is that some "private" definition
of the situation tends to interfere with the official one. A life
history of the boy confirms this view. Briefly put, he cannot
spear frogs because they are equated in his phantasy with
persons and eventually with himself. Under these circumstances we would not expect him to be a good spearman;
theoretically put, he has a private version of the situation
which differs from that of the other boys and from that of
the community at large. It is this private version that dis-
turbs his behavior.

The same point can be beautifully made in the case of an
agoraphobia. Here the person fears with a deadly fear to go
into a certain street, or across a certain square. To the rest
of us this street or square has an average culture meaning
which we will not elaborate at this point; the phobiac, however, sees, or correctly expressed, unconsciously *feels* matters
to be otherwise. To him our innocent street is a place of
danger where he will go only with the greatest reluctance, if
at all. He, too, has a private view of our object "street"
which makes the street different for him.

This is a point of very great importance because the difference between our official or average or cultural expectation of action in a "situation" and the actual conduct of the person indicates the presence of a private interpretation. Where the private version equals the official one we have normal conduct. There are, of course, minor differences in people's versions of a "situation" even where they react in the culturally expected manner, but these differences are disregarded. However, once we have discovered a private and affectively toned version of the "situation" in some persons we may then go back to our normal interpretations and find that they, too, are affect-laden; however, in this case the affects are disposed in a sense favorable to carrying out the situation in the culturally expected manner. Not only the boy who could not hunt is affectively reacting to the hunting situation, but also those who could and did; the boys who could hunt, however, have found a normal cultural outlet for their affects; the boy who could not hunt could not utilize this situational outlet and had to resolve his conflict in another manner (in this case, but not necessarily, by neurosis).

We can now come back to the question of the situation as it is related to the life history. In the adequate life history we must constantly keep in mind the situation both as defined by others and by the subject; such a history will not only define both versions of the situation but let us see clearly the pressure of the formal situation and the force of the inner private definition of the situation. One of the acutest needs in cultural theory is to specify the series of situations through which the average organism in the culture must come; this specification will probably turn out to be a more specific view of the culture patterns, a view of culture as it is actually experienced by emerging members of the group.

The usual error in regard to this criterion is to count only with the formal social situation and to overvalue it by assuming that all persons come into the formally defined situation with the same experience and define it in the same way. Only "normal" persons are able to do this. The mistake of over-valuing the existing situation is the sociological error *par excellence*. Let me remind you at this point of the example of the suicide already discussed. It is, however, equally errone-ous to value too lightly the pressure of the existing situation and to deal only with the former experience of the individual as though the current situation were a mere recapitulation of past experience. With such a view one might well overlook, for example, the whole existence of the economic order and its pressure on an individual while reveling in his recollec-tions of a childhood experience.

Both views must be held and that simultaneously. The "life" of the person is a series of such objective "situations" and the life history is a record of how they are reacted to and what tendencies to further action are bedded down in the organism by them and therefore brought into the next "situa-tion" as defining tendencies to react toward it. It seems easier for individuals to expect the standard cultural behavior from others and to count more heavily with their own motivations and private views in the case of themselves.

Criterion VII. The life-history material itself must be or-ganized and conceptualized. The utility of this criterion is not self-evident; many workers seem to feel that if you can once get the subject to tell his own story that he will auto-matically give you material of scientific character. This can only very rarely be true because the material he gives naïvely is already conditioned and limited in a great number of ways, not least by the taboos which every culture has on communi-cating certain kinds of material. It is safe to accept the pos-tulate that the naïve material will never have scientific va-lidity. Another way of stating the matter is that the life-history material does not speak for itself; the subject is un-able to give us explanatory theoretical paragraphs making

sense of the material. He may, on the contrary, and usually
does, do the very best he can to disguise it. This fact makes
necessary that the life-history worker play an active role
over against his material; he must do the critical work of
fashioning the necessary concepts, of making the required
connections and of piecing the whole life history together to
make sense plain and scientific communication easy. It is surprising how many social scientists do not use their knowledge
of the power of taboos over individual communication in approaching the subject of a life history; they appear to think
that if they merely ask him to tell all, he will be able to spin
it right off the reel and they may sit peacefully by and accept
the result as a valid life history.

Let us take the case of a young social scientist who has
heard by some accident of the curriculum or vagary of his
reading that it is important to gather life-history materials.
He will certainly have heard that there is much confusion in
interpretation of life-history materials and that he does not
have to believe anything if he does not want to; but we will
assume that his favorable conviction persists and he determines to get a life history. Without more training, for there
is hardly any to be got at present in the social science field,
he goes forth to gather such a document and comes back
presently with several volumes of material written or reported by a subject. He then dumps this material on our
desks with the proviso that we are to make sense out of it, not
he. He may give us a few very scanty theoretical pages, but
we find that he has not attempted to integrate the material
and to describe in detail the progress of the organism through
the cultural "maze." Such material could hardly be of much
value and it is not of much value. It may substantiate various
points about the structure of the culture seen on a cross-sectional level; but it will hardly give us a vivid dynamic sense
of the growth of the individual in a cultural milieu because

the subject himself, just because of his acculturation, cannot give us a valid theory of his own growth.

The life historian will develop concepts from his material and view his next life-history material with those concepts until he can improve them; if he pretends not to have any conceptual patterns through which he sees his material, we will merely conclude that he has unwittingly used the current personality theory of his culture and has blocked out of his account, or his analysis of the material, all of those facts which the culture declines to acknowledge officially. It is better that the concepts used be explicit and subject to examination. In this case the procedure of further elaboration of a conceptual system will follow the scientific movement from provisional hypotheses to the material and back again from inductive experience to the refined concept.

The future conceptual system of the life history will be sufficiently elaborate to manipulate *all* of the life-history material; we may not glide around troublesome facts with evasions or elisions here any more than in any other potentially scientific field. It is assumed that here, as elsewhere, empirical experience with life-history material will be the guide to concept formation and that the orienting concept must possess incisive relevance to the material. It is not just a question of how anyone "likes" to look at it; individual preferences are necessarily taboo, although in the present state of the art individuals do have preferences and recklessly broadcast them. "How it works" in a scientific sense will be the warrant of the adequacy of the concepts, that is, how well the conceptual formulations govern, relate, and integrate the material observed.

Like any scientific conceptual scheme this one will possess coherence and an ordered character; in the end one will be able to step conceptually from any one concept in the system to any other; each term will imply the necessary existence of the others and unlinked or contradictory concepts will be recognized as defects in the system and will invite research urgently.

The scientific formulation of the future adequate life history, that is, adequate for social science ends, will necessarily take count of our other criteria. It will recognize the pre-existing totality of the culture, give a relevant organic formulation, show the power of the family form, explain in detail how the organic life is welded into social action, indicate the continuity of the life history, define the "situation" and handle many minor points not indicated here. It will probably also give us a basis for prediction under defined and limited conditions.

Any stranger to this conceptual system will find it difficult to master, but we must stress that he can come by knowledge of its value only in the precise task of collecting and ordering life-history materials.

CHAPTER III

THE CRITERIA APPLIED:
*THE CASE OF MISS R**

WE will consider here a book entitled *The Case of Miss R* which was published under Adler's name in 1929; it represents, therefore, a recent and mature exhibit of Adler's method of analysis. The book contains an introduction by the translator, the autobiography of "Miss R," and a running fire of comment and interpretation by Alfred Adler.[1] As Adler states, he has never seen the patient and knows nothing of her except what her autobiography tells.

As I said in my preface I have never seen this girl. All that I know about her has been written by her and by me in the present book.[2]

There is little doubt but that Adler could make a still better case for his views if he had collected the life history directly from the girl herself; but, from our point of view, the document is quite adequate since it enables us to see Adler's system in the light of our criteria.

In the case of Adler, as in the case of Freud, Rank, Shaw, and our other life historians, we are not making therapeutic effect on the subject our test of adequacy. Adequacy of the concept system in our sense means the degree of "fit" with the facts reported and with knowledge derived from the field of cultural studies. The therapeutic test is too precarious for

---

* Adler, Alfred, *The Case of Miss R,* Chicago, The International Journal of Individual Psychology. All of the extracts in this chapter are taken from this book with the consent of the publisher. The permission thus granted is warmly appreciated.

1. A translator's preface and some theoretical statements are given by Dr. Friedrich Jensen.

2. *Ibid.,* p. 305.

our ends, though ultimately it should be a valuable one since a correct description of life-history events should result in some degree of direct control of those events. "Control" here means the possibility of influencing the person in the direction of adjustment to his cultural norms, providing that they are not destructive of his life. However, so many claims are made for therapy and they come from such varying sources that we must reject this criterion of adequacy for the moment. We will now turn to Adler's system and see how it scales up before our criteria, using specific citations from *The Case of Miss R* as our points of reference.

Criterion I. The subject must be viewed as a specimen in a cultural series.

It would seem reasonable that all the clinical psychologies will be deficient in respect of this criterion. After all, these clinical psychologies come out of the context of psychiatry and ultimately of mechanistic biology. This method of thought is built up specifically to exclude the idea of culture and to fix its attention on the organic aspect of man. The concept of culture was not discovered in this field and it is indeed very little known there up to the present time. It is simply a bit of knowledge which has not gotten around to the clinical psychologists and one which they could come by only with the greatest difficulty through their particular method, that is the study of the individual in our own culture.

To say, therefore, that any one of the clinical psychologies, and Adler's in particular, does not count adequately with the concept of culture is hardly a reproach. We should rather ask, how could it? The clinical psychologists have discovered that their patients have parents, but they have not effectively "discovered" that their parents have grandparents and great-grandparents. That is a discovery that could be made only when two cultures are compared; then it can be seen how culture traits and behavior forms spin on from generation to generation.

Our reading of *The Case of Miss R* produces very useful citations which recognize that the new organism comes into a highly fixed system of living; our eyes are fixed by Adler's analysis on the individual and his reaction to an intense wish to gain a superior position in the eyes of his fellows. The danger of this system from the scientific standpoint can be seen if we ask, suppose the new organism is born into a culture where there is less intense individualism and competition for status than in our own? Would it then react with the same frantic urge toward superiority and the same devious compensations in the case of the neurotic as it does in ours? The fact of culture must be "wittingly" present in the mind of the life historian; if this fact is not present, it will be easy to mistake for general principles of human nature what are actually features of the particular culture in which the person is immersed. We will indicate later that Adler has probably made this error.

Adler is not lacking, however, in appreciation of the importance of the immediate social milieu; rather he is outstanding among clinical psychologists for his recognition of its reality. In the preface to the book it is stated by Jensen, "Every human problem concerns not only one individual, but also the society in which that individual lives. Every person is tied by intangible threads to his community."[3] In the same preface we learn of three broad classes of social problems which the individual must face: first, interhuman relations; second, work; and third, sex. We note, therefore, that Adler understands very well the importance of the immediate community life for the individual, and in this sense he meets our criterion in part. What seems missing is an acute realization of the fact that this "community" is an historical fact and that the problem which it puts to the individual is an arbitrary and traditional one.

3. *Ibid.,* p. vii.

This point can be well illustrated by Adler's interpretation of the masculine protest.

However, if we had an opportunity to uncover more of what went on in her mind, we should doubtless find a wish to change into a boy. It is the small remainder of a great, general trait: it is the protest against being a woman in a world where men are generally considered superior; where they have the more advantageous positions, greater freedom and apparently greater physical strength. I have termed this manifestation the masculine protest.[4]

This attitude in Miss R is explained as "the protest against being a woman in a world where men are generally considered superior; where they have the more advantageous positions, greater freedom and apparently greater physical strength." Such a "protest" is certainly possible in a culture where the above statements are true. We should doubt, however, that it is only a "small remainder of a great, general trait," as Adler states. We should rather say that it is a reaction to a specific culture complex in our own society; the question might also be raised that there is still a mystery since our society does not recommend the same goals to men and women, but appears to set special goals for women in which their superiority is unquestioned.

In general, clinical psychologists carry their culture as an unacknowledged power which they bring to their patients; it enables them to understand the patient's reactions because they, the psychologists, bred to the same culture, unconsciously react in the same way. This is not enough, however, for scientific theory. The cultural mass which the clinician brings to his patient must be clearly and conceptually formulated, else he will interpret as general human what is actually only shared by the members of his own group. Aggressive and masterful as our culture may be and wide as its

4. *Ibid.,* p. 40.

sphere of influence is, it is from the comparative point of view just *one* other culture. A group of five hundred people in New Mexico may be able to show us just as valid and well articulated a way of life and one different from our own. Only the shock of comparison with other cultures can show the clinical psychologists how parochial their interpretations and concepts often are.

Our judgment must be, then, that Adler stresses the importance of the society in which the individual lives but he does not give us the feel that this society is arbitrarily and historically determined and that it is the result of a unique historical evolution. We begin, in the case of Adler's psychology, with the individual and not with the group which existed before him.

Criterion II. The organic motors of action ascribed must be socially relevant.

When we put the spotlight of this criterion on Adlerian psychology we find very little to say. What the body is able to do at birth and what kind of problem it presents to the culture into which it is to be incorporated does not seem to have struck Adler as important. When the individual is older and already enmeshed in the strivings of his cultural milieu we do find Adler positing bodily tendencies to react, but at the outset we draw a theoretical blank. To use a football metaphor we begin in Adler's psychology at about the thirty yard line, rather than at the goal line, so far as the biological contribution to the development of the individual is concerned. This must be seen as a defect in his view of the individual.

In the Adlerian view the child is seen as determined to master its milieu, the persons surrounding it, and to secure from them "attention," and later recognition, superiority, and status. We must assume, therefore, that a craving for "attention" is assumed by Adler to be a biological fundamental, not further explicable. The difficulty of this view is that it does not begin with a specific physical mechanism which can be identified first on the organic level and which produces results of relevance in the social sphere. Compare it with the stomach-hunger series, for example. This reaction does not seem to be identifiable until it is already involved in cultural influence. A good case in point is that of bodily defect.

Adler proceeds from the fact that bodily defects are not only to be considered as signs of physical deterioration but also frequently give rise to attempts at compensation and overcompensation. As soon as there is a physical disturbance the body attempts to compensate for it. Since every bodily disturbance makes an impression on the mind a mental striving sets in concurrently with the compensatory efforts of the body, with the aim of overcoming or, at least, making up for this defect in some way or other.[5]

We learn from the preface that as soon as a bodily defect appears a physical effort to compensate for it appears, and that with this physical effort also a mental striving sets in with an aim of overcoming and making up for the defect. Plainly such compensatory efforts can be significant in a psychic sense only when the defect is already evaluated by others as a defect and is perceived by the individual through their eyes. The child is already socialized when Adlerian psychology begins to deal with it theoretically. The other visible centers of motivation are presumed to be of no importance, except as they fall within the sphere of a socially evaluated defect. This law of compensation is called "biological" and is Adler's attempt to base his psychology on biological premises. We have shown that while it is biological, it is not original and that it can only function in the Adlerian sense after social influence has intervened.

The biological law of compensation, as a phenomenon of all

5. *Ibid.,* p. ix.

living matter, plays just as important a role on purely psychical as on physical ground. It is the motor of psychic preservation and development; the propelling force of the motor is life itself.

Adler has termed such defects "organ inferiorities." According to him every inferiority produces an urge for betterment, for an adjustment to the demands of the environment which will compensate for the inferiority.[6]

There is a case, however, in which Adler deserts this plateau of evaluation of inferiority.

There are cases where this vegetative nervous system is abnormally sensitive (an organ inferiority) and as a result it functions more strongly than usual. We might add, however, that the source of irritation lies in the psychic structure of such persons, in their style of life. In such cases a small irritation produces a great reaction in those organs which are attached to this nerve system—the heart, the bladder, perspiration glands or digestive apparatus—as in the case of this girl.[7]

This is where he indicates that should the vegetative nervous system be abnormally sensitive it can be viewed as an organ inferiority and reacted to. It is difficult to see how others could aid the individual in making the judgment that his vegetative nervous system was inferior, and still more difficult to see how, if this aid be lacking, the individual could make it for himself.

We should emphasize that the concept of organ inferiority and compensation is undoubtedly a useful one, but we must say that monistic pursuit of it may take our attention from other equally useful, and more primitive, concepts of organ function, such as hunger cravings, aggressive reactions, and needs for sleep and warmth. The only craving we perceive through Adler's eyes is one that seems to develop when the individual is already partly socialized, and it seems to follow the single idea of psychic compensation for physical defect.

6. *Ibid.*, pp. x–xi.   7. *Ibid.*, p. 299.

For example, in the case of Miss R her reluctance to be weaned is interpreted as a wish for attention.

"I never had any appetite, never liked to eat anything. I could not stand the taste of food and I chewed the morsels as if they were paper or grass. I remember vaguely that my parents complained of me to our physician. The only thing that had any taste was mother's milk; I am said to have fought desperately every attempt to wean me."[8]

The organic fact of the wish to suck and the pleasure derived from the activity is disregarded. The relevant wish for sucking pleasure, easily demonstrated in every child, is replaced by the wish (already socialized) for attention. Unless children are assumed to be born with this wish for attention apart from its direct physical service to them, it is hard to see how this assumption is realistic.

As the individual grows older and he is geared more efficiently into the social machine, we find a wish for "superiority" appearing. This wish in the case of the neurotic is said to invest every psychic phenomenon in the individual's life.

The neurotic thus has the fictive goal to strive for in order to make safe his ostensible superiority. His actions are directed from this point and maintain a typical pattern. The compulsion to secure superiority is so powerful that every psychic phenomenon constitutes, aside from its outward appearance, an attempt to get rid of the feeling of weakness or inadequacy, to gain the height, to rise from below to above.[9]

For example, it is at the bottom of our imitative tendencies.

There is no such thing as an imitative instinct. We imitate something because it pleases us, because it appears efficacious in our attempt to achieve superiority. Imitation, therefore, belongs in the realm of the striving for recognition and must be so

8. *Ibid.,* p. 9.   9. *Ibid.,* pp. xvi–xvii.

understood. The imitation of her older sister indicates that the child imitates only that which fits into her style of life.[10]

We imitate that which supports our feelings of superiority. In this case the craving for superiority is assumed to be a straight natural fact about man; he does not wish to be superior in order to "get something" or guarantee something which he has, but for its own sake. There seems to be no doubt that there are some adults of this type in our culture, but the question is whether they are *the* type of human being which exists in our society or some sort of specialization of a more generalized type. We doubt whether this concept alone will carry the load of accurate description of our nature.

Adler rejects inherited or inheritable traits as a necessary concept and sees the new-born infant as completely and plastically accessible to social influence.

According to Adler, it is unnecessary to believe in inherited or inheritable character traits. Every one can achieve everything in life, even his own misfortune. For the alleged neurotic disease is nothing but the price which the cowardly, asocial egotist has to pay for offending the "logic of life."[11]

In this he would seem to be quite in accord with the best results of the comparative study of culture. In rejecting any rigid trait or instinct hypothesis he also seems to reject the activities which the new-born infant is plainly set to carry out and prefers instead to jump, in theory, the whole organic nature of man and to accept motivational concepts that are already within the sphere of social influence, such as wishes for attention and superiority. The organic individual in Adler's psychology appears as a kind of ghost up to the time when it can psychically respond to the motivations of others; further the exact nature and relationship of physical and psychic compensation are unclear, now seeming to be pro-

10. *Ibid.*, p. 48.   11. *Ibid.*, pp. xv–xvi.

cesses that set in automatically and without reference to the social milieu and again seeming to be results of the individual's awareness of the negative evaluations of him by others.

The normal individual is not exempt from such feelings of inferiority but is compensating for them on "the useful side of life," that is, to phrase it our way, they correspond with the preferred scheme of life of his culture.

One can, however, think of inferiorities which are to be found in a healthy body and normal mind and which arise solely out of the fact that this body and mind are comparatively less developed than the majority of human beings. This is the situation which every child meets in early life.

On account of his limited abilities, every healthy child feels himself inferior, consciously or unconsciously, in a world of gigantic and apparently self-sufficient adults. That is the relative feeling of inferiority which is compensated under favorable conditions by a striving for recognition on the "useful side of life."[12]

Children are said to feel inferior because of their small size in comparison with the adults with whom they deal. This inevitable "inferiority" may itself be a sufficient background for a conduct disorder or for a powerful and useful type of behavior. It is not especially, according to Adler, that children want to *do* what adults *do*, or *have* what they *have*, but in some way they wish to be as adults are for its own sake and for the egoistic gratification which it brings.

The neurotic, for Adler, seems to be a person who has failed to work out his wishes for attention and superiority in relationships with the wider community and who attempts to control his family in order to secure in this intimate milieu the gratifying sense that he is afraid to compete for outside the guaranteed family milieu. Adler seems to feel that the

12. *Ibid.,* p. xi.

neurotic achieves his neurosis with some kind of malevolent will and is responsible himself for his own rejection of the "logic of life." This leads him to take a certain denunciatory tone in respect of the neurotic person, regarding him as a malingerer rather than as a victim of his culture or biological inadequacy. Organic differences between people seem to exist only when they fall under the principle of compensation for what is evaluated as defective by the community.

Under-functioning of an organ, as in the sense of smell or sight, may lead to compensatory reactions which make the individual in adult life especially skillful in the use of such senses.

"Once in a while I found red spots in mother's bed or on her nightshirt."

Interest in what is visible.

"When I asked her, 'Mama, why do you bleed from your back?' she replied that she had piles from which she actually suffered at times. Then I crept to the seat where mother had sat and sniffed around it. Very soon I knew this smell so well that I could detect it on every woman."

A good sense of smell may signify an organ inferiority, but it would be a mistake to assume that only the under-functioning of an organ indicates a defect. Overfunctioning is just as much an inferiority and can give rise to exactly the same difficulties as when the organ operates badly.[13]

For example, an organ inferiority in respect of sight is posited for Miss R and it is frequently remarked how much of her behavior is distinguished by special visual sensitivity. In this case it is clear that sight and smell and the other senses are granted as organic capacities of the body, but again they are seen as important only when they differentiate the individual from others in some way; what the child actually saw and smelled in the citation given seems to have been

13. *Ibid.*, pp. 67–68.

neglected in favor of a judgment about the organ. From the theoretical standpoint the organs might as well not be there unless they lead to compensation in some way. Over-functioning of an organ can also be an inferiority.

In some ways we may say that Adler neglects the ground plan of the body except as it comes under later social evaluation and gives rise to feelings of inferiority which must then be compensated in some manner. He has stressed the useful fact of compensation for perceived organic defect. He has shown us organic motivation in the specialized form of a wish for attention and superiority. We have noted that there seems to be no identifiable organic base for these assumptions and that they seem rather elaborations of organic capacities than primitive and structural aspects of the body. We see them first when they are already involved in the responses of others. We note that many of the cravings and motor impulses of the body which are plain to be seen and easily described are not included as a basis for the development of this psychology. We feel that the response of Adler's psychology when questioned from the point of view of our criterion is unsatisfactory.

Criterion III. The peculiar role of the family group in transmitting the culture must be recognized.

The material on the recognition of the family in our case study is very scattered and spotty. For example, Adler makes very little use of the idea that in our culture it is the patriarchal family into which the child comes, nor does there seem to be any systematic concept of the influence of this family as a form on the life of the child. The view of the mother which we get is that she "usually" pampers the child.

The mother represents to the child her first connection with the world. The mother helps her and usually pampers her. The second phase sets in later when the child has become somewhat more independent. She seeks to attach herself to those persons who treat her best; that is to say, she either remains attached to her mother or turns to others. Here the mother had started to pamper the child but apparently could not compete with the father in the child's attention.[14]

It is not stated how "pampering" differs from nursing, feeding, cleaning, dressing, and otherwise caring for the helpless infant. The child is assumed to turn to the parent who gives it the most "attention." This concept of "attention" evidently does not mean just looking at or noticing the child, but we cannot be very sure in using it just what it does mean in addition to this.

The parents are seen, in the main, as lay figures in the child's determined plan for getting attention from the milieu and it manipulates them as well as it can to this end. One might say that in Adler's view the parents are seen entirely from the child's point of view. The idea that they are culture surrogates who have a specific social structure to transmit to the child is difficult to discern. The parents are dealt with and are present in the life history but rather as individuals to be worked around according to the child's need for attention than as surrogates of an imperious culture. He seems to show some partial appreciation of this view when he says that a given trait is not inherited "but lies in the atmosphere of the house."

"I was very happy about my first shoes; they were hardly put on my feet when I opened the door and tried to run away with them."

That is an attempt to insure their possession. Her father is a tailor; the whole family is prone to appreciate the external. This is therefore not an inherited trait but lies in the atmosphere of the house.[15]

This atmosphere of the house is a tentative toward describing the structure of the culture and the family.

14. *Ibid.*, pp. 5–6.   15. *Ibid.*, pp. 12–13.

It is indicated that Miss R, as a little girl, identifies with her parents at various points, as when, in the case given, she imitates her father, who is a tailor, and patterns a dress.

"I liked still more to play with a beer bottle."
We know that children would rather employ their own fantasy than play with mechanical toys. . . . The child learns by imitation. That, however, she can do only when she identifies herself with others, when she plays a rôle which she has assumed from her father and mother. She imitates her father when she patterns a dress.[16]

We must remember, of course, that this imitation is assumed to take place only when it gratifies the child's sense of superiority. No finer psychological differentiation is made with regard to the concept of imitation and it is used pretty much as in lay speech. However, in endeavoring to give a correct interpretation of Adler on this point we have scoured the text for any illustrations which would show the awareness of the family form. The instances seem rather unsystematic and are not frequent. In a number of cases he seems to show a definite indifference to the family form. For example, when he discovers in the autobiography of Miss R that she is a Roman Catholic he makes no use of this concept in interpreting the material.

"I was awake at about five o'clock and peeped through the window to see if the weather was good. When I heard the hammering which accompanied the fastening of the little trees and saw flowers spread over the walks, I was overjoyed. At half-past eight father brought me to the gathering place of the procession. I wore an angel costume with a crown and wings. Then I was placed under my little canopy and permitted to carry an image of the Holy Virgin."
These recollections show the girl's interest in external beauty.[17]

16. *Ibid.*, p. 13. 　　　　　　17. *Ibid.*, p. 56.

It would certainly seem to be a fact of relevance in her milieu that she grew up in a Roman Catholic family. Instead he comments on the paragraph which reveals that she is a Catholic by pointing out her interest in "external beauty." He shows at this point a marked lack of sensitivity to the cultural implications of the family form.

Another rather shocking type of indifference to family organization is contained near the end of *The Case of Miss R*. The girl has recited her difficulties and compulsions throughout the book. Then we learn that her parents were not married during her entire childhood, that Miss R is technically an illegitimate child, and that her parents were married at the time when her father was at the point of death.

"My parents were still not married. Mother was much troubled lest I remain an illegitimate child. When the doctor left her in no further doubt as to father's condition—I only learned about this afterward—and prepared her for the worst, mother talked matters over with Olga's mother. This woman ran straight for a priest."[18]

This would seem to be a fact of utmost importance about the organization of the R family and yet Adler has no comment to make on this fact. Certainly it casts a light on the often reported jealousy of her father and must have seriously affected the girl's life. It is hard to feel that Adler takes family life very seriously when he can omit to evaluate such a fact. It does indeed seem that the family in the cultural sense does not exist in Adlerian theory; the parents are rather viewed as pawns in the status and security scramble of the child. Their behavior toward the child is revealed as "pampering" or in some way ministering to the child's need for attention and status; they are not, however, seen as having highly configurated cultural roles in terms of which they manage the child. This point is so crucial in theory that it could not help

18. *Ibid.*, p. 297.

but appear in the analysis of such a case as that of Miss R if it were a part of the conceptual structure of Adler's psychology.

Criterion IV. The specific method of elaboration of organic materials into social behavior must be shown.

We have observed under the discussion of criterion II that the organic underpinning of Adler's system consists of two facts: first, organ inferiority; and second, a biological and psychic attempt to compensate for such inferiority. We were compelled to conclude that "compensation," in the psychic sphere, involves evaluation of the defect by others and is therefore already a concept in the social sphere. It is difficult, we found, to find a statement of the organic assumptions in the Adlerian system apart from the fact of physical defect. We are still puzzled on the question as to whether a "need for attention" does not need to be postulated as an organic fundamental in the Adlerian system; very likely, we feel, it does, but Adler himself does not seem to make such a specific postulate, much as the system needs it from the logical standpoint. We will find in this section that, if we attempt to describe how the organic is socially elaborated in Adler's system, we will be confined to the responses of the subject to organic inferiority and to "attention" from others.

We find that for Adler "every wish is a wish to rise" and that other wishes or organic demands are seen as secondary to this wish.

But every wish is a wish to rise, to win more power and security, to improve one's situation and position in the community. When sexuality shows itself a suitable means for this purpose, it is adapted to the striving for power and serves as a weapon to achieve success.[19]

The sexuality of the individual is viewed as subserving his need for power and status; this is also true of fear, as was

19. *Ibid.*, p. 251.

shown when Miss R went to a hospital as a child and disliked having her throat examined.

"I remember being brought to the children's hospital. I disliked having some one look into my throat and I was afraid of the tongue depressor."

There is a tendency to reject the doctor. The pampered child is anxious to be an object of pity.[20]

She manifests fear in order to be seen as a pitiable object, not because she is actually afraid. Jealousy also is a phenomenon that appears in the quest for superiority and its relationship to the love impulse is not important.

The fact that jealousy is to be found so frequently in love relations does not justify its being classed as an exclusive expression of sexual love. Jealousy is very often a matter of prestige.

"When my mother caressed my father, I frequently interfered, stroked his hair, rolled up his shirt sleeves and kissed his arms."

I do not believe that this is an expression of sexual love. Any explanation based on sexual considerations is fallacious.[21]

In this system we do not need to be concerned, therefore, with how sexual craving, jealousy, or fear are elaborated in human relations because we see them as by-phenomena to the powerful craving for superiority and status.

We have a good example of the social elaboration of a physical defect in the case of eye defects; this seems one of the most useful aspects of Adler's theory and shows how he handles the social elaboration of biological factors.

Many dramatists have had eye defects; their training has sprung from such defects. One must be able to see before one can visualize the presentation of a stage scene. This is easier for those who have placed seeing in the foreground. Such a training is a disadvantage when the difficulties are over-emphasized; on

20. *Ibid.*, p. 18.　　　　21. *Ibid.*, p. 16.

the other hand, an advantage can be seen in our appreciation of art.[22]

He believes that many dramatists have had eye defects and that in compensating for them they have somehow acquired the type of vision characteristic of their craft. We must note here, however, that eye function is taken by itself and that the emphasis is put on the fact of seeing and not what one sees. This stands in parallel to Adler's emphasis on the wish to be superior for its own sake, not for what one gets or does by being superior.

A much used concept in Adlerian psychology is that of "courage."

Pampered children always suffer from a strong feeling of inferiority because they grow up like hot-house plants, and therefore dread the raw reality of life as soon as they are brought in contact with it. But not only that. In order to retain their favorable position of security they will purposely exaggerate the harshness and difficulties of life and thereby lessen their courage. Their feeling of inferiority, which is nothing more nor less than the result of a wrong interpretation, becomes absolute and the urge to rule, as compensation for the inferiority sting, is intensified in direct ratio to the deepening feeling of inferiority. Thus the deplorable retreat of the neurotic is developed out of cowardice and excessive lust for power.[23]

Such a personality fact as courage must be one that is somehow elaborated in the growth of the organism; we are not told on what it is based; but we must note that it seems important. The neurotic, for example, will avoid conflict, retain a favorable and secure situation and thereby lessen his "courage." Since courage is a personality characteristic which could only appear in social relationships, it also must have a history, but we find nothing in the organic arsenal in Ad-

22. *Ibid.,* p. 99.   23. *Ibid.,* p. 21.

lerian psychology out of which it could develop. The antony-
mous concept of "cowardice" is used, but this also is introduced without footing in the organic life of the person.

A very important concept in the Adlerian psychology is
that of "social feeling," and an example of its use is given
here.

Now that we have seen that all neurotic characteristics are
distinctly opposed to the social feeling, that the neurotic strives
in a supremely egotistical manner for personal power at any
price, we can well assume that his devotion to his family is not
based on sincere affection, but is used as a means to obtain an
object to feed his lust for power. A nervous person needs the
family which pities him, which believes in him, and thinks he is
ill, as he needs his daily bread. He knows that he would be an
absolute nonentity without his family, abandoned without hope
of salvage to his feeling of insecurity and insufficiency.[24]

The neurotic is said to be defective in social feeling. It is obvious that this quality is developed in social interaction and
is not assumed to be a primitive characteristic of the organism; here again we reach for the organic substratum of the
concept but are not informed as to its genesis. The concept
seems to mean the person possessing it is useful and that his
behavior is serviceable to others. Apparently very young
children are lacking in social feeling; they are not receptive
to the restrictions which adults put on them and frequently
defy these limitations in order to show their superiority over
their parents.

"When we had cutlet, I imagined—that was my own invention
—that the fork was a woman and the morsel on it her hat; then I
let the hat-morsel on the fork-woman walk around the plate several times and afterwards ate it."

These are the well-known tomfooleries of children. They always have to listen to, "Eat now; otherwise you won't grow up!"

24. *Ibid.,* pp. 96–97.

They see clearly of what importance it is to the adults that they (the children) eat well. A child that feels inferior or oppressed— and only such a child comes upon the idea of protesting—can hardly find a better way by which to manifest an apparent superiority than by not yielding to the demands and commands of the adults, or as here, to laugh at them.[25]

The child apparently perceives the clamping down on him of cultural limitations as a continuous diminution of his feeling of superiority; if this is a correct paraphrase of Adler's point of view, it seems a very good point to be made. However, we are still at a loss as to how "social feeling" develops and we cannot find its organic roots.

Adler seems to evade this problem with a circumlocution, and a surprising one since it seems to attribute no importance to social impacts.

It does not matter what happens in the environment. What does matter is that the child attaches itself to its surroundings, that it develops social feeling, and then difficulties cannot produce negative results.[26]

The terms, social feeling and superiority striving, which are polar concepts in the Adlerian system, seem to be about equivalent to altruism and egoism, as they are used in ordinary speech.

In general, it may be said that the final judgment of every human attitude and action may be based, on the one hand, on this attitude's content of social feeling or altruism, and on the other, on the content of the superiority striving or egoism. One and the same action can therefore be useful or useless, depending upon whether it works with, without or against social feeling.[27]

We can see more clearly at this point the value of criterion II; without it we would not be able to state so decisively that

25. *Ibid.*, p. 61.   26. *Ibid.*, p. 93.
27. *Ibid.*, p. 96.

the two polar concepts seem dubious because they are not pinned down to identifiable organic facts. They seem rather descriptions of behavior which begin to be pertinent at some considerable time after the individual is born and when the maturational process in society has already been completed in part.

When we recur, however, to the matter of organ inferiority, we can find an account of how the organic is developed into socialized motivation. Adler tells us that he occasionally finds an organ inferiority of the digestive apparatus and that in such cases the later recollections of the person concern themselves principally with eating and food.

We hear a good deal about eating which permits the assumption of an organ inferiority of the digestive apparatus. Experience has taught us that those memories which are retained over a period of many years and remain particularly clear, frequently point to bodily deficiencies either acquired or congenital. . . . When recollections concern themselves principally with eating or food, they intimate a weakness of the digestive apparatus.[28]

Whether or not this conclusion is valid in fact, it is theoretically justifiable and accords with the demand of criterion IV. It would, of course, be necessary to stipulate carefully how the "inferiority of the digestive apparatus" made itself manifest in the behavior of the individual and what responses it elicited from the social "others" to enable the bearer to judge himself as inferior. If this could be done, the statement would be quite adequate from the theoretical standpoint and would be quite different from the case of the superiority urge or the "social feeling" impulse which do not seem to have an organic point of reference.

It is interesting to note that Adler specifically rejects the natural science explanation of glandular activity as a base for temperament and regards it as an unproven assumption.

28. *Ibid.*, p. 66.

Pure forms of temperament seldom occur; what we usually see are mixtures. A human being, during the course of his life, can also change from one temperament to another. The representatives of the natural sciences believe that temperaments are produced by the various activities of the inner glands, such as the thyroid gland, the sexual glands, the suprarenal glands and so on. This assumption is quite mechanical and has not been proved. We, on the contrary, regard the temperament as an expedient safety device, the development of which is determined by the degree of the feeling of inferiority and discouragement.[29]

He feels that temperament is variable and that a given individual can change his temperament in the course of his life. Temperament, for Adler, is related to the degree of inferiority feeling. The concept of temperament is loosely used here and it is very difficult to make out just what is meant by it, but we can see that Adler rejects to an extraordinary degree the usually assumed organic facts as the initiation point of his psychology and posits a very great plasticity in the organism. This may be the reason why he does not feel the need for making a firm conceptual statement of what the organism contributes to culture. The concept of compensation for organic inferiority is systematically stressed to account for the personality type of the individual.

We have learned from long observation and considerable study that the type to which an individual belongs is not mere chance. In very many cases it can be conclusively proven that the type to which a person has elected to train himself represents in reality a compensation for a defect in the functioning of one or more of the five senses, or a deficiency in the organs of motion (limbs). A congenital or acquired inferiority of the eyes, for example, calls forth a compensatory endeavor to overcome the inferiority in spite of the inadequate eyes and therewith starts a permanent training in the direction of the visual. Even if the

29. *Ibid.*, p. 153.

original organic inferiority vanishes completely in later years, the individual still pursues the same training pattern.[30]

The character form is set by the effort to compensate and is maintained even though the organic inferiority on which it is based has disappeared. The individual has "trained" himself to the compensation and goes on compensating.

We have observed in this section a series of concepts that deal with motivation; only in the case of the compensatory reactions to organic deficiency have we had specific reference to the organism. In the case of the other concepts, such as "social feeling" and "cowardice," we have not been able to discern how such characteristics arise and have viewed this fact as a logical failure in the Adlerian system.

Criterion V. The continuous, related character of experience from childhood through adulthood must be stressed.

Adler is quite as specific on this point as anyone could wish; indeed, it is from his work and that of other clinical psychologists that this criterion presents itself as imperative. Adler states his conviction that the development of a human being is largely determined in the first four or five years.

We go back to the very early years, because it is my belief that the development of a human being is largely determined in the first four or five years.[31]

He has provided us with the concept of a life goal toward which the person's actions are directed, a goal based on the balance of inferiority and superiority feelings. He speaks of a "style of life" which is determined in childhood and which is characteristic of all of the person's later adjustments.

A psychologist may commence the study of a life story where he will; he will always find that the particular life he is investigating is directed toward a certain goal. In order to understand a person's life, it is necessary to discover the thread which runs

30. *Ibid.*, p. 28.　　　31. *Ibid.*, p. 5.

through all his symptoms and which can be traced directly to his goal. We can also call this thread the style of life of a human being. The style of life is the special manner in which a human being faces life and answers the challenge of existence; how he feels, thinks, wants, acts; how he perceives and how he makes use of his perceptions. The style of life is formed by early childhood influences, developed in early childhood, and is guided by the goal of the person who follows it unquestioningly.[32]

He notes the manner in which an adult neurotic person selects his perceptual world in terms of his unconscious goal and style of life.

We must remember the extraordinary ability of the psyche to arrange, correct, choose, exclude and purposively apperceive. When we remember this, we can then understand that where the psychical apparatus has become the instrument of a neurotic goal, the intellect, governed by feelings, arranges, chooses and purposively apperceives such facts as will not disturb the neurotic development, or the neurotic goal, and the neurotic finally appears to us as a poor, pitiable victim of circumstance. He plays a trick and is fooled by it himself.[33]

We might remark at this point that unconscious mental activity plays some role in Adler's psychology, although he seems to refer to it occasionally when in need rather than use it systematically as a concept; there is, for example, no coherent theory as to why certain trends are said to function in behavior without the scrutiny of consciousness.

Underlying and unifying the acts of an individual, as we have seen, is the goal of superiority which the person has set for himself.

The sum total, in a cross section, of all forms of expression of an individual is called his behavior pattern; his method of approaching his personal goal of superiority is termed his style of

32. *Ibid.*, p. 50.   33. *Ibid.*, p. 207.

life. When we discover the goal of an individual, we are then able to trace his behavior pattern and style of life and to disclose and modify his entire life scheme.[34]

He approaches this goal via his style of life. If a normal person, the individual gratifies his craving for superiority in a useful way in the real world and balances it by altruistic tendencies. If the individual is a neurotic, he may set a false goal of superiority, one not to be achieved in reality, and comfort himself for his failure to actualize it in the wider environment by stressing his control over persons in the indulgent family group.

The neurotic's style of life and the arrangement of his particular neurosis are closely connected. The feeling of inferiority, arising from actual facts, then inflated and later on maintained for certain tendencies, drives the patient to set his goal in early childhood far beyond all human proportions. In order to intrench this goal he surrounds himself with a widely ramified net of precautions, all of which tend to maintain his superiority. In a case of washing-compulsion the goal in view is to be the cleanest human being on earth, an entirely useless enterprise, of course. What really happens is that this superhumanly clean person neglects the simplest duties of social life (including cleanliness), avoids responsibilities, exerts pressure on others, retreats from reality with many excuses, but still retains a well-fed feeling of superiority ("No one is as immaculately clean as I am . . .")—at least in the small circle of the family.[35]

A washing-compulsion is interpreted as the wish to be the cleanest person in the world, and therefore superior in this point; we should welcome a reference at this point to the cultural prescriptions which stress cleanliness in childhood and to the organic tendencies which these prescriptions meet.

Adler feels so strongly the configurated, unified quality of the individual's life that he believes himself able to interpret

34. *Ibid.,* p. xii.   35. *Ibid.,* pp. xviii–xix.

the life of the person on the basis of a single particularly clear remembrance from childhood. He tells us that individual psychologists are able to interpret the speaker's life to him once they have such a memory.

And so when an adult tells us of an early remembrance (it matters little whether it is the first or not) which is particularly clear to him, we are able to interpret from it the speaker's personal attitude toward life. This is, in essence, the attitude he has retained up to the moment of telling, even should that be twenty, thirty or forty years later. If his attitude toward life has changed in the course of years, the childhood memories which occur to him before and after such a change will differ.[36]

The attitude revealed by the memory is felt to be continuous during the life of the person from childhood on. We find at this point that Adler accepts our criterion in a very extreme form and would probably state it more rigorously than we do. In several cases Adler gives us autobiographical bits about himself, but he does not interpret them in the line of his theory, nor indeed would we put this demand upon him.

When I was two years old, my parents took me to hear some singers of popular songs. I heard good and bad things. I saw some operettas at the age of five or six. Who knows what might have become of me if they had not taken me along? I hope my power of resistance is appreciated since I had to swim through such turbid waters. These things are not so harmful as they seem; the anxiety of parents is exaggerated.[37]

They seem to show that he attaches great importance to the actual events of childhood and to the specific pressure of the social milieu in developing the life style of the individual.

Adler's acceptance of criterion V is quite complete and leaves nothing to be desired in point of specificity.

36. *Ibid.*, p. 6.   37. *Ibid.*, p. 71.

Criterion VI. The "social situation" must be carefully and continuously specified as a factor.

We have seen that Adler places tremendous stress on the manipulation of the environment by the individual in the service of his superiority cravings. He tends to see the social situation confronting the patient as an opportunity for intensifying or damaging his evaluation of himself in this sense. For the neurotic person the presented social situation is something to be shunned, since he always fears that a contact with the culturally stipulated outside world will result to his disadvantage or will fail to confirm his exaggerated claims for precedence.

The futility of all neurotic efforts to master, without an appropriate justification, the world in which we live, induces such individuals to retreat farther and farther until they reach that vast region where responsibility for their activities is no longer required. I mean the region of disease.

The sick are exempted from duties, the sick are irresponsible, especially when they are supposed to be mentally sick. To use the cloak of disease as a means to attain one's goal is a dangerous deception, for the patient himself, who does it unconsciously, as well as for every one who is taken in by it.[38]

We note, however, that Adler does not take much pains to specify the situation apart from the subject's interpretation of it. He does seem to be aware in a general way of the significance of social rank, as he comments that Miss R wishes to out-rank everyone else in the outside community; but it is a very general way and the impression is clear that the social situation is uniformly undervalued.

Her father was a tailor. We see how significant social rank is to her. If her father had been a shoemaker, and his a tailor, she would have argued in the same way; that is to say, the shoemaker would then have been better. From this one sentence we can de-

38. *Ibid.*, p. xv.

duce that this girl wants to surpass every one, not only in the family, but in the outside community as well. As a consequence, she can give but little to the community.[39]

For example, a man says he wants to get married and have a child. He falls in love with one girl after another and each one rejects him. The result is that he is in exactly the same spot after twenty years as he was when he started; namely, unmarried. The world pities him since he obviously makes every effort to win a wife. The world does not bother to examine the sincerity of his efforts very closely. If it did, it would see that he probably always approaches a type which he knows in advance will refuse him; or that he makes his courtship so clumsy an affair that he is sure to be unsuccessful; or that his behavior toward the woman makes him impossible as a prospective husband; in short, that he does everything to prevent the actual steps leading to a marriage in order that he may remain within the fortress he has built because of his fear of women.[40]

The sense of a structured communal life against which the neurotic works out his attempts toward compensation is quite lacking; rather the external situation is a mere shadow played upon by the compensatory strivings of the individual. It is not that Adler is altogether unaware that even neurotic persons live in a culture; he is aware of this fact and he points out how they fail to consider "the general human purpose of the community."

We find this form of private intelligence throughout the reflections of all kinds of persons with conduct disorders, such as problem children ("because I don't want to . . ."), neurotics as in the present case, insane people ("because I am influenced by electric currents"), criminals ("because he has better clothes than I"), suicides ("because life has no meaning"), perverts ("because perversions are a higher form of love culture"), drunkards, morphinists ("because I cannot live without these

39. *Ibid.*, pp. 119–120.   40. *Ibid.*, pp. 207–208.

remedies"), superstitious people ("because something brings good luck or bad luck") and so on. All are justifications to the attainment of personal goals, but not one considers the general, human purpose of the community. And that is why they all belong in a neurotic system.[41]

It is just in this failure that the neurosis lies, according to Adler. This "general human purpose" can only be the culture itself because these are the only formal ends that individuals can be expected to serve. But in the concrete use of the social situation we find that Adler attributes very little potence to it and does not see the value of accurately specifying it. It is quite probable that this is a defect in his system which we will find also to be shared by the other clinical psychologists; they are bound to be limited in that they were created in our own culture and their creators are subjected to all the limitations of concept and insight which our culture imposes. In establishing the integrated character of the mental life of the individual they have tended to react against the current overvaluation of the social situation in sociological thought.

Criterion VII. The life-history material itself must be organized and conceptualized.

It must be quite clear from the foregoing that Adler does stand off against the life-history material and give conceptual form to it. His analysis of the case of Miss R is a good example in point. He takes the material, paragraph by paragraph, sometimes sentence by sentence, and exposes its systematic content according to his conception. We cannot challenge him with failing to organize and systematize his observations.

It must be clear by now that in proposing these criteria for the life history we are not trying to attack his scheme of interpretation. For example, we have no objection to Adler's

41. *Ibid.*, p. 275.

interpretation of neurosis as such, nor do we contrast it with, say, Rank's and make a choice of points of view. The writer does not feel that the present state of the life-history field justifies this attempt. Every "competent" person must approach Adler's analysis for himself and decide as to its usefulness. We are here concerned only with this question, Does Adler give systematic intellectual form to the life history material and adopt a consistent position? And we answer that he does. Almost any one of the citations already indicated will convince the reader of this point of view. We have only to remind ourselves of his concepts of organ inferiority, physical and psychic compensation, striving for superiority, inferiority feeling, social feeling, life goal, style of life, behavior pattern, masculine protest, and others, to realize the force of this point. They constitute a conceptual apparatus which is at least workable whether it be the most adequate way of formulating the data or not.

THERE are a few things to be said about Adler's psychology which do not fit easily into the framework of the criteria cited above and which are not directly relevant to them. We will, however, take the liberty of making a few of these points. Adler does not consider a neurosis to be a disease in the usual sense of that word but defines it rather as a "mistaken way of living," that is, as a deviation from the culture of the neurotic individual. On the other hand, he does consider that the neurotic is "responsible" for his neurosis in some sense.

We do not believe a neurosis to be a disease per se, but hold it to be a mistaken way of living. Therefore, in that which does not exist we cannot take refuge. I have no objection to using the terms illness or disease as figurative expressions, but the mechanism is different. One must never lose sight of the fact that a human being is not responsible for an infectious disease of which he is the innocent victim (diseases such as pneumonia, diphtheria, typhoid, etc.), but he is responsible for a neurosis. Disease is accompanied by damage to parts or to the whole of the organism; neurosis in itself is not.[42]

By this responsibility he seems to mean simply that while organic disease is accompanied by organic damage, neurosis is a result of a reaction of the person's superiority craving to the responses of others. This seems a valuable distinction which Adler shares, to be sure, with the other clinical psychologists. Therapy takes place when the individual is made to see his fictive unconscious goal of superiority and to take the responsibility for a life which is actually his. The criterion of cure lies alone in the efficiency with which the individual later manages his cultural world.

Symptoms are small parts, but we are interested in the whole human being. A criterion for a cure lies alone in how the entire individual reacts in the future to life and to the demands life makes of him.[48]

We cannot fail to note in Adler's psychology a certain contemptuous and denunciatory attitude toward the neurotic person. There is a certain robust color about Individual Psychology and a husky contempt of the strong man for the weak one which reminds us much of the older theories of the disease. The reference to parental care as "pampering" is an example, and in the same citation we observe that Adler's comments often sound like an indictment of Miss R.

"Mother made some sandwiches for me to take along to school; sometimes I had chocolate too. But I rarely touched my breakfast. I either gave my sandwiches away or took them home with me again. I felt a dislike for other children, for their hair, for their smell."

42. *Ibid.*, pp. 83–84.   43. *Ibid.*, p. 274.

This is to be expected from this type of spoiled child. In the parks one often sees children who make gestures warding off the others. That means the exclusion of others. Such a gesture indicates a pampered child who abjures strangers and wants to be only with the familiar, yielding members of her family.

"And I often wondered how they could eat anything in that smelly atmosphere."

Her superciliousness increases.[44]

At this point we tend to take more seriously his statement that the neurotic is responsible for his neurosis and we are puzzled when we think back to another contention of Adler's, namely that real events in the life of the child bring about the neurotic reaction. The latter idea would seem to place the responsibility for the neurosis with the culture. However, we cannot solve this dilemma; we can only point it out. We find a constant reference in Adler's comments to life as a "battlefield" and the picture of the neurotic which comes to mind is that of a "slacker" from this battlefield.

So-called logical arguments are of no avail in attempting to free this girl of her compulsion ideas and compulsion acts. She must be shown, step by step, the real construction of her behavior as we see it. She would have to learn to recognize what the purpose of her symptoms is and what she achieves thereby; that she wants unconsciously to detach herself by compulsion from the compulsion of communal demands; that she has built a secondary battlefield in her intense desire to avoid the principal battlefield of life; that she wants to fritter away her time so as to have none left for the accomplishment of her daily tasks; that she intends to evade life's demands with excuses, curses, alibis or ostensibly good reasons.[45]

Such a citation as this one leaves little doubt of this attribution of personal willfulness to the neurotic. The character-

44. *Ibid.*, p. 64.   45. *Ibid.*, p. 290.

istic that seems to identify the normal person and the cured neurotic is a determination to "go the way of general usefulness."

And still there is a principle which convinces me that overemphasis does not have to disturb life, and that is the principle of social feeling. When I keep to the standpoint that, under any circumstances, I will go only the way of general usefulness, I can make no important mistakes. No one has yet been able really to disprove this principle.[46]

An unusual power seems to be attributed to this conscious determination to be useful, and it is implied that any one can do this if they only will. Altruistic feeling, apparently, can be developed in a fiercely compensating neurotic; how it is linked with the "socially relevant organic" is not theoretically designated.

Perhaps the clearest picture of the normal person is implied in the following citation.

The most satisfactory compensation for the feeling of inferiority is the development of courage, objectivity and social feeling. An individual compensating satisfactorily, approaches life in a sincere and fearless manner, tries to solve his problems and accomplish his tasks as they come along, and adapts himself to the smaller or larger community in which he lives. He trains in an upward direction, toward a superiority which is concerned with progress, improvement, adjustment to the world; in short, with useful things.[47]

There we learn that the striving for "useful superiority" is the essential and valuable characteristic, as opposed to the neurotic who presumably strives for useless superiority.

More should be made in our analysis of the way in which Adler's psychology is related to our current culture; it seems directly modeled on the competitive nature of current West-

46. *Ibid.,* p. 118.   47. *Ibid.,* pp. xii–xiii.

ern European society, and more specifically on the recent
movement upward of middle-class groups. We have referred
to the representation of life as a battlefield. This metaphor
is repeatedly used. A compliment to Miss R is represented as
a call to go to the "front of life."

Picture this girl: a compliment to her eyes works like a call to
go to the front of life. Now a compliment has been paid her teeth
and she is going to attack them.[48]

The motive of individual economic competition, so characteristic of our culture, is stressed repeatedly and we see the normal person as a climber for increased status in a real social
sense, and the neurotic as just the same climber but using
devious and unfair techniques.

She describes her suffering with much skill and penetration. An
antisocial, selfish life never leads to pleasure in the power which
has been won over a few people at the expense of so much exer-
tion. She sits like a tyrant on a throne which can be overturned
at any moment; she rules by fear and is herself ruled by fear.
She has to make her position in the "enemy country" secure by
cunning and brute force.[49]

At some points Adler describes the ethos of our culture with
great simplicity and power.

What matters is to make progress in life, to make oneself useful.
One does not make oneself useful by declaring that everything is
dirty and then resting on one's oars.[50]

Here he says "what matters is to make progress in life, to
make oneself useful." To be sure, these two ideas can easily
be incompatible, but the idea of progress is repeatedly
stressed. It seems to the writer that Adler's psychology could
be characterized as peculiarly bound by our culture and as

48. *Ibid.*, p. 189.   49. *Ibid.*, p. 289.
50. *Ibid.*, p. 205.

emphasizing in psychology the motive which is most characteristic of it. This is certainly a value which will recommend it to many observers, but it also imposes a limitation on its use as a generalized social psychology which must be adapted to use in cultures which do not exhibit our powerful status and money competition and which do not put such a premium on fighting. This close identification with the overhead structure of our culture may tell us why Adler puts so little emphasis on the organic life which is presented to the culture. This organic life is not immediately visible in terms of our formal cultural theory and it is the latter which Adler has taken as the model for his psychology. Some cultures might lend themselves very well to Adler's view, such as the West Coast Indian cultures,[51] while for others it would be a very inaccurate description. We have stressed, however, that the social psychology needed in social science will be applicable in general principle to any society and will not reflect too carefully the peculiarities of our own culture, as Adler's view seems to do.

We must note also the fact that Adler's psychology is in no sense a critique of our culture; it is a pro-cultural psychology. This is what we should expect from its apparent derivation from the cultural ethos of a moving middle-class group, striving to make itself superior to a dissolving upper class. Adler's scheme swims the tide with our culture and seems likely to arouse very little resistance. This may be why it takes a rather contemptuous view of the neurotic person and implies that it is the neurotic's own fault that he is sick; this is also the view of our wider society, which makes the same charge against the person who is out of work. We cannot help noting a certain moralistic note, that of preaching courage and confidence to the neurotic and attempting to

51. Sapir, Edward, "The Social Organization of the West Coast Tribes," *Transactions of the Royal Society of Canada,* Third Series, Volume IX, Toronto, 1916.

shock him out of his neurosis by exhortation. This is, of course, not a well-formulated part of Adlerian theory, but it is an impression that one receives from reading the case of Miss R and from the often contemptuous reference to her life-evasive behavior.

Adler wins our admiration for the boldness with which he takes a document, such as Miss R has provided, and gives us his free-running comments on it. He himself has enabled us to evaluate his system because he has taken concrete material, which any of us can read, and attempted to analyze it. Often he seems to write with knowledge that is not accessible to us and some of his inferences are not immediately convincing; but we reserve the possibility that lack of familiarity with his system is at fault. From the logical standpoint, apart from the theory of Individual Psychology, the writer often has difficulty in following Adler's arguments. They seem to have at some points an irrational quality which makes it difficult to put your finger on the point. Often he seems to exhibit a too great skepticism about what the patient actually says and feels, and disregards not only the expressed reaction of the patient but also the real situation as well. This is only an impression which I offer tentatively and it comes as a by-value of my reading of his book for other ends.

We must stress again that we are not applying the test of therapeutic efficiency to Adler's system, that is, how it works in a practical sense; rather we are applying the test of "how it works" in a scientific sense, that is, how it hangs together logically and how it fits into our knowledge from other fields.

CHAPTER IV

THE CRITERIA APPLIED: "THIRTY-ONE CON-
TACTS WITH A SEVEN YEAR OLD BOY."*

THIS book by a prominent follower of Rank will offer us the needed material for a review of his life-history theory and practice. Its publication is sufficiently recent (1933) so that it should give some kind of indication of Rank's views; it may well be that he has altered his position still more recently, and it would in any case be preferable to use a document by Rank himself. Unfortunately there seems to be none available in print.

We must note the aim of Dr. Taft's book; it is not a systematic attempt to present Rankian theory but is a contribution to the study of the therapeutic process. This does not invalidate it for our uses because there is, as we would expect, a close relationship between Rankian theory and therapeutic practice. Indebtedness to Rank is of course acknowledged. In endeavoring to explain "how she did it" Dr. Taft presents in this book two documents and adds a theoretical discussion of the material from point to point throughout the book. This case differs from the one selected to represent Adlerian psychology because Dr. Taft herself wrote down the material directly during the interview situation. The document discussed here is not a "life history" in the formal sense of the word, because very little attention is paid to specific incidents in the career of the subject apart from his birth and the continual emotional reinterpretation of his life in terms of the birth experience. In the sense of a longitudinal record of the

* Taft, Jessie, "Thirty-One Contacts with a Seven Year Old Boy," *The Dynamics of Therapy*, New York, The Macmillan Company, 1933, pp. 113–274. All of the extracts in this chapter are taken from this book with the consent of the publisher. The permission thus granted is warmly appreciated.

life of a person Rankians do not seem to gather life histories. This peculiarity of Rankian psychology will be discussed at length later. Such a record as this of a specific therapeutic situation is what we would expect, according to Rank's theory, from this school in lieu of a life history, and it will serve us for an examination of his theoretical structure as well as any document now available.

Dr. Taft has presented the case of a seven-year-old boy who offered a problem in permanent placement. His personality difficulties, including enuresis, were such that it was difficult to keep him settled in a foster home. The author of the book felt that some therapeutic interviews might be helpful to the end of making him a more suitable person in a foster home. Accordingly she gave him thirty-one interviews, took notes during the interview hours and reports the results, hour by hour.

We must express our admiration and gratitude to Dr. Taft for her courage and honesty in writing out and reporting the material of these interviews. It enables one to get a good picture of her theoretical as well as therapeutic practice and to get the feel of the Rankian approach to personality. It may well be that even the account presented by Dr. Taft does not give an altogether fair picture of her method or of the therapeutic situation in which she was involved with Jack; but her attitude and care in reporting the material convinces us that her reports give as complete a picture as she was able to give of what seemed to her relevant in the situation. Such care and honesty as she has exhibited makes scrutiny of her system possible and enables us to undertake a measured examination of it.

A disturbing question intrudes itself. Is it fair to examine a document which purports to be a discussion of the dynamics of therapy and in which theoretical presentation is only incidental? My answer is that it is fair, because the theoretical system is constructed in the first place only to manage such

materials as are presented in the therapeutic situation in the
case of these clinical psychologies. Certainly if theory is not
idle speculation and is really meant to master specific materials, it should be in evidence whenever a systematic account of a therapeutic situation is given. Furthermore, the
essential characteristics of the theory are bound to reveal
themselves in the treatment of specific materials. Very often,
as we shall show, the treatment of some casual bit of data will
reveal a whole theoretical perspective. One might say with
justification that in a consistent scientific theory the whole
implicative structure of the theory is present by inference in
every observation made. This is due to the coherent character
of a scientific concept system which does not tolerate frag-
mentary insights without recognizing them as defects in the
system and problems for research. We will now see what is
revealed about this system in the light of our criteria.

*Criterion I. The subject must be viewed as a specimen in a
cultural series.*

There are no statements which I can find in this document
that indicate a clear conception of Jack as an individual
added to a *group*, nor of the concept of a systematic habit
context to which he was added. We can afford to show the
same indulgence here that we have exhibited in the case of
Adler and state that we would hardly expect to find it since
the clinical psychologists are not handed, by their training,
a clear workable concept of culture. When Jack presents material which indicates that his personal culture stands in a
kind of continuity with that of his parents and older people,
little or no theoretical use is made of such material. Of
course, it is impossible to treat a human being by any type of
therapy without realizing that he is not a mere brute, and the
case report is full of implicit, unevaluated references to the
general structure and the peculiarities of Jack's culture. At
this point we are helpless to do anything more than note that
the idea of culture is strikingly absent from Rank's psy-

chology as exhibited by this document. This systematic neglect doubtless stands in relation to a view of the birth trauma as the important event in Jack's life; when we take this point of view it seems quite natural to us that the culture is viewed as a mere screen on which the affective forces generated by the birth experience are played. It could hardly have much of a role in the formation of the individual career and it would indeed be an unnecessary explanatory principle.

We notice with surprise also that the therapist does not view herself as a surrogate of the culture in the therapeutic relationship. She seems to feel that she comes "clean" of cultural influence into the situation and that what counts is the immediate interaction between her and the subject. An example of this is the point that she does not seem to regard it as important that she stands before her patient as a woman with a woman's role, as defined in our society, that she is a "doctor" with a doctor's role, that she is an older person with an older person's role, and so on. Naturally one would not expect her to take time to elaborate such concepts theoretically with all their background, but we might expect her, if she had a clear-cut cultural concept, to utilize them in the direct situation with her patient. They can hardly be unimportant, but it would seem that they are, if we accept this view of the growth of the person. There are several terms used by Dr. Taft which seem to imply in embryonic fashion the notion of culture. One such is the use of the term "limit." The child is represented as striving to find the limit of what the therapist will stand in the way of behavior.

Once more he returns to the rug to see if he can find the limit. "Can I fight with this?"

. . . .

"Go ahead and I'll see what you do with it. If you put it on the couch, perhaps it won't slip off too much." He doesn't like that, wants it on the floor. "Jack, you are just trying to see how much you can do without my taking the rug away, aren't you?"[1]

This seems like a vestigial acknowledgment of culture because, although there would be slight differences between individual therapists as to their "limits," the therapist herself would have her notion of the "limit" given to her by her culture. If we can conceive of Rank's therapy being applied in another culture we would immediately say that the range of limits might be quite different from those imposed on Jack by Dr. Taft. The writer of this life history seems to feel, however, that she herself sets the limit and that it is somehow a personal thing with her. This, of course, can hardly be the case. What we wish to stress here, however, is that after a fashion the cultural concept is acknowledged, but after such a limited and inadequate fashion that it only serves to remind us of how much is unacknowledged. We will note later that this therapy specifically disclaims any attempt to adjust the individual to his "environment," that is, to his culture.

Another example, in itself trivial, will help to make the point.

"I'm going to smash my watch and fix it." (This is a defiance in terms of his own property, where I have no right to object but where adults frequently do.)[2]

Here the therapist allows the child to smash his own property, if he wishes, and comments that by her therapeutic principles she has no right to object, but notes that adults usually do. This is again a marginal acknowledgment of the fact that older persons, in our culture, systematically protect property against destruction by children. Conservation of material things is one of the habits that children are persistently taught by older persons who act as surrogates of the

1. Taft, Jessie, *The Dynamics of Therapy,* New York, The Macmillan Company, 1933, p. 174.
2. *Ibid.,* p. 188.

culture in this respect. We might note that **Dr. Taft** does protect her own property but does not insist that the child conserve his. She has, in the therapeutic situation, relinquished one of the roles which adults systematically take toward children; she has, as it were, altered the form of the culture presented to the child. Evidently she feels that this culture is unfavorable to the recovery of her patient, but she is not able to state her problem in a cultural form, that is, to define her behavior as a modification of the culture.

We can only say from the foregoing that Rankian psychology does not seem to utilize the cultural concept and seems to have only vague intuitions as to how the culture functions in the individual life. Perhaps we shall discover something in the psychology which is specifically opposed to the concept of culture.

Criterion II. The organic motors of action ascribed must be socially relevant.

It is difficult in treating of these clinical psychologists to avoid the common error of merely uttering a phrase. Many persons seem to feel an enviable satisfaction when they are able to couple terms in the following fashion: Adler-inferiority, Freud-sex, Rank-birth trauma. These phrases provide an easy victory over the difficulties of mastering the theories in question. We will strive to avoid this over-simplification and to determine what of value there is in the above slogans. It seems that Rank views the organism as organized by the experience of birth; this experience with its organic reverberations and the attendant psychic attitudes is what the culture has to work on, even though, as we have seen, the role of the culture is not highly evaluated. By "birth trauma," of course, Rank does not mean only or chiefly the physical injury of the child during birth, but views the experience as one to which the child can react, ultimately psychically, and one which sets a reaction form to later experiences which may seem at first blush to be quite alien to birth itself. The fundamental view seems to be that of an organism utilizing its culture according to the exigencies of a psychic form established at birth, rather than that of a culture molding an organism into a preferred form and utilizing its organic propensities for this end. Other organic aspects apparently do come into play in the maturation of the individual, but their role is viewed as slight in comparison with the birth experience.

We cannot change the fundamental biological and psychological conditions of living for others, nor for ourselves, but somewhere within each individual is this same life process which can go on for and of itself, if the fear which has become excessive primarily in birth and the earlier experiences can be decreased in quantity sufficiently to permit the inherent normal ambivalence to function and hence to provide its own checks and balances.[3]

The concept of the fear originating in birth plays an extraordinary role in this psychology. Later experiences, such as the genital sexual experience, are seen to have their role primarily in diminishing the fear attendant upon the "grim organic memory" of the birth experience.

Even sex may fail as a natural therapy for fear if the grim organic memory of that first too forced and violent introduction to autonomous living has not been softened by the tenderness and restoration of union at the mother's breast, followed by some sense of ego achievement in the weaning and early habit training.[4]

We may assume that this memory, and the affects attendant upon it, is the organic fact most stressed in Rankian theory. Culture and its influence on other bodily capacities may play the role of intensifying or lessening this fear.

The concept of fear as a reaction to an external danger situation is specifically rejected and fear is assumed to be "inherent in individuation and self-consciousness."

3. *Ibid.,* p. 14.   4. *Ibid.,* p. 289.

Fear is a necessary part of all experiencing, a consequence not so much of immediate external danger as of the inherent ambivalence of the human being who must always be pulled in two directions, must always long for and avoid the problematic situation, must fear stagnation even while he resists his own impulse to growth. In other words fear is inherent in individuation and self-consciousness, in the necessity to be both part and whole.[5]

The individual is said to be inherently ambivalent and has two incompatible wishes, the one to individuate himself, the other to remain part of a larger whole. Fear is manifested when either wish threatens to be actualized.

We will note repeatedly the use of the term "will" in Rankian psychology. This is evidently a primary organic datum and is discovered in operation from birth on.

Guilt, as I have been using it in the Rankian meaning, is an inevitable by-product of self-conscious living, not a symptom of which one may be cured. It arises from the fundamental dualism of life itself as expressed in the ambivalence of will; that human capacity for wanting and not wanting the same thing at the same moment, and the bi-polarity of fear, on the one hand the fear of becoming a separate individual, on the other the fear of dying without having lived.[6]

The "will" is said to be ambivalent in the above sense. We will find frequent reference to this concept.

According to the author, each of the thirty-one hours of her therapeutic contact with Jack reveals this conflict between "the desire to come and the fear of coming, and second, of the struggle of the will to go and the fear of going."

The record of Jack, because it is longer and because Jack is a more self-conscious, verbal, emotionally sensitive child, is more difficult to follow as a whole than the first record but contains

5. *Ibid.*, p. 284.   6. *Ibid.*, p. 103.

the same general movement which consists first of the conflict between the desire to come and the fear of coming, and second of the struggle between the will to go and the fear of going. In each single hour one can trace a miniature therapeutic experience with its minor acceptances and resistances, its fears and its satisfactions.[7]

The movement of the therapeutic situation is traced in terms of the acceptance of both of these wishes and the domination of the impulse toward individuation. If we accept this system we must see "will" as a primary organic datum which is not further definable or referable to anything else.

Apparently various aspects of a fear experience generated at birth are subject to modification by the culture and are therefore "socially" relevant; we note that the patient has taken over an aspect of the birth fear and "transformed it into an ego achievement."

In the symbolic birth struggle of the 20th hour, "I'm getting born, I don't get hurt," Jack strikes the key note of a therapeutic experience with a favorable outcome. He has taken over the birth fear and transformed it into an ego achievement. . . . This is as it should be, the patient goes on to a new world which needs him as he needs it. It is the therapist who is abandoned, who, like the scapegoat, takes upon himself the death aspects of the birth process, and becomes the repository of the outworn self.[8]

This concept of the "ego" might well lead us in a new direction, but no systematic implication is given as to what the ego is or how birth fear is transformed into one of its achievements.

The concepts of birth trauma, fear, and ambivalence of the will evidently indicate organic propensities which are to some degree culturally modifiable and in this sense Rank's theory does meet our criterion. We have noted that guilt and

7. *Ibid.*, p. 274.   8. *Ibid.*, p. 282.

fear are modifiable through the later experiences of the individual of a direct organic kind, such as nursing and sexual contact, and still more significantly by the practice of psychotherapy which does not imply physical contact with the subject. In saying this we do not imply, of course, that Rank's description of the relevant organic factors is adequate as a basis for life-history theory, but we have specifically rejected the responsibility of discussing a theory from that standpoint. So far as criterion II is concerned Rank's organic assumptions *could* be adequate.

Criterion III. The peculiar role of the family group in transmitting the culture must be recognized.

The culture is made concrete for the child by the family; just because the family is this kind of out-post of the culture, the first to meet the organic life of the child, it plays a peculiarly important role in personality development in every society. This is true in a general sense of the "form of the family," by which we distinguish such characteristics as the roles of father and mother and their positions in the family, as well as the peculiarities and details of the structure of the given family. Our criterion is therefore of peculiar importance for evaluating any psychology which aims to be of service in cultural studies.

We have already noted that Rankian psychology seems not to be highly conscious of the cultural aspects of the individual with which it deals; its attention is centered on a single, probably very important, organic fact. We must now see what kind of justice it does to the fact of family organization.

In general we may say that Rankian psychology seems to be conscious of only one of the parents. If we were to judge family organization by the picture which it presents we should be inclined to make a very low estimate of the role of the father in our culture. It would seem that only the mother and the child's organic and other types of connection with her come in for systematic evaluation. Even then, she seems, after the child's birth, like a target for its affective life rather than like a real actor in the drama that forms the child's personality. We do not see a specific acknowledgment of her very important role in transmitting various types of taboo to the child. It would seem that she has done what she can when she has given the child birth. All of the other well-known aspects of her role as an acculturated person seem to be systematically neglected or undervalued. The awareness in Rankian psychology of the roles imposed on parents by their culture would seem to be very low and the significance of the father seems almost infinitesimal. If we were to judge by this psychology we would hardly suspect the existence of the type of relationship which we know to be a fact between parents in our culture.

We do learn various facts about Jack's home life, such as that his parents had quarreled frequently during his first six years of life, that his father was a hard drinker and beat his mother.

Mrs. H. requested that care be given John since she could not keep him any longer. She and Mr. H. had separated a year and a half ago after six years of continual quarrelling, drunkenness and fighting. The real difficulty between the two started when Mrs. H. was carrying Jackie. Mr. H. came home drunk night after night and beat her. Mrs. H. and Paul, the older boy, went to live with her mother. Jackie stayed with her sister who had three children.[9]

We also know that Jack had an older brother and that when the parents separated Jack was sent to live with an aunt. All of these facts seem to point to a family milieu significant for the fact of his difficulties. Very little use is made of these facts in understanding Jack's case or in the theoretical formulation of his problems, though they would seem to be natural

9. *Ibid.,* p. 127.

enough points from which to undertake an evaluation of the family life. We are told that he had an "apparently destructive attachment to his own mother," but are left to infer that the destructive nature of the attachment is to be connected with his reaction to organic separation from his mother.

When the record of this boy was sent to me by the reception worker for suggestions as to a permanent foster home, I was so dubious over the possibility of giving him a satisfactory home in view of the apparently destructive attachment to his own mother, and so impressed with the picture of extreme fearfulness and resistance to growth, that I proposed an experiment in preliminary therapeutic interviews with myself as an outside person unrelated to John as far as Children's Aid authority was concerned.[10]

We are told that his mother "failed to give him any real return in care or feeling" in response to his fixation on her and that this was one of the causative elements in making him a child difficult to place in a foster home.

In the picture of John H., as presented to me, I saw a comparatively young child of potential promise likely to prove impossible for placement because of the extreme fear, the excessive fixation on a mother who failed to give any real return in care or feeling, and a number of habits so hard to bear that any foster home placement could easily be broken up by them if John himself were resisting the situation inwardly, while accepting it outwardly.[11]

There is no attempt to account for this attitude on the part of his mother or no implication that such an understanding would be relevant to the life history, and incidentally to the therapeutic problem. There are certainly enough instances in the material which refer to the family to make us curious as to its role in Jack's life. For example, he seems to respond to loud voices in the hall which indicate people quarreling.

10. *Ibid.*, p. 125.   11. *Ibid.*, p. 126.

As he is getting the dolls out, the janitor and his wife talk noisily in the hall outside. He is all attention instantly.

"Is him and her fighting?"

"No, I think it's just that she has a loud voice. She sounds cross even when she isn't!"[12]

In view of the relations between his parents this would not seem surprising and we might expect our therapist to make theoretical use of this fact. However, she does not. This is unquestionably a defect in therapeutic knowledge as well as insight because if Jack were particularly alarmed by quarreling between older people, on the basis of his in-family experience, it might be well to have this fact in mind in selecting a foster home. Incidentally, in these quarreling scenes the father gets one of his few opportunities for theoretical recognition; it is not, however, accorded him.

Jack's mother evidently is a person who is indifferent, if not actually hostile, to him. At least she constantly breaks her promises to him and administers severe frustrations in actual current life.

Jackie is very attached to his mother. He looks for her to come every week and is continually disappointed by her not appearing. He does not want to go to another home. He wants to go back to his mother. On the other hand Mrs. H. is not so interested in Jackie. She visits him but once a month. She tells him she is coming and then does not appear. She promises him she will phone every day, then does not fulfill her promise. He never cries as a result of these disappointments, but seems crushed and resorts to infantile behavior as bed-wetting, being unable to dress himself, etc.[13]

In response to these frustrations he "seems crushed and resorts to infantile behavior." This information raises questions as to what kind of a person this mother can be. Cer-

12. *Ibid.,* p. 158.　　　　　13. *Ibid.,* p. 128.

tainly she does not conform to cultural expectation, though her type may be far more frequent than cultural ideals would lead one to suppose. If she had, for example, a chronic hostility toward this child, it might well be that this would be an immediate explanatory principle for the boy's behavior that would be quite useful in addition to the one offered. The fact that no such questions occur to the analyst of these materials indicates that the family organization is not taken very seriously by the writer of this document. At one point it seems that the therapist recognizes her own role as a mother surrogate, though she does not recognize that the mother in turn is a surrogate of the culture.

"I'm going to move in four more Saturdays."

"Oh, are you?"

"But I'll still come here," hastily.

"When you are in your new home, perhaps you won't want to come here."

"Oh, yes, I will. Mrs. T. will still bring me. When I go home for good, then I won't come any more." (This shows the rôle the therapist plays at this point as the child's most important relationship, but one he won't need once he is at home.)[14]

The picture of the mother that is maintained throughout is that of a kind of "organic" mother, not the person with a configurated role whom we think of as a mother in cultural studies.

We are informed also that the mother, when she does see him, treats him like a very small child, "dresses him, bathes him and even carries him round in her arms."

He continually wants to be babied and told what to do. His mother, aunt and grandmother always ask how the baby is and treat him like a two year old. His mother, when she visits in the foster home, dresses him, bathes him and even carries him around in her arms. The foster mother is at her wit's end about him. She

14. *Ibid.*, p. 225.

thinks she has made no progress with Jackie. She feels that she has tried everything to get him to change his behavior but has failed to bring about any good results.[15]

This would seem again to be a cue which would lead to an investigation of the attitude of this particular mother and a comparison of her behavior with the standard mother role in our culture. Such a comparison would, however, necessitate a live and vital concept of the family and would lead in directions not marked out by Rankian theory. It would seem, too, as though his actual mother had done for him some of the time just what he wanted and had reciprocated his fixation, and that her pampering of him must stand in some kind of relationship to the frustrations and disappointments she imposes upon him. However, such considerations would tend to direct attention to the parents and their role in the life of the child. Apparently one is not led by Rankian theory to discover the role of the parents.

We have several times noted that the mother's role in the character formation of the child is apparently skimped in Rankian theory; we must now repeat that the father's role in the child's life is elided altogether. While this may be true of the theory, it is not true of the boy.

"This is going to be a cute little table." He sets it with great enthusiasm. "The mother is going to sit here, and this is going to be the father's place, and the little doll will have to wait."

. . . .

He goes on with his playing.
"The dolls are going to eat in bed."
"Then they aren't father and mother, are they, Jack?"
"No,"—looking at me very shyly. "I'm the father"—pause— "and you are the mother, and they are the two babies." He collects enough articles to serve as sugar bowl, creamer, pepper and salt.[16]

15. *Ibid.*, p. 129.   16. *Ibid.*, p. 149.

We find him carrying out actions in which father, mother, and children as concepts are all required. We find him also putting the therapist in the mother's role and himself in the father's role. Such facts would seem to point to a vivid awareness of the fact of his father in his life; and why not, we ask, since his father has been a factor in the home situation for the first six years of his life. No use is made of these clues by the author and the father remains undiscovered, from the angle of this theory, as a factor in the life of his son. It must be clear from the foregoing that we would hardly suspect the nature of the Western European patriarchal family from the picture presented in this analysis, and we must conclude that the role of the family in Rankian psychology is greatly undervalued.

Criterion IV. The specific method of elaboration of organic materials into social behavior must be shown.

We will face in the data relating to this criterion a peculiarity of Rank's system of thought. Since he puts so little stress on the role of the culture in determining personality (via parental actions, of course) we will see very little in the way of elaboration of basic organic material into anything we might call "attitudes." That is, Rank makes very little use of the possibility that there is a social element added to the organic tendency which is then called an attitude or wish.

We have found in discussing criterion II that the concept of "will" plays a very important role in Rankian theory. This "will" with its full ambivalence is in action at the beginning of extra-uterine life and it is found continuously through the life of the patient, without modification by the culture, so far as we can see. It is a difficult concept to deal with because it does not seem to be related to any specific organic apparatus; we must, however, work with what Rank gives us to work with. We see that therapy itself depends on a conflict of wills between the therapist and the subject.

Since for the child as for the adult, it is no particular goal which is desired but the process of striving and testing one's strength, any set up no matter how carefully guarded will be utilized eventually for the will conflict on which therapy depends.[17]

This conflict of wills is shown at many points in the study in mischievous acts on the part of the patient, as where he throws a ball against the wall of the interview room violently, and where by begging for a little pamphlet he gets it and breaks the rule of not taking things home from the interviewing room.

After a good many violent throws, looking at me anxiously, "Do you think the ball makes a spot?"

"I don't think so, Jack." He tries it out thoroughly, finally almost rubbing the ball against the wall. "It doesn't seem to, does it? I guess you wish it would, don't you?" (The old will conflict is a relief from the inside pressure.)

"No, I don't want to dirty the pretty wall."[18]

"And can I have that little book?" The book is only an advertising book, and I decide to give in and let him have it. This is a terrific victory, and he kicks up his heels and stamps around at a great rate, throwing the window open.

"*You* had your way that time, didn't you, Jack?" He grabs a pillow and begins fighting. "Listen here, you shut up. Here comes a man. I'll lock the tent so he can't come in." (Begins to feel the fear of success.)[19]

This will can be "unconscious," destructive, and negativistic.

Her will is too unconscious, too impulsive, too negative. It is determined largely by a need to resist someone else rather than a pressure to be itself. It takes no responsibility for itself, finds no planned constructive expression but is content to defeat and

17. *Ibid.,* p. 124. 18. *Ibid.,* p. 184.
19. *Ibid.,* p. 178.

destroy in opposition to other wills. What saves her is the comparative absence of strong hatred.[20]

The will of the patient can also take over responsibility for the "cure," and the patient is cured when he is able to leave the analytic situation.

The analyst in this view has no goal, has no right to one. He *is* passive in the sense that he tries to keep his own ends out of the situation to the extent of being willing to leave even the "cure" so-called, to the will of the patient. The patient is there to work out his own will and to use the therapist as he can, even to the final overthrow and destroying of the analytic situation.[21]

The term "will" which is used here as some kind of an element becomes more and more indispensable to Rank's system but does not become clearer as one finds further uses for the term. We will note again that the will has both positive and negative aspects and may manifest itself both by the desires to be free and to be bound, and by resistance to both desires; both may be exhibited in the transference situation.

Transference, like resistance, is accepted for what it is, a stage in the growth process, in the taking over of the own will into the self. It is the point at which the will is yielded up to the other, is worshipped, if you please, in the other and kept in abeyance in the self.[22]

The analyst must be able to tolerate the patient's "will to leave" and be resigned to be the person left behind at the end of the treatment.

Both aggression and what is more or less its equivalent, the negative compensatory reaction are recognized.

The therapist by bringing out unfailingly the aggressive intent which such reactions mask and not allowing these slight unrec-

20. *Ibid.,* p. 104.   21. *Ibid.,* p. 108.
22. *Ibid.,* p. 97.

ognized hostilities to mount to proportions which cannot be handled therapeutically, can usually help the patient to feel them in embryo and to accept them responsibly as part of the self however painful, without the necessity to put them out blindly in a truly injurious form.[23]

He hates to stop, and delays as usual.

"You won't see me for a long time, Jack."

"I'll still be happy."

"You won't care a bit? Well, that's good. You let me be the one to care. I'll have to be sorry. Let's see when you are coming again, Jack. Next Tuesday, isn't it?" He looks a little doubtful. "Maybe you are tired of coming?"

"Yes, I am tired," he says.*

"Well, you don't have to come any longer than you want to, but I think you'd better come once more anyway, so you come on Tuesday and bring the key back, and then we'll see if you want to come any more." He looks a little startled with himself for having said this. Perhaps the key was taken to insure return.

* *n.* Here we get the full negative compensatory reaction to my desertion.[24]

In the latter case the negative reaction seems to be due to a frustration imposed by the therapist. Both of these affective factors seem to be present from earliest life on.

We find that many terms indicating affective states are used, such as fear, guilt, hate, love, jealousy, but we do not find any systematic attempt to define them or to indicate how they are related to organic life, apart from the one important consideration that they circle around the experience of birth and subsequent experiences of parting, losing, and individuating the self.

23. *Ibid.,* p. 120.

24. *Ibid.,* p. 205. (NOTE: The symbol "n" indicates that the comment which follows appears as a footnote in the book from which the extract as a whole is taken. The asterisk is used when the footnote refers to a statement in the body of the extract. No asterisk is used when the footnote refers to the extract as a whole, or to the final statement in it.)

The content, however, the symbols chosen to express the deepening emotional experience, might have taken on a more intimate personal character, might possibly have turned to sex differences, to the various aspects of the physical relation to the mother or social relation to the father, to the details of toilet training or what not, in order to express the growing intensity and gradual acceptance of the fear, guilt, hate, love and jealousy which the analytic situation calls out.[25]

The idea of "love" as an impulse is treated here primarily in its infantile form, and we are told that some patients realize a kind of "cosmic ecstasy" in the therapeutic situation "far beyond the sexual."

Many patients realize in this relationship for the first time a kind of cosmic ecstasy far beyond the sexual like that which the mystics describe, a oneness with life, an harmonious flowing into reality. That such an intense emotional realization of one human impulse should arouse equally intense fear goes without saying. It is the final overcoming of fear, fear of loss of the self, and fear of the loss of the other, to the point of taking the experience regardless of consequences, that constitutes the first victory for therapy.[26]

Such a passage calls attention to the little recognition that is given to the natural history of the "love impulse." Love seems something that appears when you are leaving persons rather than while you are with them.

Hides his head and in tones I can hardly understand says, "Say you love me truly," looking at me with much embarrassment but considerable emotion.
   "Well, how about you, Jack?"
   "I don't want to kiss *you*."
   "You don't? Jack, I think you must be fond of me."
   "What does that mean?"

25. *Ibid.*, pp. 105–106.   26. *Ibid.*, p. 290.

"I think you like me because you are going away. You always like people when you are going away from them."

"But I'm coming to see you just the same. Tuesday and Thursday and Saturday."[27]

We have learned also that great fear is a regular accompaniment of a powerful gratification of a love impulse; just why is not clear.

In a number of instances Jack shows signs of curiosity about birth, as in the case of babies, but this impulse is brought into relation to his anxiety over his impending separation from the therapist and is not regarded as a real curiosity to know what he asked about.

"They come from their mothers. Just like kittens."
"From big mothers like you?"
"Yes. Only not nanny goats, but little babies."
"Well, how do they get out?"
"They come out of a hole."
"Does the mother die?"
"No. Why should she?"
"Because the nanny goat comes out of her."
"But that doesn't kill her," getting a little mixed myself.
"Is she sick?"
"Yes, she is sick."
"How sick?"
"She goes to the hospital sometimes."
"Does the mother goat go to the hospital?"
"No, just people go to hospitals."
"What do they do with nanny goats when they are sick?"
"There's no hospital for goats, Jack."
n. This interest in origins seems to me the child's way of expressing his anxiety over separation, which, as with adults, is likely to come in terms of curiosity or fear about birth.[28]

Again, an interest in the body of the therapist and of a pic-

27. *Ibid.*, pp. 253–254.   28. *Ibid.*, pp. 208–209.

ture of a nude woman on the wall does not suggest anything
as regards a curiosity about these matters for their own sakes.

"We do have to clear up this room, Jack. See if you can't
help."

Reluctantly he picks up a few papers. "I have to take a nap,"
seating himself on the couch. "Tie my shoe." I pay no attention.
"Tie my shoe. Please tie my shoe." I finally decide it is easier to
do it as the time is getting short. As I bend over, he points to
my necklace, "What's that?"

"Amethysts." He repeats it after me.

"You have something like the lady."

"Yes, of course I have, Jack. All ladies have breasts. Didn't
you know that?"

"Yes, but I didn't know milk came from them."

"Your mother has breasts, too, and when you were a baby,
that was how you were fed, probably."[29]

Erotic motivations and interests are not taken seriously by
this psychology, as judged by the evaluations of such interview materials. We must confess that the Rankian theory
does not seem to be well worked out at this point and does not
offer us very clear-cut conceptions. We can only conclude
that the theory does not asume it to be important to show
how the organic life of the person is modified and organized
in social experience.

*Criterion V. The continuous related character of experi-
ence from childhood through adulthood must be stressed.*

From the standpoint of a theory of the life history Rank's
psychology meets this criterion admirably. We have noted
repeatedly how the current situation is seen as related to the
individual's past, especially and overwhelmingly to the experience of being born. The psychic effects of this experience
are assumed to set a mold for character upon which any later
experiences and even this therapeutic situation have limited

29. *Ibid.*, p. 267.

effects. We see, therefore, that Rank views the individual life as a unit in a thoroughgoing and somewhat surprising sense.

We have noted that it is sometimes difficult to understand the terms which are used to describe unity and indicated the term "will" and the term "limit." But whatever their exact definition may be they are used constantly to identify processes going on within the individual. For example, we find that Jack exerts his will against an opposing limit "in every hour of this record" and presumably has been doing it during the course of his life before the therapeutic experience began.

In every hour of this record, if you look closely, you will see Jack feeling his way against an opposing limit, resisting, teasing, coaxing, pleading, fighting fiercely, exerting his strength to the utmost to overcome my refusal and then after a burst of rage, hate or despair, accepting it as just or at least inevitable and turning afresh to the free creative possibilities or the emotional satisfactions which the situation does afford despite its rejections and deprivations.[30]

We see the patient rolling on the floor and punching a pillow which he asserts is a man.

"A man. He can't hardly breathe. Just look! Here's his face." There is more punching and rolling. "This is a man. See me! See me!" He rolls over and over the full length of the room, with more violent punches and contortions. "The man's nearly dead. He's knocked out."

"You do feel pretty good this morning, don't you, Jackie?"

"Yes, I do. But I've got to bathe my head off."

"Because you've been fighting so hard?"

"Yes, I'm hot." He goes to the toilet and I can hear him talking loudly. As soon as he returns he falls to with the pillow once more.

"Oh, he's knocked out." He seizes the pillow and bats the floor with it so violently that I sneeze from the dust.[31]

30. *Ibid.*, pp. 276–277.   31. *Ibid.*, p. 161.

A footnote commenting on the instance explains that "we seem to have here in symbolic activity the overcoming of the rival (father, brother or sister) who stands between him and the complete possession of the mother, in this case the therapist." We seem to see, therefore, in the patient's behavior the appearance of an old primal wish to reunite himself actually with the mother, and the struggle against the limiting father is a means thereto. Genital sexual union is excluded as a goal and only possession as defined before birth or immediately after birth is admitted as the object. We are glad to have, however, as a tangible example of a "limit" the father, sister, or brother who may stand between the person and his reunion with his mother.

It was made clear under criterion II that we deal (in Rankian psychology) not only with a desire to return to the mother's body and escape individuation, but also with a desire to be an individual and to resist a "too entangling situation," again, apparently, a reference to the birth experience. Here the therapist attempts to mobilize the wish to leave by suggesting that Jack will someday want to leave.

"All right, Jack. I think maybe you are a little tired of coming."
"No, I'm not."
"Well, someday you will be."
n. This is an effort to recognize and pave the way for the natural impulse to withdraw from a too entangling situation, which begins to make itself felt as the contrary impulse toward union with the "other," the giving up of self in yielding and dependence approaches a climax.[32]

Such a response as this can be posited only on the theory as Rank formulated it, and is evidently an interpretation of the current situation in terms of the affects mobilized at birth. Such a wish, appearing in a social situation like the therapeu-

32. *Ibid.,* pp. 184–185.

tic one, has a history which runs through the whole life of the individual and is somehow related to an "organic" wish to be free of an entangling, cramping situation,—that is, possibly that of the developing child in the close embrace of the mother's body.

In view of the foregoing utilization of the birth trauma concept it will puzzle us to note that Dr. Taft specifically rejects the idea that "the worker is being used in the present but only as a lay figure on which to project experiences and feelings from the client's past."

According to this concept, the worker is being used in the present but only as a lay figure on which to project experiences and feelings from the client's past. An utter confusion results, a practical denial of the reality of the present which is functioning for the sake of the past. Once more the worker is effectively hidden behind the screen of father, mother, brother, sister, while all the time her value for the client is that she is none of these and he knows it. He may be using patterns which were developed by him in birth, nursing, weaning, toilet training, Œdipus situation and what not, but he is using them now, with all the changes wrought by years of living, using them afresh as they are in the present hour, in immediate reaction to someone who behaves as no one has ever behaved to him before; someone who understands and permits a use of herself, which determines for the client a new experience valuable, if at all, in and for itself.[33]

We would have expected a quite different formulation of the matter on the basis of our findings in examining the life history and the use which is here made of it. It would seem that nothing is clearer than that the current situation is being interpreted as a repetition of Jack's experience in birth and that the therapist herself sees the interview material in this form and so interprets it. We do not know how to view this discrepancy in theory and must simply record it with puzzlement. We do not gather that Dr. Taft believes she is

33. *Ibid.,* p. 9.

"merely" the mother of the day of Jack's birth or the mother of his nursing period, but we do gather that Jack himself is reacting to the current situation in terms of his experience in these older situations and that while the situation is, to be sure, "different," it is also in striking respects similar; at least similar enough to warrant reacting to Jack "as if" he were facing still an unsolved emotional situation resulting from his very earliest experience. If this unnecessary and contradictory rejection of the summative value of past experience were withdrawn, the stress on the importance of the current situation would have greater validity.

Despite this confusion we must conclude that Rank does stress the unified and continuous nature of the life history and views the current situation as determined in part by the affects mobilized at the time of organic separation from the mother.

Criterion VI. The "social situation" must be carefully and continuously specified as a factor.

The attempt to see Rank's psychology in relation to this criterion offers a number of problems and seeming contradictions. This criterion requires that the immediate social situation be carefully differentiated from the subject's interpretation of it. This means that we must divide up our picture of the current situation into two parts, one the subject's picture of it, and, two, the average cultural picture of it; the second view of "the situation" is what we are stressing here as desirable, since it reveals the standard cultural interpretation of the situation against which the subject's reaction to it can be differentiated.

Rank does not appear to make this distinction. We have already noted that his theory does not give an account of the systematic role of culture in the life of the individual but sees it as a kind of frieze which is vitalized only by the individual's affects as they are organized in the birth situation. We have sensed in the concept of the "limit" a certain reference to the culture, since the limit is evidently a cultural definition of the situation which the therapist imposes.

It is at the same time true that Rank's psychology is very specific in emphasizing the current situation in therapy and in stressing the reality of the interrelations between the therapist and the subject. This very valuable emphasis is not, however, capitalized from the standpoint of the culture and it is hard to tell what is meant by the "present realities" of the therapeutic situation which are so often referred to. It seems to us that this emphasis on the current situation is a point "against" something rather than a definition of a positive character. We are warned against evaluating the actual therapeutic situation simply in terms of the subject's past.

Whether such individual treatment as this is often advisable where children are concerned is for me a very grave question but I think there is no use to deceive ourselves as to what we do when we undertake direct contacts with a child, no use to disguise present realities of which we are a vital part under the veil of intellectual interpretation of the past which after all is gone forever and can never again be utilized for therapy.[34]

This past is said to be gone and not accessible for therapeutic purposes. Despite this valuable emphasis on the actuality of the relationship between the therapist and subject, we can hardly believe that the past is so thoroughly gone; it may well be gone as a real situation but it is not gone in the sense that it has left no deposit or pattern in the character of the subject. We cannot hold Rank's view unless we maintain that culture is not being "laid down" in our subject, and this proposition is hardly defensible in view of our knowledge of comparative cultures. Individuals, even of seven years of age, already embody a large part of the fundamental claims of their culture; indeed, were this not so there would be no possibility of therapy at all and the current situation would

34. *Ibid.,* p. 107.

not exist. One has only to think of exchanging Dr. Taft's American patient for a Navajo child to surmise that the latter patient's past would play a tremendous role in the situation. It would seem that the whole cultural factor is here simply taken for granted in fact, but not indicated in theory. We cannot differ with the view that "analysis of the Rankian variety is nothing but an opportunity to feel in the present and gradually to begin to accept responsibility for one's own feelings."

In fact, from one viewpoint, analysis of the Rankian variety is nothing but an opportunity to feel in the present and gradually to begin to accept responsibility for one's own feelings and impulses in all their ambivalence, with as little denial, rationalization and justification as may be.[35]

But it is hard to admit that one's own feelings are so little patterned by the massive and pervasive cultural structure to which one is exposed from infancy on. The "present" in which the subject feels is not only a moment of time and a physical relation in space to persons and things, but it is also a cultural situation full of understandings and implications; and it is an event which will leave its own future mark on the person. Else what is therapy for? Somehow the therapeutic situation itself must differ from the usual experience of the subject. These differences must be definitive of the character and social world of the subject in a new sense or else there is no therapy. The serious attempt to formulate these differences between the therapeutic situation and the usual life situation of the subject might open the way to a more careful scientific definition of the therapeutic relation.

The therapeutic value of the hour lies in its immediacy and spontaneity, but the spontaneity of the therapist must of necessity be unfailingly oriented and reoriented with reference to the patient, as the central and dominating figure of the relationship,

35. *Ibid.*, pp. 94–95.

with a prior, never to be forgotten claim. Which is one reason, perhaps *the* reason, why therapy is non-scientific, and the therapeutic relationship not open to research at the moment.[36]

Certainly no scientific views about a person can be formulated if he is separated from his cultural past and from the emotional reactions he has developed in specific cultural situations. We might say that Rankian psychology stresses the value of the immediate real situation between the therapist and the subject, but fails to note that the "real situation" is a cultural situation, that is, that the subject attributes preferred roles to the therapist, that the therapist himself has a chronic, formal role and that both persons are irremediably actors in a social situation in addition to being physically and temporally present in it. For example, the average social situation between adults and children is modified in this case, as Dr. Taft recognizes, by her greater lenience and indulgence toward the child. This fact seems to be an admission that the culture (persons) with which Jack has been faced has been unduly harsh and that a milder policy will be of therapeutic value. Indeed, we are informed that a therapy consists primarily in "this fear-reducing heightening of the value of the present."

Perhaps the ending of a long-time therapeutic relationship, agreed to by the patient from the beginning, takes on more of this compelling quality than any other situation where threat of death is entirely absent; hence its therapeutic worth, which consists primarily in this fear-reducing heightening of the value of the present and the releasing discovery that an ending willed or accepted by the individual himself is birth no less than death, creation no less than annihilation.[37]

It would be worth defining specifically just what alteration of the usual relationship between adults and children takes

36. *Ibid.,* pp. 118–119.   37. *Ibid.,* p. 16.

place in the Rankian therapeutic situation to give this result of reducing fear. One modification which seems to be obvious is that the therapist in this case is not a fearsome person, and does not threaten the individual so sternly as do others in his social milieu.

Despite this emphasis on the value of the concrete situation, it seems to be constantly interpreted, not culturally, but in terms of the birth situation. For example, the ending of the analysis is believed to stand in relationship to the patient's acceptance of his own birth and individuation.

He now begins on a story of suicide. "Did you hear about the man who killed himself? He was a friend of my Uncle Billy. He made a fire in his auto and burned himself and his dog. He didn't have any father and mother. The funeral is going to be Monday."* No other indication of feeling or interest was given.

* *n.* While the relation of this story to the situation is certainly not evident, the fact remains that I have never known a patient to fail to bring in reference to death, at the point where the ending of the analysis is being faced.[38]

Whether or to what degree this is true is not our problem. We merely note that the current situation *is* interpreted in terms of the "grim organic memory." This seems to be one memory that functions even if more recent ones are not very important.

In Rankian psychology we find a constant reference to time as an important consideration. Through the case history the acceptance of time limits and units is constantly stressed both in theory and in the response of the therapist to the patient.

This time he accepts the decision, which is to leave the box in the office.

"That must mean that you are coming back, Jackie."

"Yes, I am."

38. *Ibid.,* p. 246.

"Well, when is it going to be?"

"Maybe Monday."

"I think Mrs. T. can come only on Tuesday."

"I could come Saturday."

"That's too far off. How would you like to come three days next week—Tuesday, Thursday and Saturday?" He seems willing to do this, and wants to know just exactly how many times that will be. "Jackie, how would you like to keep on coming to see me for quite a little while, maybe a month or two, until you get tired coming and it's such nice weather that you wouldn't want to stay inside?" He seems to think this a good idea, but has already begun to think of how he is going to get on the street car all by himself. His whole attention is now concentrated on getting himself across the street to meet Miss Y. "Good-by, Jackie. See you Tuesday."[39]

Time is one of the limits which the subject must learn to accept since time is the essence of all maturational processes and of course involves limits on gratification and the necessity of parting. It is not unfair to note, however, that time is also, and perhaps strictly speaking, a concept with relation to society and that especially in our culture it is one of the most vigorously felt and imposed basic concepts. The therapist, like the subject, must accept it and it has certainly "social" as well as organic factors. This concept of time is one which might well be discussed in Rankian theory from the standpoint of society.

"Have I got a long time yet?"

"Fifteen minutes. Do you know how long that is? Are you tired? Do you want to go?"

"No, I just wanted to know how long."

"Well, you can do quite a little in fifteen minutes."

"Could I do something in ten minutes?"

"Yes, quite a little." Once more he is absorbed in the cutting.[40]

39. *Ibid.*, p. 145.　　　　　　　　40. *Ibid.*, p. 143.

The therapist does this constantly in actual life when she explains to her patient that she cannot spend more time with him because she has other things to do.

We seem, however, to get the sense from this case history that the concept "time" is used with reference to some fundamental biological quality, very difficult to define, and the impression suggests itself that "time" really refers to some kind of unconscious biological pacing of the intra-uterine period. But this is a speculation developed in the effort to master this exceedingly difficult idea.

We are surprised to note that the therapist does not feel that her work is designed to adjust the subject to norms of current society. It is no plea for ruthless imposition of our culture standards when we say that she can hardly do anything else. The only other thing she can do is to adjust the child to some personal variant of our culture which she embodies and prefers. This point is brought out in connection with a discussion of another case study which is reported in the same volume.

Reports from the Farm to which Helen went for three weeks indicate no behavior problem but as I see it therapy in the sense of socially desirable behavior can never be the goal of this type of analytic relationship. It is a purely individual affair and can be measured only in terms of its meaning to the person, child or adult; of its value, not for happiness, not for virtue, not for social adjustment but for growth and development in terms of a purely individual norm.[41]

Therapy is said to be a "purely individual affair" and not to be measured in terms of social adjustment. Such a statement seems to reject the concept of culture altogether and to substitute for it some "purely individual norm." Our cultural knowledge tells us that such a norm can only be a fiction and that the cultural norm is present whether acknowledged or

41. *Ibid.*, p. 109.

not. This is a point at which the effort to identify the current situation of the patient would be invaluable, because only when it was defined could we understand how his behavior is changed by it.

This psychology cannot be said to do justice to the culture concept as expressed in the definition of the immediate situation which the life history subject faces.

Criterion VII. The life-history material itself must be organized and conceptualized.

We have discussed the technical apparatus of Rank's psychology in such detail that it is needless to indicate that he meets the above criterion. The material of the life history is systematically managed and conceptualized, and Rank is very far from the supposition that the patient can give us an adequate theory of his own life. Indeed, by definition he cannot, in the view of Rankian psychology. The life-history taker must stand off against the material and evaluate it theoretically. This is done satisfactorily from the formal standpoint. It is not in our province to suggest whether or not his concepts give the best possible picture of a life when they are used.

THERE are a few more things to be said about this psychology which do not fit well into our criteria. For example, we should be glad to know a little more about the pre-history of the child. The few bits of knowledge that we have are very enticing.

In preparing for a child I did nothing except to clear the upper part of my desk and the lowest drawer. I bought two fifty-cent dolls, which might pass for a boy and a girl, and a tiny baby doll in a bed, because I had heard that John enjoyed playing with dolls. I added to this a small baby carriage that would hold the little doll, and a few dishes with which to set the table. These were all put away in the lowest drawer together with some boxes that might be utilized in playing. In the top part of the desk there were pencils, crayons, drawing paper and a few little odds and ends that a child might be interested in.[42]

We learn, for instance, that Jack was fond of playing with dolls and with this in mind the therapist provided a few dolls in the interviewing set-up. In this sense she does anticipate and create a situation in which the child can express itself, but the fact that a seven-year-old boy wishes to play with dolls seems to point to some aspects of Jack's character which should be further investigated. The social situation is remodeled in his favor without any questions asked as to why his behavior is different from current expectation.

The case history was written down apparently during the time of the interviewing hours when the therapist was directly in the interviewing situation. This certainly has advantages in reporting the acts of the child and helps to give the case record a lively and realistic character. The writing by the author does attract the child's attention and serves to give her a definite role in the situation. Occasionally the child questions her on the point, but she manages to avoid admitting that she is actually writing down observations on the interview.

By this time I have seated myself on the couch and taken up my pencil and paper. "Let's see. Four more Saturdays, you say, Jack? How long is that going to be?"

He goes over it carefully. "Are you writing that down? What are you writing?"

"Oh, just some things I want to write." I divert him by asking whether he can write, and whether he is learning to read.[43]

We cannot help but note that in this case the therapist is not completely candid in her responses to the child and he shows that he suspects what she is doing. This could be a damaging factor in the situation from the child's standpoint since it

42. *Ibid.,* p. 132.   43. *Ibid.,* pp. 225–226.

might raise doubts as to her veracity. But so far as the record goes it does not seem to have been destructive. Needless to say the observation and comment of the therapist are directed by Rankian psychology. There can be no possible objection to this fact and we do not state it as an objection; if objection were made it would have to lie on the ground that Rankian psychology does not afford an adequate perception of what was going on.

The therapist at one point disavows the intention to "subject such a child to the pressure of one more powerful will" and believes that she has managed to keep her own will out of the therapeutic procedure.

To me it seems a very doubtful procedure to subject such a child to the pressure of one more powerful will actually directed upon him and his behavior, however benevolently. . . . It relieves the other of all responsibility for himself and permits of unlimited negative exercise of the own will.[44]

From a relative standpoint this may be true, but the necessities of defense of herself and her property indicate that she cannot avoid imposing her will on the child. She cannot avoid it because she is acting in a cultural situation, because she is herself acculturated and because she must represent to some degree the cultural taboos. If this point were stated as a relative point, it would be much more effective.

The writer makes very modest therapeutic claims.

Report from Visitor, November 5, 1932:
Jack has made a good adjustment in his foster home. Enuresis is lessened. There has been no rejection of school thus far. Visitor's inquiry regarding Jack's attitude toward coming to Philadelphia brought out the following response from the foster mother. "You're the forgotten woman. He never mentions you or Dr. Taft or any of his old friends any more."[45]

44. *Ibid.*, p. 110.   45. *Ibid.*, p. 273.

The boy has apparently gone to school and is living in the new foster home. Apparently also he has forgotten the therapist. His enuresis is said to have lessened. We must note how carefully the author avoided stressing the fact that the child is "adjusted" to anything. We also cannot help noticing that he has a reality situation to adjust to and the points mentioned seem to indicate that he is doing well at it. The effort to deny cultural situations and implications must prove always to be as difficult as it does for this author.

In surveying Rankian psychology we have had repeated difficulty in defining his practice and concepts clearly. It may be that the theory has not had time to jell and it is to be hoped that our review will aid in a more serviceable definition of it.

CHAPTER V

THE CRITERIA APPLIED: "ANALYSIS OF A PHOBIA IN A FIVE-YEAR-OLD BOY."*

THIS case was published in 1909 and is a significant section of the life history of a small boy who developed a phobic reaction for streets, horses, and trucks. It is, in many ways, unfair to Freud to use as an example of his work such an early case history because since that time he has refined his concept system in many ways and changed the stresses at many points; not least important in this connection is his more conscious and systematic formulation of cultural factors. Furthermore, the case history is of a small boy and covers a relatively short period of his experience. The fact, remains, however, that it proves to be a perfectly serviceable exhibit of Freud's work and that we will find in the "little Hans" case all of the central structure of Freudian theory; in many instances this structure is concretely exemplified in relation to the materials, in other cases it can only be inferred. It is a definite advantage that the case is so widely known that most readers will not have to make special reference to it to follow the points in this discussion. The age of the child does not seem to be important, since the principle of continuity of the life history holds in this case quite as well for a five-year-old as it does for an adult.

We are not working here on a document which is a naïve production of the subject, who, indeed, at this time could not write. The father of little Hans, a close adherent of Freud, makes the observations which Freud comments upon and

* Freud, Sigmund, "Analysis of a Phobia in a Five-Year-Old Boy," *Collected Papers,* Volume III, London, Hogarth Press, 1925, pp. 149–289. All of the extracts in this chapter are taken from this book with the consent of the publisher. The permission thus granted is warmly appreciated.

helps to systematize. We must note also that the culture of little Hans differs in at least one respect from that of the ordinary child of his period, i.e., his parents had agreed to bring him up with as little coercion as possible. This seems to have had the result that the boy was able to express his fantasy with relative freedom to his father and that there was less necessity for relegating it to a private life of his own. Freud tells us plainly that the case history is designed to exhibit the "sexual" life of the child and that it has the advantage of exhibiting these impulses directly, whereas in the case of adults we are dependent on inference with respect to motivational factors at earlier age levels. There is no doubt that the material on which Freud works is selected by the systematic expectations of the father and of Freud; this is theoretically admissible and even necessary in a scientific work, but it is not our province to decide whether or not the principle of selection is a correct one. We are concerned rather with the formal structure of the theory as a possible contribution to social science knowledge. It is very striking how seriously and earnestly Freud takes the social life of his little patient and with what linear detail he follows it from day to day and week to week. He saw Hans only once in person and the rest of the time his organization of the material is based on the reports of the father.

Criterion I. The subject must be viewed as a specimen in a cultural series.

It can hardly be said that at this time Freud has the culture concept in a systematic sense and views his subject as a specimen in a cultural series. Nor can it be said that he is totally unaware of the culture, even at this time; he seems rather to perceive how the attitudes of the parents affect Hans, but always in a concrete sense, and he does not go behind the attitudes of the parents in any systematic manner. He does not show by statement or implication a realization that the difficulties of little Hans are in part the result of a persistent stream of tradition hostile to his impulse life, but seems always to stop with the immediate fact that Hans' parents interfered at one point or another with his drives. On the other hand, we observe an unusual and realistic sensitivity to the immediate milieu and that Freud's views are in no sense antithetic to cultural knowledge. We might say that he knows Hans has parents but does not stress that these parents in turn have parents. Such a fact as a taboo on masturbation is treated as an action of the parents, not as a culture pattern which they share and exemplify. Freud shows in a clear-cut manner that what the parents *do* is often determinative of the child's character; he seems, however, to have no systematic perception that what the parents do is traditionally determined for them also. It might be said that he has shown tradition in action without "knowing" it in a clear conceptual sense. Since this identification of the role of tradition in the individual's life is one of the primary values of the culture idea for the student of the life history, it must be explicitly acknowledged at every point if the life-history system is to be serviceable to us. Freud's system would indeed require rephrasing and change of stresses at many points, if the attempt were made to naturalize it in the social sciences. We will now take up a detailed discussion of this point on the basis of the material derived from our case.

There are some statements in the document which would seem explicit enough to satisfy any student of culture, as where Freud speaks of "the unavoidable difficulties by which a child is confronted when in the course of his cultural training he is called upon to overcome the innate instinctual components of his mind."

I can therefore well imagine that it may have been to Hans's advantage to have produced this phobia; for it directed his parents' attention to the unavoidable difficulties by which a child is confronted when in the course of his cultural training he is called upon to overcome the innate instinctual components of his mind, and his trouble brought his father to his assistance.[1]

It would seem, however, that Freud is not able to maintain systematically the point of view expressed in this phrase since there are many points at which the parents act as cultural surrogates and their behavior is not so designated. We understand, for example, that the father is a physician and this would seem to imply a particular position in his group and possibly a specific role for his son, but we receive no implications of this possibility. We learn again by chance that the family had servants, which would certainly differentiate it from lower class families and might offer explanatory cultural references for the particular behavior of his parents toward him.

'Once, when the little girl failed to make her appearance at the window at her usual hour, Hans grew quite restless, and kept pestering the servants with questions—"When's the little girl coming? Where's the little girl?" and so on.'[2]

We have already noted that this middle-class culture was, in Hans' case, modified by a "Freudian culture" of non-aggression toward the child. At one point Freud refers to the Oedipus situation as "destiny" for little Hans, but he does not indicate how this "destiny" functions; it is certainly quite a different thing if it is intimately related to the family configuration and to the roles and culture of the parents than if it is viewed as a kind of biological fate.

'Hans: "I know. I was their Mummy before, *now I'm their Daddy*."
'I: "And who's the children's Mummy?"
'Hans: "Why, Mummy, and you're their *Grandaddy*."

1. Freud, S., *Collected Papers,* Vol. III, London, Hogarth Press, 1925, p. 284.
2. *Ibid.,* p. 159.

'I : "So then you'd like to be as big as me, and be married to
Mummy, and then you'd like her to have children."

'Hans: "Yes, that's what I'd like, and then my Lainz Grand-
mamma" (my mother) "will be their Grannie." '

Things were moving towards a satisfactory conclusion. The
little Oedipus had found a happier solution than that prescribed
by destiny. Instead of putting his father out of the way, he had
granted him the same happiness that he desired himself : he made
him a grandfather and let him too marry his own mother.[3]

The cultural "destiny" is alterable and there remains the
scientific probability that the Oedipus situation will be developed with markedly different coloring in different cultures. It seems clear from the materials that Freud *could*
have taken the position that this situation is a specifically
cultural one, cultural in the sense that it presents an arbitrary and traditional pattern to the impulse life of the child.
We see also that Hans' mother had a "predestined part to
play" in her treatment of Hans and this is indicated both
by her excessive affection for him and her rejection of his
advances.

His father accuses her, not without some show of justice, of
being responsible for the outbreak of the child's neurosis, on
account of her excessive display of affection for him and her too
frequent readiness to take him into her bed. We might as easily
blame her for having precipitated the process of repression by
her energetic rejection of his advances ('that'd be piggish').
But she had a predestined part to play, and her position was a
hard one.[4]

One recognizes an imperative element of truth in this statement, but it is again open to the modification that her role in
both respects may be a cultural role and that what is accepted as "human" destiny is actually the specific way in
which the child's instinctual life is handled in our culture.

3. *Ibid.*, pp. 238–239.   4. *Ibid.*, p. 171.

We cannot allow ourselves to be impressed by the vigor with which the mother feels her role; it is quite characteristic of acculturated beings that they feel the "naturalness" of their actions with the same intensity. For example, Hans' mother refuses to touch his genital when she is bathing him and rejects his suggestion that she do so with the information that it would be "piggish."

'Hans, four and a quarter. This morning Hans was given his usual daily bath by his mother and afterwards dried and powdered. As his mother was powdering around his penis and taking care not to touch it, Hans said: "Why don't you put your finger there?"
'Mother: "Because that'd be piggish."
'Hans: "What's that? Piggish? Why?"
'Mother: "Because it's not proper."
'Hans (laughing): "But it's great fun." '[5]

This is, of course, a way of classifying Hans' love for her as extremely disagreeable, aligning it with animal behavior and calling up impressions of filth and dirt. We can only stress that such classifications are features of our own inherited habits and that they derive their meaning only from this system. Hans' demand is therefore opposed not only by his mother as an individual, but by the whole system which she embodies and represents.

In the case of the little boy's sexual curiosity we see him again as the antagonist opposed not only to his mother as a concrete reacting person, but also to the whole cultural system. For example, he is thwarted in his efforts to observe her "widdler" because she wears clothes, which is certainly not a "natural fact." Apparently also he hears no frank discussion of sexual matters and his egocentric belief that all persons have a genital organ similar to his own is heavily assisted by the parental attitudes. He believed, indeed, that his mother

5. *Ibid.*, p. 162.

had a penis and that it was a large one, an error which certainly would rapidly have been corrected had he grown up in some cultures.

Another time he was looking on intently while his mother undressed before going to bed. 'What are you staring like that for?' she asked.

'Hans: "I was only looking to see if you'd got a widdler too."

'Mother: "Of course. Didn't you know that?"

'Hans: "No. I thought you were so big you'd have a widdler like a horse." '[6]

Since this misunderstanding is an important element in the maturation of his Oedipus complex, we must charge up to the culture an important share in generating his anxiety and fear. It is also quite clear that Hans' father, impersonating the culture, forced him to falsify his perception as to the pregnancy of his mother by transmitting the stork fable.

The most cogent evidence of this is furnished by the phantasy (which he persisted in with so much obstinacy, and embellished with such a wealth of detail) of how Hanna had been with them at Gmunden the summer before her birth, of how she had travelled there with them, and of how she had been able to do far more then than she had a year later, after she had been born. The effrontery with which Hans related this phantasy and the countless extravagant lies with which he interwove it were anything but meaningless. All of this was intended as a revenge upon his father, against whom he harboured a grudge for having misled him with the stork fable.[7]

This "fable" is obviously a cultural device for confusing the child and inhibiting his sexual interest, as is exemplified in the case of little Hans. His real antagonist here, therefore, is his father only in one manner of speaking about it, that is, his father as a member of a deceitful and suppressive culture.

6. *Ibid.*, p. 153.   7. *Ibid.*, p. 270.

Hans clings, however, at least unconsciously, to the reality of his perceptions and revenges himself on his deceitful parents by inventing ironic stories for them in turn. In one case he informs them that a calf is not born out of a cow but comes out of a cart.

'I: "Can you remember how the cow got a calf?"
'Hans: "Oh, yes. It came in a cart." (No doubt he had been told this at Gmunden; another sally against the stork theory.) "And another cow pressed it out of its behind." (This was already the fruit of his enlightenment, which he was trying to bring into harmony with the cart theory.)
'I: "It isn't true that it came in a cart; it came out of the cow in the cow-shed." '[8]

It would be interesting to know in the comparative study of cultures how vigorously people cling to their actual perceptions despite the overpowering force of the structured theory of the culture. Hans certainly puzzles himself about many points which are important to him but which are not covered adequately by the stork explanation.

'Hans: "Does Hanna belong to me or to Mummy?"
'I: "To Mummy."
'Hans: "No, to me. *Why not to me and Mummy?*"
'I: "Hanna belongs to me, Mummy, and you."
'Hans: "There you are, you see." '
So long as the child is in ignorance of the female genitals, there is naturally a vital gap in his comprehension of sexual matters.[9]

It would seem that if the culture does not provide, as in this case, a theory which satisfactorily controls the child's actual perceptions there is bound to be an element of conflict on such a point from that time on. Nor are his parents ever able to brace themselves to giving the child the concepts it wishes

8. *Ibid.,* p. 231.   9. *Ibid.,* pp. 229–230.

and needs in regard to the nature of the parental genitalia and of the sex act.

'An unsolved residue remains behind; for Hans keeps cudgelling his brains to discover what a father has to do with his child, since it is the mother who brings it into the world. This can be seen from his questions, as, for instance: "I belong to *you*, too, don't I?" (meaning, not only to his mother). It is not clear to him in what way he belongs to me. On the other hand, I have no direct evidence of his having, as you suppose, overheard his parents in the act of coitus.'[10]

Freud wished them to do this and felt it would resolve the conflict permanently, but they were not able, because of their own *culture* conflicts, to accept his recommendation, and this despite the fact that both had worked with him as *analysands*. One might say that the parents could not accept Freud's bold modification of the culture, but insisted on transmitting the traditional version of it.

Freud was certainly able at this time to think of the possibility of the biological transmission of ideas, a possibility which stands the cultural argument exactly on its head and which is not in accord with the views of comparative students of cultures. We note that it is possible for him to think of a "deep and universal connection" between two ideas as a way of explaining a similarity between two words.

'In the light of this, we may review the interpretation of Hans's earlier phantasy to the effect that the plumber had come and unscrewed the bath and had stuck a borer into his stomach. The big bath meant a "behind," the borer or screwdriver was (as was explained at the time) a widdler.'

n. We may perhaps add that the word 'borer' was not chosen without regard for its connection with the words 'born' and 'birth.' If so, the child could have made no distinction between 'bored' and 'born.' I accept this suggestion, which

10. *Ibid.*, p. 242.

comes from an experienced fellow-worker, but I am not in a position to say whether we have before us here a deep and universal connection between the two ideas or merely the employment of a verbal coincidence peculiar to German (and English). Prometheus (Pramantha), the creator of man, is also etymologically 'the borer.' (Cf. Abraham, *Traum und Mythus*, 1908.)[11]

He does not make this judgment but neither does he reject it. This is the type of thing that makes us suspicious when he speaks of destiny in connection with the Oedipus situation. If his views are to be acceptable to students of culture, he will have to resolve this dilemma in favor of the traditional transmission of the ideas in question.

A very important idea for students of culture emerges in Freud's discussion of this material. He is able to show that a person, even so small a boy as Hans, is not merely the passive recipient of the cultural print, but also that he "works over" his culture, perceives independently and attempts to resolve contradictions between his perceptions and the formal cultural schema. This is a most important idea because too frequently we get the picture of the individual in culture studies as a passive recipient of the stamp of culture and we do not count sufficiently with his opposition and reservations, often unconscious reservations, to the formal pattern. If the culture is solidly united against the child's investigations and protests, it must be that such protests are frequently not expressed at all but rather repressed and that little Hans constitutes a happy exception in that he faced a father acculturated to a more tolerant attitude.

Our conclusion must be that Freud meets our criterion only in a very limited sense. He seems to recognize the cultural point in the concrete, but he is not able to formulate it in any systematic sense. We shall not be surprised at this

11. *Ibid.*, p. 240.

since, after all, he is working totally within our own culture and not using the comparative view or materials. We would also stress the fact that if his views are to be serviceable to students of society, he would have to recognize specifically that Hans' real antagonist is not the family situation in the concrete, that is, the one he actually confronted, but that it is the vast controlling framework of the culture itself which the family impersonates.

Criterion II. The organic motors of action ascribed must be socially relevant.

Freud's statements with regard to the organic side of man seem to stress capacities of the organism which are socially relevant. Although he frequently uses the term "instinct" and refers to egoistic instincts and a sexual instinct, he does not use the term in the same sense that it is used for lower organisms. In the Schreber case he refers to instinct as "the mental representative of organic forces," that is, the inner perception of tension or the urge to act.

It would be otherwise if we could start out from some well-grounded theory of instincts; but in fact we have nothing of the kind at our disposal. We regard instinct as being a term situated on the frontier-line between the somatic and the mental, and consider it as denoting the mental representative of organic forces. Further, we accept the popular distinction between egoistic instincts and a sexual instinct; for such a distinction seems to agree with the biological conception that the individual has a double orientation, aiming on the one hand at self-preservation and on the other at the preservation of the species.[12]

It is quite clear from the study of the case of little Hans that he does not regard the instincts as having a fixed social goal; rather, indeed, in the case of the sexual instinct he has stressed the vague but powerful and impulsive nature of the drive and has emphasized that its proper social object is not

12. *Ibid.*, p. 461.

picked out in advance. His seems to be a drive concept which is not at variance with our knowledge from comparative cultural studies, since his theory does not demand that the "instinct" work itself out with mechanical certainty alike in every varying culture.

We must now examine the specific arsenal of drive forces which Freud has postulated as a result of his study of persons. First we will begin with a negation. He disclaims specifically the existence of a special aggressive instinct which operates in a unitary manner and allots instead a dynamic character to all instincts and impulses, a character which is proper to the type of gratification demanded by it.

I cannot bring myself to assume the existence of a special aggressive instinct alongside of the familiar instincts of self-preservation and of sex, and on an equal footing with them. It appears to me that Adler has mistakenly hypostatized into a special instinct what is in reality a universal and indispensable attribute of all instincts and impulses—their 'impulsive' and dynamic character, what might be described as their capacity for initiating motion. Nothing would then remain of the other instincts but their relation to an aim, for their relation to the means of reaching that aim would have been taken over from them by the 'aggressive instinct.' In spite of all the uncertainty and obscurity of our theory of instincts I should prefer for the present to adhere to the usual view, which leaves each instinct its own power of becoming aggressive; and I should be inclined to recognize the two instincts which became repressed in Hans as familiar components of the sexual libido.[13]

This is tantamount to stating that one is not aggressive in general but always in relation to something, and more specifically to some type of tensional release. Where there is aggressive behavior that seems to function by itself it has become separated in the course of development from its instinct component on the pleasure side.

13. *Ibid.*, pp. 281–282.

We need hardly labor the point that pleasure or the avoidance of pain is, in Freudian theory, the goal of all instinctual manifestations. This pleasure goal is taken to be a chronic aspect of organic function in the human and a permanent guide to activity, appearing in its clearest form in childhood and gradually circumscribed as to its execution by the conditioning structure of the culture.

. . . it therefore seems impossible to avoid the assumption that during the period when he himself had been looked after as an infant these same performances had been the source of pleasurable sensations for him. He had obtained this pleasure from his erotogenic zones with the help of the person who had looked after him—his mother, in fact; and thus the pleasure already pointed the way to object-choice. But it is just possible that at a still earlier date he had been in the habit of giving himself this pleasure auto-erotically—that he had been one of those children who like retaining their excreta till they can derive a voluptuous sensation from their evacuation.[14]

Freud has distinguished three "erotogenic zones" from which children obtain their chief gratification. The first of these, the lip-mouth-stomach integration, is barely hinted at in the case of Hans. We see that Hans is excited by perceiving the care and satisfaction which his infant sister now derives from his mother and tends to live over in some manner his own infantile experience.

The most important influence upon the course of Hans's psycho-sexual development was the birth of a baby sister when he was three and a half years old. That event accentuated his relations to his parents and gave him some insoluble problems to think about; and later, as he watched the way in which the infant was looked after, the memory-traces of his own earliest experiences of pleasure were revived in him.[15]

14. *Ibid.*, p. 250.   15. *Ibid.*, p. 255.

In the case of Hans, Freud apparently found very few identifiable traces of his earlier oral phase, except his jealousy at
the care given to his tiny sister who was in this phase at the
time of the study.

Hans does, however, show clearly his interest in excremental functions and gives evidences of the satisfaction
which he derived from their performance.

Thus in little Hans's sexual constitution the genital zone was
from the outset the one among his erotogenic zones which afforded him the most intense pleasure. The only other similar
pleasure of which he gave evidence was excremental pleasure,
the pleasure attached to the orifices through which urination
and evacuation of the bowels are effected.[16]

He is interested in the feces of horses and gives evidence of
concern about his mother's underclothes on the basis of their
relationship to excrement.

'Later on, I asked: "Have you ever seen a horse doing lumf?"
'Hans: "Yes, very often."
'I: "Does it make a loud row when it does lumf?"
'Hans: "Yes."
'I: "What does the row remind you of?"
'Hans: "Like when lumf falls into the chamber."
'The bus-horse that falls down and make a row with its feet
is no doubt—a lumf falling and making a noise. His fear of
defaecation and his fear of heavily loaded carts is equivalent to
the fear of a heavily loaded stomach.'[17]

'He: "Only when I saw the black ones—when she bought them
—then I spat. But I don't spit when she puts her drawers on or
takes them off. *I spit because the black drawers are black like
a lumf and the yellow ones like widdle, and then I think I've got
to widdle.* When Mummy has her drawers on I don't see them;
she's got her clothes on over them."

16. *Ibid.*, p. 249.   17. *Ibid.*, p. 208.

'I: "And when she takes off her clothes?"

'He: "I don't spit then either. But when her drawers are new they look like a lumf. When they're old, the colour goes away and they get dirty. When you buy them they're quite clean, but at home they've been made dirty. When they're bought they're new, and when they're not bought they're old." '[18]

At the end of the analysis he is still much concerned with the problem, has indeed achieved some freedom to deal with it in a socially acceptable manner, as shown by his care for his fantasy children whom he treats as still in the period of cleanliness training.

'Hans: "This morning I was in the W. C. with all my children. First I did lumf and widdled, and they looked on. Then I put them on the seat and they widdled and did lumf, and I wiped their behinds with paper. D'you know why? Because I'd so much like to have children; then I'd do everything for them—take them to the W. C., clean their behinds, and do everything one does with children." '

After the admission afforded by this phantasy, it will scarcely be possible to dispute the fact that in Hans's mind there was pleasure attached to the excremental functions.[19]

Freud has attached an importance for character formation to these aspects of nursery behavior which is certainly novel and original.

A third source of pleasure of great importance in Freudian theory is that of genital excitation in the small child.

Meanwhile his interest in widdlers was by no means a purely theoretical one; as might have been expected, it impelled him to touch his member. When he was three and a half his mother found him with his hand to his penis. She threatened him in these words: 'If you do that, I shall send for Dr. A. to cut off your widdler. And then what'll you widdle with?'[20]

18. *Ibid.*, p. 205.　　　　　　　　19. *Ibid.*, p. 239.
20. *Ibid.*, p. 151.

This constitutes the third or phallic phase of the development of the young male organism in our culture; this excitation is met by some kind of stimulation of the organ by the child, either by the hand or in some other way, and is accompanied by fantasies, often vague fantasies relating to other persons, usually the parents. It is presumed to be an instinct component bedded down in the organism and one which becomes especially intense during the age period of three to six years. Gratification of this impulse is believed to meet uniformly with discouragement on the part of culture surrogates. In addition to this auto-erotic interest in the genital Freud postulates for the male child a vague wish toward some kind of union with the mother.

Some kind of vague notion was struggling in the child's mind of something that he might do with his mother by means of which his taking possession of her would be consummated; for this elusive thought he found certain pictorial representations, which had in common the qualities of being violent and forbidden, and the content of which strikes us as fitting in most remarkably well with the hidden truth. We can only say that they were symbolic phantasies of coitus, and it was no irrelevant detail that his father was represented as sharing in his actions: 'I should like,' he seems to have been saying, 'to be doing something with my mother, something forbidden; I do not know what it is, but I do know that you are doing it too.'[21]

Apparently this wish is developed in social interaction, as illustrated at least by little Hans, but also represents a kind of blind organic excitation. Hans is shown as intuiting the genital act by exhibiting a fantasy and wish toward "making an opening into something, of forcing a way into a closed space."

But his father not only knew where children came from, he actually performed it—the thing that Hans could only obscurely

21. *Ibid.,* p. 264.

divine. The widdler must have something to do with it, for his own grew excited whenever he thought of these things—and it must be a big widdler too, bigger than Hans's own. If he listened to these premonitory sensations he could only suppose that it was a question of some act of violence performed upon his mother, of smashing something, of making an opening into something, of forcing a way into an enclosed space—such were the impulses that he felt stirring within him. But although the sensations in his penis had put him on the road to postulating a vagina, yet he could not solve the problem, for within his experience no such thing existed as his widdler required. On the contrary, his conviction that his mother possessed a penis just as he did stood in the way of any solution.[22]

He does not have clear images of what he wants to do but struggles with vague stirrings in this direction. This is assumed to be one of the facts with which culture has to deal in the case of male children.

Sexual curiosity seems to be a derived instinctual component which is present in little Hans. We find him wrestling with the problem and attempting a solution of the riddle (for him) of birth.

As his parents still hesitated to give him the information which was already long overdue, little Hans had by a bold stroke taken the conduct of the analysis into his own hands. By means of a brilliant symptomatic act, *'Look!'* he had said to them, *'this is how I imagine that a birth takes place.'* What he had told the maid-servant about the meaning of his game with the doll had been insincere; to his father he explicitly denied that he had only wanted to see its widdler.[23]

Apparently he has already solved the problem in some respects on the basis of direct observation of his mother, but in his ignorance of the vagina supposed that a baby was born

22. *Ibid.,* pp. 275–276.   23. *Ibid.,* p. 228.

by the act of defecation. We note in the case history also the impulses to show himself as well as impulses to see.

Love of others, that is, object love, is not represented in itself as an instinctual force, but is rather represented as derived from the care of the child while it is still small; the child learns to love those who give it gratification and are useful to it.

The boy had found his way to object-love in the usual manner from having been looked after when he was an infant; and a new pleasure had now become the most important for him—that of sleeping beside his mother.[24]

The center of stress is here on the problem of gratification and object love is viewed as conditional upon service and pleasure given to the child.

Freud has marked out with a fair degree of clarity a series of bodily capacities on which the culture may count and with which it works in the induction of the individual to group life. In a formal sense these capacities seem quite satisfactory since they permit of social elaboration according to the exigencies of the culture into which the individual comes.

Criterion III. The peculiar role of the family group in transmitting the culture must be recognized.

We will find in this discussion that Freud puts tremendous stress on the interaction between the child and his family and that he views the character of the child as a precipitate, in large part, of the family experience. So far as the recognition of the importance of the concrete family is concerned, no more could be desired. We will note again, however, that Freud's eye is on the patient and not on the parents, and that he does not carefully distinguish between the parents as physical beings who are simply put down face to face with their particular child and the parents as surrogates of a wider cultural order. Certainly in Freud's earlier writings,

24. *Ibid.*, pp. 252–253.

including the one we are studying, the latter view is not systematically stressed. To say it in another way, we might state that Freud has "discovered" the family as the matrix of character formation and we might add that he could have stated, but did not, that the family is also the institution in which certain basic aspects of the culture are transmitted from one generation to the next. This latter point is of extremest interest to the student of culture, since the nature of cultural transmission remains such an arid spot in cultural theory. It is just on the central situation in Freudian theory, namely that of the Oedipus complex, that we are left in doubt as to the efficient circumstances conditioning it. We cannot tell from the theoretical statement whether difficulties in this respect are inevitable human biological facts or whether they occur in the stipulated form as a function of our culture.

It must be, I told him, that he thought his father was angry with him on that account; but this was not so, his father was fond of him in spite of it, and he might admit everything to him without any fear. Long before he was in the world, I went on, I had known that a little Hans would come who would be so fond of his mother that he would be bound to feel afraid of his father because of it; and I had told his father this.[25]

Freud is apparently puzzled by this point and although he is willing to predict before Hans' birth that he would face this conflict, he does not commit himself on the reason for its inevitability. It would seem from the evidence adduced by Freud himself that cultural factors played no small role in Hans' case. We have seen that many impressions which were traumatic in the development of the phobia have arisen from conditions imposed by the parents and from things specifically said and done by them as good members of our Western European culture group.

If the theory at this point be somewhat uncertain, the evi-

25. *Ibid.*, p. 185.

dence with regard to the importance of the immediate family life and the scenes and relationships connected with it is inescapable. Hans, for example, transposes a current family situation which he faced into one of his dreams which is decoded by Freud.

'The whole thing is a reproduction of a scene which has been gone through almost every morning for the last few days. Hans always comes in to us in the early morning, and my wife cannot resist taking him into bed with her for a few minutes. Thereupon I always begin to warn her not to take him in bed with her ("the big one called out because I'd taken the crumpled one away from it"); and she answers now and then, rather irritated, no doubt, that it's all nonsense, that one minute is after all of no importance, and so on. Then Hans stays with her a little while. . . .

'Thus the solution of this matrimonial scene transposed into giraffe life is this: he was seized in the night with a longing for his mother, for her caresses, for her genital organ, and came into our bedroom for that reason. The whole thing is a continuation of his fear of horses.'[26]

The big giraffe is the father, the crumpled giraffe is the mother, etc. Through the dream a wish which could not be realized in daily family life was put through as a reality. The great role of the family is stressed again by the patient's reaction to the arrival of a baby sister; indeed, this event along with what preceded and followed it seemed to be at the core of the little boy's neurosis.

'Hans is very jealous of the new arrival, and whenever any one praises her, says she is a lovely baby, and so on, he at once declares scornfully: "But she hasn't got any teeth yet." And in fact when he saw her for the first time he was very much surprised that she could not speak, and decided that this was because she had no teeth. During the first few days he was naturally put very much in the background. He was suddenly taken ill with a

26. *Ibid.,* p. 182.

sore throat. In his fever he was heard saying: "But I don't want a little sister!" '[27]

A definitely hostile reaction is aroused in him by the experience of being moved from the center of affection in the family, a fact which he perceived as a severe frustration.

'April 14th. The theme of Hanna is uppermost. As you may remember from earlier records, Hans felt a strong aversion to the new-born baby that robbed him of a part of his parents' love. This dislike has not entirely disappeared and is only partly over-compensated by an exaggerated affection.* He has already several times expressed a wish that the stork should bring no more babies and that he should pay him money not to bring any more *out of the big box* where babies are. (Compare his fear of furni-ture-vans. . . .)'[28]

* *n.* The 'Hanna' theme immediately succeeded the 'lumf' theme, and the explanation of this at length begins to dawn upon us: Hanna was a lumf herself—babies were lumfs.

Pregnancy, birth, and sex relationships seemed to be presented with renewed intensity as problems by the birth of the sister. Hans is shown constantly as wrestling with problems as they were defined for him by his parents, or, failing a definition which corresponded with his perceptions, falling into confusion and perplexity. Freud's description of little Hans represents him as in the grip of the family situation at every point and brings his behavior continuously into relation with family attitudes and taboos.

The parents as surrogates of a repressive culture are shown at many points; some of these, such as the mother's condemnation of his onanistic activities and the stork story, have already been shown. Another example is the manner in which they tabooed his expressed wish to have one of the neighborhood girls sleep with him at night.

27. *Ibid.,* p. 154.   28. *Ibid.,* p. 211.

' "I want Mariedl to sleep with me." On being told that would not do, he said: "Then she shall sleep with Mummy or with Daddy." He was told that would not do either, but that Mariedl must sleep with her own father and mother.'[29]

He was simply told that "it would not do." This seems to be an extension of the taboo on sleeping with his mother to one of the other females in the environment.

Even with all his influence over these parents whose child he was helping Freud was not able to overcome their resistance at one point; not even at the end of the treatment could they bring themselves to tell Hans of the "existence of the vagina and of copulation."

If matters had lain entirely in my hands, I should have ventured to give the child the one remaining piece of enlightenment which his parents withheld from him. I should have confirmed his instinctive premonitions, by telling him of the existence of the vagina and of copulation; thus I should have still further diminished his unsolved residue, and put an end to his stream of questions. I am convinced that this new piece of enlightenment would have made him lose neither his love for his mother nor his own childish nature, and that he would have understood that his preoccupation with these important, these momentous things must rest for the present—until his wish to be big had been fulfilled. But the pedagogic experiment was not carried so far.[30]

We are not raising at this point the question as to whether or not this would have been wise, but only calling attention to the reluctance of the parents as being associated with their own cultural prohibitions. There are certainly many cultures where such knowledge is as accessible to small children as any other kind of knowledge, and the inference is that here Freud had impacted a cultural taboo which he could not overcome. He does not state the matter in this way but simply com-

29. *Ibid.*, p. 160.   30. *Ibid.*, p. 286.

ments that the parents withheld from the child "one remaining piece of enlightenment."

It is truly astonishing that Freud could have achieved such knowledge of the power of the family while working solely within his own culture. Even trained students of culture are often very poor at delineating our own society. Freud seems to have the most vivid perceptions of what parents actually do, although he does not formulate what individual parents do as an aspect of transmission of culture forms.

Criterion IV. The specific method of elaboration of organic materials into social behavior must be shown.

Freud is able to give a very definite account of the way in which biological impulses are elaborated into social action. Some of the main principles of this process are illustrated in the case of little Hans. For example, we see how a "longing for his mother" is elaborated first into a generalized morbid anxiety which replaced the repressed longing; this anxiety is then attached to a shifting series of social objects, such as horse, street, moving van, and others.

His morbid anxiety, then, corresponded to repressed longing. But it was not the same thing as the longing: the repression must be taken into account too. Longing can be completely transformed into satisfaction if it is presented with the object longed for. Therapy of that kind is no longer effective in dealing with anxiety. The anxiety remains even when the longing can be satisfied. It can no longer be completely retransformed into libido; there is something that keeps the libido back under repression. This was shown to be so in the case of Hans on the occasion of his next walk, when his mother went with him. He was with his mother, and yet he still suffered from anxiety— that is to say, from an unsatisfied longing for her. It is true that the anxiety was less; for he did allow himself to be induced to go for the walk, whereas he had obliged the nursemaid to turn back. Nor is a street quite the right place for 'coaxing,' or whatever else this young lover may have wanted. But his anxiety had stood the test; and the next thing for it to do was to find an object.[31]

The trail is clear, straight back from a nonsensical phobic object (street) to a biological craving manifested directly in the family situation. This process is itself a type of direct definition corresponding to our criterion. The process of repression which initiated the change from desire to anxiety is certainly related to the behavior of the mother in rejecting the overtures of the boy; the repressive dynamism is a device for remoulding a biological impulse, usually for ends which are socially valued.

A similar example can be given from the side of the excremental interests which Hans is said to have exhibited in his early childhood.

We have seen how our little patient was overtaken by a great wave of repression and that it caught precisely those of his sexual components that were dominant. He gave up onanism, and turned away in disgust from everything that reminded him of excrement and of looking on at other people performing their natural functions.[32]

By the time of the analysis these had already been repressed and what was once a pleasurable sphere of interest had become toned with loathing and disgust. Such a transformation of an instinctual component under the pressure of the (cultural) cleanliness training is again a model of the elaboration of the biological life into character and socialized attitudes. The culture-wide presence of some kind of interference with interest in anal functions makes this transformation of particular interest to the comparative student of culture.

A similar elaboration occurs in other aspects of the boy's behavior, as in the case of his propensities toward cruelty and

31. *Ibid.*, p. 169.   32. *Ibid.*, p. 279.

violence. Their transformation into feelings of pity apparently had already taken place at the time of the analysis.

But Hans was not by any means a young blackguard; he was not even one of those children in whom at his age the propensity towards cruelty and violence which is part of human nature still has free play. On the contrary, he had an unusually kind-hearted and affectionate disposition; his father reported that the transformation of aggressive tendencies into feelings of pity took place in him at a very early age.[33]

We assume, according to Freud's theory, that these tendencies were already paired with particular instinct aims of a positive kind and that they appeared when these positive trends were prohibited; it was the rejection and repression of these hostile instinct components which gave rise to socialized feelings of pity. Since feelings of pity are of such tremendous importance in social life, it is valuable to have this indication of how they may arise; presumably the original hostile feelings are repressed in the child with the aid of parental opposition to their expression. We find the same state of affairs in respect of the genital wish for some kind of nearer traffic with his mother.

A most suitable continuation of the giraffe phantasy. He had a suspicion that to take possession of his mother was forbidden; he had come up against the incest-barrier. But he regarded it as forbidden in itself. His father was with him each time in the forbidden exploits which he carried out in his imagination, and was locked up with him. His father, he thought, also did that enigmatic forbidden something with his mother which he replaced by an act of violence such as smashing a window-pane or forcing a way into an enclosed space.[34]

In this case the wish, blocked in reality, is elaborated in a dream and disguised there by being displaced onto an animal fantasy. The wish is also believed to have the power of ex-

33. *Ibid.*, p. 254.   34. *Ibid.*, p. 184.

pressing itself symbolically in such acts as smashing a window pane or forcing a way into an enclosed space, such as a forbidden area of a park. Again we find the same clear trail from the immediate biological life of the child to social objects and impressions. In yet another example we see how the sadistic component of the genital wish is displaced onto a fantasy of beating horses.

> 'Hans: "It was just a horse from the stables."
> 'I: "How did it get to the trough?"
> 'Hans: "I took it there."
> 'I: "Where from? Out of the stables?"
> 'Hans: "I took it out because I wanted to beat it."
> 'I: "Was there no one in the stables?"
> 'Hans: "Oh, yes, Loisl." (The coachman at Gmunden.)
> 'I: "Did he let you?"
> 'Hans: "I talked nicely to him, and he said I might do it."
> 'I: "What did you say to him?"
> 'Hans: "Could I take the horse and whip it and shout at it. And he said 'Yes.' "

. . . .

'In the street Hans explained to me that buses, furniture-vans, and coal-carts were stork-box carts.'

That is to say, pregnant women. Hans's access of sadism immediately before cannot be unconnected with the present theme.[35]

In all these cases Freud has clearly indicated that the instinctual life is defined and in part determined by the milieu. We see in the case of the homosexual person that Freud does not take stock in a special homosexual instinct.

A homosexual may have normal instincts, but he is unable to disengage them from a class of objects defined by a particular determinant. And in his childhood, since at that period it is taken for granted that this determinant is of universal application, he is able to behave like little Hans, who showed his affection to little

35. *Ibid.,* pp. 222–223.

boys and girls indiscriminately, and once described his friend Fritzl as 'the girl he was fondest of.' Hans was a homosexual (as all children may very well be), quite consistently with the fact, which must always be kept in mind, that he was *acquainted with only one kind of genital organ*—a genital organ like his own.[36]

Freud attributes normal sexual impulses to the homosexual male, but believes that his behavior is determined by a fixed requirement that he can love only a being with a genital organ like his own. This requirement is assumed to develop in considerable part through the ignorance of the child of the nature of the female genitalia and his later refusal to accept this fact because of its dangerous implications for himself. In this case, as in others in Freud's theory, the argument does not run directly from a social act to an instinctual force, but postulates intermediate social elaboration. Social acts, per Freud, derive their energies from the instinctual life of the individual but are not defined directly by it. In cultures where different social results occur Freud's theory would work satisfactorily since it would posit different intermediate (i.e., cultural) conditions. For this reason it is a handy tool in the grip of a student of society.

Criterion V. The continuous related character of experience from childhood through adulthood must be stressed.

We need hardly affirm that Freud's system meets this criterion since in a very real sense the fact of the continuity of mental life is one of his discoveries. As he says picturesquely about an adult neurotic, "a continuous and undisturbed thread of mental activity, taking its start from the conflicts of his childhood, has been spun through his life."

When, however, an adult neurotic patient comes to us for psycho-analytic treatment (and let us assume that his illness has only become manifest after he has reached maturity), we find

36. *Ibid.,* p. 252.

regularly that his neurosis is connected on to an infantile anxiety such as we have been discussing, and is in fact a continuation of it; so that, as it were, a continuous and undisturbed thread of mental activity, taking its start from the conflicts of his childhood, has been spun through his life—irrespective of whether the first symptom of those conflicts has persisted or has retreated under the pressure of circumstances.[37]

Even in the case of little Hans at the age of five years we already find him with a life history in this sense; he is seen to be reacting in terms of his former interest in excretory matters long past the time when he was directly facing his cleanliness training. At five years, however, his reaction is one of shame where it had formerly been one of pleased interest and satisfaction.

I have a few comments to make at this point on the business of the drawers. It was obviously mere hypocrisy on Hans's part to pretend to be so glad of the opportunity of giving an account of the affair. In the end he threw the mask aside and was rude to his father. It was a question of things which had once afforded him *a great deal of pleasure*, but of which, now that repression had set in, he was very much ashamed, and at which he professed to be disgusted. He told some downright lies so as to disguise the circumstances in which he had seen his mother change her drawers. In reality, the putting on and taking off of her drawers belonged to the 'lumf' context.

.   .   .   .

Nevertheless, it is worth bearing carefully in mind the desire, which Hans had already repressed, for seeing his mother doing lumf.[38]

The same thing is true of other aspects of Hans' behavior, as where he reproved his father for making "such a row with your feet."

'I asked him why he was afraid, and whether perhaps he was

37. *Ibid.*, p. 283.   38. *Ibid.*, p. 200.

nervous because the horse had done like this (and I stamped with my foot). He said: "Don't make such a row with your feet!" Compare his remark upon the fallen bus-horse."[39]

He complained also because a bus-horse had fallen down and made a row with its feet. This seems to have been connected also with excretory sounds and images exerting their influence long after the time when Hans was directly in conflict over them. In the case of the adult person, according to Freud, these childhood determining incidents would be more remote and less easily visible than in the case of Hans, but they would be no less active determinants of behavior. We will recall also that little Hans is said to have reacted to a threat on the part of his mother to cut off his penis a full year at least after it was made. Apparently this threat was, as it were, kept in reserve until a context arose in which it became applicable. The boy's phobia would be quite unintelligible were one not to include in the data this item from his still earlier experience. Freud's work gives us the most telling illustrations of unity and continuity in the individual life.

Criterion VI. The "social situation" must be carefully and continuously specified as a factor.

In common with Freud's other references to cultural matters at this period, he seems to handle the culture quite well in a practical sense, but not to utilize the concept in a systematic sense. He shows plainly that little Hans' phobia can only be identified if compared with the normal behavior expected of a child of his age.

Hans evidently collected the material for the particular disguises adopted by his fear from the impressions to which he was all day long exposed owing to the Head Customs House being situated on the opposite side of the street. In this connection, too, he showed signs of an impulse—though it was now inhibited

39. *Ibid.*, p. 195.

by his anxiety—to play with the loads on the carts, with the packages, casks and boxes, like the street-boys.[40]

He shows that the phobic fear is an element added to the culturally defined objects, street, horse, bus, and so on. Hans' interpretation of these objects after the phobia set in can certainly be referred to as a private version of culture. Freud stresses also the effect of the current situation in the origin of the phobia. It does not grow out of thin air but is solidly implemented by the behavior of others toward him. To let one example serve for many we refer again to the effect of the castration threat pronounced by his mother and acting with deferred effect a year and a quarter later.

'It does grow onto me': if the motives of the thought were solace and defiance, we are reminded of his mother's old threat that she should have his widdler cut off if he went on playing with it. At the time it was made, when he was three and a half, this threat had no effect. He calmly replied that then he should widdle with his bottom. It would be the most completely typical procedure if the threat of castration were to have a *deferred* effect, and if he were now, a year and a quarter later, oppressed by the fear of having to lose this precious piece of his ego.[41]

We remember that at this time the mother threatened to call the doctor to cut off his penis in case he masturbated; the doctor in question turns out to be Hans' father, both in fantasy and in the real actual life situation. His father was also a physician. This at first "external" situation is psychically incorporated and becomes a motor element in the instinct renunciation which led to the traumatic anxiety. Freud informs us that anxiety is judged as morbid when it can no longer be dissipated by gratification in a real world.

It is perhaps only on the question of formulation of the problem that we can challenge Freud here. If the external

40. *Ibid.*, p. 266.   41. *Ibid.*, p. 178.

situation were more critically defined it would certainly lead him out from the exigencies of the psychic life of the person to status and economic situations in the wider group and the effect on the individual life. The study of an individual life may become a study of the culture at any time if one attempts to state adequately the current life situation of the person. It does not mean that one always has to do this, but this possibility should remain as a constant frame of reference, at least for the social scientist who deals with life-history materials. Freud seems to have dealt quite adequately with the problem of the current situation in a practical sense; he has not evaluated the many clues which it offers for an understanding of the wider society in which the person lives. Indeed, it is only by reference to the cultural structure already precipitated in the psyche of the analyst that one can understand *how* he follows the action and fantasy of his patient. Put him in another society where the social situation is not continuously and automatically defined by his own unconscious mental life and he will not understand anything until he has mastered the formal structure of the culture. The type of understanding required is not given by any degree or formal status tag; it can only be acquired by participation in the group life in question. There seems to be a tendency among analysts to disavow or make little of this structure of the culture which they carry and which makes understanding of neurotic patients possible for them. It leads to a conviction that the culture which they share need not be explicitly pointed out, and to an acceptance of this culture as "given" and basic. The adequate theoretical definition of the current situation and the differences between it and the patient's private view of the same situation is an important step in acculturating such a psychology as Freud's to social science uses.

Criterion VII. The life-history material itself must be organized and conceptualized.

In conclusion we cannot help commenting upon the singular consistency and beauty of Freud's concept system. It hangs together firmly and organically and revolves around a few central concepts. There is a bottom to it as well as an integrated texture and no essential question within its field is left unacknowledged in a conceptual sense. Although it lacks the cultural perspective and exhibits biases from the organic field at times, there is nothing in it which is antithetic to cultural knowledge. What the technical student of culture has to add can be added without essential damage to the system, and what it brings to cultural studies is most urgently needed.

CHAPTER VI

THE CRITERIA APPLIED: "LIFE-RECORD OF AN IMMIGRANT."*

PARTICULAR interest attaches to the analysis of the treatment of personal life-records by Thomas and Znaniecki because these writers designate such materials as the *perfect* type of sociological material.

We are safe in saying that personal life-records, as complete as possible, constitute the *perfect* type of sociological material, and that if social science has to use other materials at all it is only because of the practical difficulty of obtaining at the moment a sufficient number of such records to cover the totality of sociological problems, and of the enormous amount of work demanded for an adequate analysis of all the personal materials necessary to characterize the life of a social group. If we are forced to use mass-phenomena as material, or any kind of happenings taken without regard to the life-histories of the individuals who participate in them, it is a defect, not an advantage, of our present sociological method.[1]

They believe indeed that the only limitation to the use of such materials for sociological ends is the difficulty of acquiring them and that the use of other materials is a "defect," not an advantage of our present sociological method. They seem to feel that statements made by social informants are invariably fragments of a life history, but one that is inadequately defined; the more complete, therefore, the life his-

---

* Thomas, W. I., and Znaniecki, Florian, "Life-Record of an Immigrant," *The Polish Peasant in Europe and America,* Volume II, New York, Alfred A. Knopf, 1927, pp. 1831–2244. All of the extracts in this chapter are taken from this book with the consent of the publisher. The permission thus granted is warmly appreciated.

1. *Ibid.,* pp. 1832–1833.

tory, the more adequate is any single statement, such as a questionnaire answer made by an informant. It would be interesting if we could carry this view over to ethnological materials and regard such materials as fragments of life histories which are still inadequately seen. The problem of the adequate life history is all the more important if we are to regard it as a fundamental of sociological research. We are informed again that individuals must be seen in their "entire personal evolution" if data derived from them are to be used for the determination of social laws.

The use of individual life-records as material for the determination of abstract social laws must be supplemented by a sociological study of these individuals themselves in their entire personal evolution, as concrete components of the social world.[2]

The emphasis that Thomas and Znaniecki have put on the life history has been evaluated as an important contribution to sociological research and has not ceased to influence research method and thought, including, of course, that of the writer.

We deal here with an autobiography written by a mature Polish immigrant to the United States, a baker by trade, married at the time of writing. The document is a long and in some respects a very detailed exposition of the writer's life. The writer was a man of meager education, and in view of this fact, has written a surprisingly expressive autobiography. He has not attempted to give us a theory of his own life in any systematic sense. This theory is supplied by the authors in the form of footnotes to the text and a final chapter discussing the materials.

As is clear from the autobiography the writer was in extreme need of money and wrote at the outset because he was paid to. The authors believe, however, that "ambition, lit-

2. *Ibid.,* pp. 1835–1836.

erary interest and interest in his own life probably became at once the main motives."

We must add a few remarks about the document itself. Wladek was first induced to write his autobiography by a promise of money, but ambition, literary interest and interest in his own life probably became at once the main motives. He wrote with an astonishing rapidity.[3]

Very likely they have supplementary experience with Wladek himself to confirm this statement although economic motives would provide quite a sufficient and indispensable explanation. We should have been grateful for some detailed discussion by the writers as to just how this sale of his autobiography had influenced these specific materials; it seems hardly possible that it can have failed to be a factor.

In the comments of the authors upon the material at least two scientific ends are served. In the first case they attempt to give a theory of Wladek's life on the basis of the material which he produces and to present it as a unified enterprise; in the second case they derive the facts from it which serve to define social groups. For example, in a case where Wladek had played cards for an evening it is noted that such amusements were typical of the lower-middle class but are not needed in the primary peasant community.

So I amused myself (card-playing) on the first evening in Mokrsko.

n. The party was typical for the lower-middle class, and also to some extent for the classes from which it is imitated. The general basis upon which people meet and enjoy each other's company depends of course upon the common interests they have. In the primary peasant community there is no need of creating any particular basis of entertainment, for all the main interests of life are common because of the similarity of the

3. *Ibid.,* p. 1912.

occupations and the identity of the social milieu, which is an object of a permanent interest to all of its members.[4]

It is perfectly possible to utilize life-history materials for both purposes, that is, to explain the subject and to identify his group. If there may be said to be any preference for either of these objectives by the writers, it would seem to be the second rather than the first.

Criterion I. The subject must be viewed as a specimen in a cultural series.

If we cannot say that our authors invented the point of view out of which the above criterion is derived, we can agree that they have stated it most clearly and emphatically. They recognize and use the notion that the individual organism comes into a group which exists before him, which has an organized method of living already in operation and which will present him with a series of defined situations to which he must adjust. After reading their evidence we will agree that the "man who grew up on a desert island" will have to be dropped from social science thinking, even as a fictive method of securing emphasis on an existing culture. The power of the preëxisting group and its frame of life is too patent.

But much more important is the positive limitation of evolution which society imposes upon the individual by putting him into a determined frame of organized activities which involves in advance a general succession of influences—early family education, beginning of a definite career with determined openings, marriage, etc.—establishes a regularity of periodical alternations of work and play, food and sleep, etc., and with the help of economic, legal and moral sanctions prescribes and excludes certain forms of behavior.[5]

The full working-out of this point will have revolutionizing

4. *Ibid.*, p. 2076.   5. *Ibid.*, p. 1842.

effects on all of the disciplines which deal directly with persons. They state again that a "personality is always a constitutive element of some social group" and that it lives and exists only in a social life, a traditional social life.

A personality is always a constitutive element of some social group; the values with which it has to deal are, were and will be common to many personalities, some of them common to all mankind, and the attitudes which it exhibits are also shared by many other individuals.[6]

Wladek is, therefore, to be viewed not as a personality in general but as a resultant of the particular concrete (Polish) culture from which he came and as constantly living in interaction with the trends of development of this society. For example, the autobiography of Wladek is not independently understandable; it has to be viewed in the context of the Polish peasant social milieu as established in the other volumes of this study by Thomas and Znaniecki. The pains which they have been at to make this definition concrete and perspicuous are alone an important contribution to social science research. In reading Wladek's autobiography we must constantly refer to this cultural frame of reference if we are to read with discrimination. As an example of this delineation of the background we find a discussion of the social hierarchy in a manorial village like that in which Wladek grew up.

n. In the manorial village all the inhabitants are more or less dependent upon the manor-owner, and there is the most minute social hierarchy from the manor-owner down, in the order of priest, steward, teacher, tavern-keeper, organist, butler, teamster, blacksmith, carpenter, shepherds, etc., and finally the common laborers. There is no real community, no unique and consistent social opinion, no permanence of tradition; servility, desire to climb, with little opportunity to climb. In

6. *Ibid.*, pp. 1831–1832.

Volume I (Sekowski series) we have characterized this milieu.
Although Wladek's parents were not really manor-servants
they fitted perfectly into this environment.[7]

This type of community is clearly differentiated from the
peasant milieux spacially surrounding it. It is important to
see, as we do here, that Wladek comes from a social group on
the march to higher status in a time of shifting class lines.
The compulsive character of the organization of the peasant
group is differentiated from that of the cultural sub-section
of Polish society into which Wladek was born.

Thus, a modification introduced into some social ceremony has
nothing to do objectively with the technique of hunting or warfare, a new technical device in constructing houses has no direct
effect upon the political organization of the group, etc. But
the common bond between all these schemes lies in the character
of sacredness which all of them possess in the eyes of the group
as parts of the same traditional stock whose unity is ultimately
founded on the unity and continuity of the group itself. The
individual must make each and all of these schemes his own in
order to be a full member of the group.[8]

Here (among the peasants) we find the sacredness of the
total social heritage insisted upon more stringently than in
the town group and we see also the indivisible character of
primary group life which gives a kind of unity to the lives of
those who participate in it.

On such a point as the reluctance of Wladek's father to
pay for the instruction of his children we find reference made
again to the preëxisting culture.

My mother had a more generous disposition, and cared more
for the instruction of her children, and this displeased my father
greatly, particularly when it came to paying for the instruction.
n. We saw in Part I that the woman has more in view the needs

7. *Ibid.*, p. 1916.   8. *Ibid.*, p. 1892.

of the individual members of the family while the man cares more for the material existence of the group as a whole. As long as the basis of this existence is the farm, exclusive interest in the maintenance and increase of the familial fortune is perfectly justifiable and efficient, for thereby the children have their future assured. But in the present case the old Wiszniewski keeps the old attitude when it is completely misadapted to the actual conditions. There is no familial property which could assure the future of the children, and in his small trade he can never hope to put aside enough to endow them. The only way to assure their existence is to give them a sufficient instruction and push them into a middle-class career. He does this, indeed, but unwillingly and incompletely, as will appear.[9]

The father had the attitude that this was an unnecessary expense, an attitude which *was* appropriate to the peasant situation where the family land guaranteed the future fortunes of the children. This attitude, however, has survived in a situation where it was disadvantageous, that is, where the social logic of Wladek's life was to push forward into a middle-class career. Such a career would imply special training and therefore expense to the father. Such a hang-over of parental attitudes is indeed part of the defining culture which Wladek faced, although he seems to view his father's attitude as a personal idiosyncrasy.

The above are only a few examples in theory and in statement of the massive and concrete manner in which Thomas and Znaniecki meet our criterion. All of the five volumes of their study are related to Wladek's autobiography, at least in the sense that they constitute a monumental definition of the society into which Wladek came. Without reference to the cultural background thus delineated, his life would seem very strange indeed and must seem so to readers who study it alone. This background is not defined, point for point, in

9. *Ibid.*, p. 1923.

following the autobiography of Wladek, but it swings like a massive frame to the document, and one finds constantly that one can bring to bear on the document itself one's knowledge of the Polish culture as defined from the other materials. Shifts in the social picture, such as the realignment of classes or break-up of older forms, are also indicated; indeed, Wladek himself is a resultant and partly a victim of such changes.

Criterion II. The organic motors of action ascribed must be socially relevant.

Thomas and Znaniecki seem to make quite clearly the distinction between the biological being as offered to culture and the same being after his biological potentialities have been elaborated in a specific cultural milieu. This distinction is made concrete in their terms "temperamental attitudes," which apply to the organism, and "social attitudes"; the latter term is used when a social or meaning component has been added to the temperamental attitude.

The biological being and his behavior represent therefore nothing but the limit dividing natural from social life; the individual is an object-matter of social psychology only in so far as his activities are above this limit, imply on his part a conscious realization of existing social meanings and require from the scientist an indirect reconstruction of his attitudes. Therefore this limit itself must be defined by social psychology in terms of attitudes, and the concept of temperamental attitudes serves precisely this purpose. An individual with nothing but his biological formation, or—in social terms—with nothing but his temperamental attitudes, is not yet a social personality, but is able to become one.[10]

They say, "We may call temperament the fundamental original group of attitudes of the individual as existing independently of any social influences."

10. *Ibid.,* pp. 1849–1850.

We may call temperament the fundamental original group of attitudes of the individual as existing independently of any social influences; we may call character the set of organized and fixed groups of attitudes developed by social influences operating upon the temperamental basis.[11]

Character, on the other hand, is "the set of organized and fixed groups of attitudes developed by social influences operating upon the temperamental basis." It is easy to see that these writers feel the need of such a statement of the biological life as will interlock with our terms from the cultural field.

They do not, however, present the temperamental attitudes as a fixed group of characters which work themselves out, despite social influence, into definite character forms. Rather they put the stress on the milieu and state that "if the proper influences were exercised from the beginning, a wide range of characters, theoretically any possible character, might be evolved out of any temperament."

We know already that the development of temperamental attitudes into character-attitudes can assume many different directions, so that, if the proper influences were exercised from the beginning, a wide range of characters, theoretically any possible character, might be evolved out of any temperament.[12]

The latter statement would lead us to believe that they posit different basic temperaments as well but do not attribute to them definitive power for the development of the personality.

The general theoretical form of statement is quite satisfactory from the standpoint of our criterion, as we have seen above; the specific identification of the temperamental attitudes is not, however, so clear-cut. Two basic tendencies which we do have to go on are those of curiosity and fear.

In the reflex system of all the higher organisms are two powerful

11. *Ibid.*, p. 1844. 12. *Ibid.*, p. 1863.

tendencies which in their most distinct and explicit form manifest themselves as curiosity and fear. Without curiosity, that is, an interest in new situations in general, the animal would not live; to neglect the new situation might mean either that he was about to be eaten or that he was missing his chance for food. And fear with its contrary tendency to avoid certain experiences for the sake of security is equally essential to life.[13]

These temperamental attitudes are pictured as present in the reflex system of all higher organisms and as essential to survival. The avoidance tendencies exhibited through fear are believed to be essential for "security." It would seem that the social wishes for new experience and security are elaborations of curiosity and fear; these relationships will be discussed under criterion IV. In another statement "hunger and sexual desire, fear and anger" are listed as basic temperamental attitudes.

Thus, hunger and sexual desire, fear and anger manifest themselves independently of each other without any conscious attempt at co-ordination. In character, on the contrary, attitudes are more or less systematized; their continuity through many manifestations makes this indispensable.[14]

The authors do not state explicitly whether they consider that "sexual desire" would be primary in a time sense as is hunger, probably not; fear and anger would certainly manifest themselves very early. At their first appearance these attitudes are more or less unsystematized; it is only through cultural elaboration that they are consolidated into social attitudes and inter-related as an organization of character. We find in another place hunger and sex mentioned as basic and are led to believe that the authors rely heavily on these impulses as the two foundation stones of their theory.

13. *Ibid.*, p. 1859.   14. *Ibid.*, p. 1846.

If a certain group of temperamental attitudes reappears from case to case in such activities as the satisfaction of hunger or of the sexual appetite, it is not because these attitudes have been consciously subordinated to a predominant attitude, but because their association has habitually brought the desired result in the given conditions.[15]

Our conclusion here must be that the authors seem to meet our criterion very satisfactorily in a formal sense. They seem to waver a bit when it comes to giving us a solid outline of the instinctual equipment of man. This will necessarily be a disadvantage when we must ask ourselves how the temperamental attitudes are elaborated into social attitudes in our fourth section.

Criterion III. The peculiar role of the family group in transmitting the culture must be recognized.

After our experience in seeing the great weight which is attached by Thomas and Znaniecki to the structure of the culture, we shall expect them to attach fundamental importance to the family institution and to the particular family of Wladek in generating his character. In the first of these expectations we shall be gratified; in the second, our approval will necessarily be more reserved. The family as a form is clearly understood and appreciated by our authors. We find them commenting on the "character of seriousness and constraint" which is typical of family organization in his class.

n. His relation with the D. family always remained more free, even if less close, than that with his own. Indeed the attitudes of personal friendship and affection cannot express themselves with sufficient freedom in the family because the traditional norms of obedience and the feeling of responsibility give the whole relation a character of seriousness and constraint. This character is not felt so much in the primary peasant family,

15. *Ibid.,* p. 1845.

where the respective attitudes are habitual. In Wladek's case
the familial connection is already felt as an unpleasant duty
and may disappear if the contrary attitudes find favorable
conditions of development.[16]

This is said to be less true of the primary peasant family.
Wladek always, indeed, feels more free in the household of
one of the neighbors. The subordination of the individual to
the family group is an important identifying character of
the Polish peasant family, though it is noted in connection
with this example that the family is unable to carry out its
traditional duty of permanent support toward the member.

Bronislaw had worked the whole summer at the manor. The girls
bought winter hats for themselves with the money he earned while
he went around as before in nothing but rags. When there was
no more work in the field, he took a rope and went to the forest
after dry wood. Sometimes he went four times a day and as he
was a strong boy he brought wood enough to keep them warm.
They had no money to buy firewood, and they could not even
think of letting him go away from home, for if he were not there
who would work for them?

n. A good example of the subordination of the individual to the
   family. In the peasant family the individual makes no sacrifice
   by his subordination, because the group embodies his interests.
   But here the familial organization is decaying, and while the
   family still demands as much as possible from the member it
   is unconscious of and unable to perform its duties toward
   him.[17]

This is given as an instance of decay in family organization.
The Polish culture sanctions the physical punishment of children by the parents, although such punishment by the father
is subject to criticism by the large family group if it goes
beyond certain bounds.

16. *Ibid.*, pp. 1944–1945.   17. *Ibid.*, p. 1960.

The way our father beat us was this: he put my head—if it was
I who was punished—between his legs so that the hind part pro-
truded, and then beat with whatever he found under his hand,
wood or iron.* Therefore none of us loved father. He could never
boast of the love of his children.

* *n.* The beating of children is sanctioned by public opinion, but
in this case we find two anomalies—the lack of measure in the
father and the lack of affection in the children. They are explicable by the isolation of the marriage-group from the rest
of the family.[18]

In the case of Wladek's family the restraining force of this
criticism was lost through the isolation of his parents from
the wider family group, and the father "acts without familial
control under the influence of passion." Such a fact can
hardly be without importance for the character formation of
the children in the family and it may be related to Wladek's
persistent inability to define disagreeable situations clearly.
The older peasant attitude of responsibility for the children
is changing in the culture of Wladek's parents and they tend
to isolate him both from family responsibility and family
protection.

"Only you, Wladzio, don't look for help toward your parents,
for we can give you no help. You will have as much as you can
earn." And we talked long this way.

n. This is evidently the first serious conversation of this kind
between father and son. The situation has not been favorable
for the development of Wladek's family attitude. He has been
told that he is to expect no help from the family, and when
the parents begin to share the family responsibility with the
other sons they do not share it with him. In this way the policy
of the family tends to isolate him as an independent individual
and to give his family attitudes the vague form shown later
and which can be characterized as complete indifference to the

18. *Ibid.,* p. 1922.

family when he is separated from it and dependence on response when he happens to be with it.[19]

We may note also that Wladek gives as his reason for his
childhood hostility toward his father the fact that he was
beaten by him and the fact that the father was harsh and
unloving.

Wladek points to a Polish peasant custom of giving each
child at Christmas time a gift "measured according to our
parents' love," and says that he and his sister Marya always
received the worst gifts.

But Christmas had more importance for us, because every
child was presented with a gift, measured according to our parents' love. Our parents did not love us all equally and so the gifts
were not equal. I and sister Marya always received the worst,
though I don't know even now how I merited this. As to my sister,
our parents said that she was very disobedient and bad-mouthed
(impudent). But as far as I remember, I never made my parents
angry (by impudence) and I even loved my mother a great deal.
And so my "little star" was always the worst. I often wept because of this.[20]

This favoritism of the parents toward the other children is
believed to have provoked a strong degree of envy in Wladek
which "occasionally became a tendency to climb." This is not
a very concrete and well-elaborated instance of family influence, but it shows how the authors believe character formation to take place in family experience.

The authors are convinced that under family influence the
primary organization of attitudes has taken place in Wladek.

The fact that Wladek feels so keenly the disruption of his home
is sufficient proof of a primary organization of attitudes. His
persistent preservation of some standards throughout his life

19. *Ibid.*, pp. 1973–1974.	20. *Ibid.*, p. 1927.

shows precisely the power of the early familial organization of attitudes.[21]

The authors comment that "his persistent preservation of some standards throughout his life shows precisely the power of the early familial organization of attitudes."

In the formal sense, therefore, our criterion is very adequately met in this case. However, we cannot suppress a craving for a concrete picture of how Wladek's character is elaborated under the impact of family situations and attitudes, especially in early life, and this need is only very inadequately met. The parents never emerge as actual personalities. We feel here as if we were facing a good theoretical statement but that the authors did not know just how to make it work; it may be said, of course, that the information Wladek gives does not permit a conclusive theory of his infamily experience. We go with Thomas and Znaniecki, as far as they go, with warm agreement, but then we find ourselves let down and fed with rather general statements about the Polish culture and family. It is, after all, the personality of Wladek that we wish to understand, and it is through his development in his family that we expect to see the Polish family culture at work. The acknowledgment of family form is quite thorough; what we miss is the sense of Wladek's developing character under the impact of family stresses. Nothing less will be adequate for social science ends.

Criterion IV. The specific method of elaboration of organic materials into social behavior must be shown.

In relation to this criterion we will meet our greatest difficulty with the analysis proposed by Thomas and Znaniecki. Our criterion requires that there should be a clear identifiable development of the assumed biological material into the social attitudes, and that we should be able to trace, point for point, how this or that organic tendency is integrated into

21. *Ibid.,* p. 2238.

character under the pressures of group life. The problem is here avoided rather than clarified. We are led to believe that somehow social attitudes develop out of less specified structures under the impact of collective life; but just what we want to know most is missing. We are given, to be sure, the concepts of temperament and character, but how temperament becomes character is the problem, and it remains a problem throughout the discussion.

Temperament and *character* are the concepts in which has been expressed the common-sense realization that there are always a few organized groups of attitudes in a personality which play a predominant part in its activity, so that for practical purposes any attitudes outside of those groups can be neglected as inconspicuously manifesting themselves in personal behavior.[22]

What we are calling for is a specific statement of how *what* temperamental potentialities are elaborated into *what* character attitudes in Wladek, since he is our subject and center of discussion. There is a theoretical recognition of the fact that a firm theory is needed at this point, as is instanced by the attempt to explain how attitudes are developed by interaction with social values.

In such a series every single link is a fact of the type: attitude—value—attitude, or: value—attitude—value, and as such, if properly analyzed, can always be explained by sociological law (or lead to the discovery of a sociological law), but the series as a whole cannot be subject to any law, for there are many possible ways in which an attitude can be developed out of another attitude, a value out of another value; all depends on the nature of the intermediary data. Thus, if we have as starting-point an attitude *a* and as result an attitude *m*, the evolution may have gone on in such a way that out of *a*, under the influence of a value *B*, is evolved the attitude *d*; out of *d*, under the influence of *J*, the atti-

22. *Ibid.*, p. 1843.

tude k, and k, under the influence of a value N, was changed into the attitude m.[23]

But this remains on a theoretical plane. No one knows how to substitute the concrete attitudes and values in the alphabetical illustration given. Such an illustration is bound to remain a verbal transaction until it is seen to control the elaboration of attitudes which can be specified.

Thomas and Znaniecki do not leave the attitudes of the individual altogether unclassified. They do come forward at this point with a group of desires or wishes which are used throughout the discussion of Wladek's case as motors of action. These wishes are called those for response, recognition, new experience, and security. We will try to decide in each case what relation they have to the temperamental attitudes assumed and how they are utilized in illuminating Wladek's life.

In the case of the desires for response and recognition we are informed that they correspond respectively to the family system in the primary group organization and to the wider social group.

The adaptation of the individual to the primary group requires therefore, that all his attitudes be subordinated to those by which the group itself becomes for him a criterion of all values. These fundamental social attitudes are the *desire for response*, corresponding to the family system in the primary group-organization, and the *desire for recognition*, corresponding to the traditionally standardized systems of social values upon which the social opinion of the community bases its appreciations. The desire for response is the tendency to obtain a direct positive personal reaction to an action whose object is another individual; the desire for recognition is the tendency to obtain a direct or indirect positive appreciation of any action, whatever may be its object.[24]

23. *Ibid.*, pp. 1839–1840.   24. *Ibid.*, p. 1882.

These wishes seem, therefore, to be identified rather by their source in group life than by reference to the organism itself. A search of the theoretical material does not reveal how these desires are elaborated from tendencies to act which are postulated as being organic and primary.

The character of the individual is apparently stabilized and unified on the basis of these two desires.

But such a stabilization and unification of character on the ground of the desires for response and recognition becomes more and more rare with the progress of civilization. Even in the still existing primary groups it tends to diminish as members of these groups get in contact with the external world. Every attempt of a member of such a group to define his situations from the standpoint of his hedonistic, economic, religious, intellectual, instead of his social attitudes, is in fact a break in his character, and such attempts become more and more frequent as, through extra-communal experiences, the individual finds before him situations that are not connected with the primary group—for example, when in the city he has the opportunity of drinking without any ceremonial occasion, when he earns money by hired labor instead of working on the family farm, when he can have a sexual experience without passing through the system of familial courtship, when he learns anything alone by reading and not in common with the whole village from a news-bearer, etc.[25]

If the environing group, family or wider community, is solidly organized and defines recurring situations adequately, the result will be a character of a unified and consistent sort. The character of the individual will possess the unity exhibited by the social group which defines his behavior. We cannot help noting, however, that the wishes in question seem to be postulated to meet the group facts as known rather than derived from the organic substratum of the individual. There is definitely a break in theory in the system at this point.

25. *Ibid.,* pp. 1884–1885.

Only where the unified character of group activity is preserved can the individual character be integrated on the basis of the general desire for response and recognition.

Therefore individual character can be no longer unified upon the basis of the general desires for response and recognition, for even if these desires always remain fundamental for social relations, they must be differently qualified in different groups.[26]

The term "social values" is regularly used here as a means of identifying the cultural facts, objects and situations external to the individual in question at any one time.

Certain social conditions being given, Wladek's evolution would depend on his attitudes toward the social values constituting these conditions, and *vice versa*, given certain attitudes toward social values, the social conditions in which he found himself would determine his evolution.[27]

The lack of pungent illustrations of the elaboration of attitudes under contact with any values is never more painful than at this point.

Suppression and sublimation are also terms which appear in the system of Thomas and Znaniecki. In the case of suppression two forms are distinguished, a negative type, in which the undesired impulse is neglected and not evoked, and a positive type, in which a mobilized attitude is resisted, perhaps punished.

The mechanism of suppression is double. A temperamental possibility not yet conscious is suppressed if given no opportunity to manifest itself in any situation, for only through such manifestations can it become explicit and be evolved into a character-attitude. This form of suppression is attained by an isolation of the individual from all experiences that may give stimulation to endeavors to define situations by the undesirable tendency. The suppression of sexual attitudes and of free thought in reli-

26. *Ibid.*, p. 1885.　　　　27. *Ibid.*, p. 2228.

gious matters are good examples of this mechanism. The second course, used when an attitude is already manifested, in order to prevent its further development and stabilization, is suppression by negative sanction; a negative value—punishment or blame— is attached to the manifestation of the attitude, and by lack of manifestation the attitude cannot evolve.[28]

This is certainly a method by which an impulse factor might be elaborated into a social attitude, but again we lack any vigorous demonstration in the life of Wladek. By sublimation a temperamental attitude may be exclusively turned toward situations "that have in them an element endowed with social sacredness."

The principle through which any attitude can be made not only socially harmless but even useful, is *sublimation*. It consists in turning the attitude exclusively toward situations that have in them an element endowed with social sacredness. We cannot analyze the latter concept now; we shall do it another time. At present it is enough to point out that an object is socially sacred when it provokes in members of the group an attitude of reverence and when it can be profaned in the eyes of social opinion, by being connected with some other object.[29]

Not much use is made of the concept of sublimation in dealing with the case material. These two concepts, however, have the earmarks of developmental concepts and might, had they been carefully delineated, have given us an idea of how the four wishes are evolved; or, on the other hand, the attempt actually to use them might have shown the authors some of the difficulties in the way of their theory.

In discussing the desire for recognition we find many points in the case material which are indicated as evidences of reaction to this desire. Wladek's life is said to be highly characterized by dependence upon society.

28. *Ibid.*, p. 1865.   29. *Ibid.*, p. 1868.

But Wladek's exclusive dependence upon society is not abnormal at all; it is, as we have seen in Part I, the typical attitude of the peasant. And, as in the peasant, it manifests itself in two ways— as desire for response in immediate personal relations with individuals, as desire for recognition in relations with a group.[30]

This dependence is not viewed as abnormal but rather as a function of primary group experience which continues after he is no longer in the grip of a primary group. This dependence phenomenon seems to be well observed, but we are interested in its history as well as in the fact that it exists, and it is this history of its genesis which our criterion demands. This account is not given us either in theoretical outline or in concrete application to Wladek's life. Slavishly responsive to his wish for recognition Wladek is not able to manifest an opposition to group norms of conduct nor any superior type of activity.

The desire for recognition expresses itself in Wladek in a facility of adaptation to any standards recognized in the group in which he finds himself, not in an opposition to those standards and not in any superior type of activity through which he might gain distinction in the group. Recognition represents the response of the group, and as Wladek never developed any distinguished intellectual, economic, aesthetic or moral qualities, and never had a career embodying any special attainments, his methods of getting distinction remain of the elementary and "showing-off" type.[31]

He cannot wait for the response of the group or endure any fracture of his immediate rapport with it. His autobiography does, indeed, give evidence of this type of behavior. There is, however, a good deal of doubt concerning the utility of postulating his wish for recognition in order to account for such facts. When we do postulate it we are still faced with the

30. *Ibid.*, p. 2229.   31. *Ibid.*, p. 2233.

question of genesis and in particular we would need to know how the family influenced or developed this wish.

Social organization can help to intensify the wish for recognition. The superior position of Wladek's family in the local church is believed to have accentuated this desire in him.

As I mentioned already, we went to church through the sacristy, but the priest did not allow everybody to do this. No one passed through the sacristy but the nobility of the neighboring manors, a few of the more prominent farmers, and my parents. My mother had her own chair on which she sat during the service. No other people were allowed to have chairs. On this account many were angry with the priest, but he did not care at all.
n. Even the church helps to develop the consciousness of social hierarchy and the desire for recognition.[32]

We find again that after a rebuke by his mother his desire for response or recognition is expressed in a day dream of growing up, establishing a business and taking care of his parents in their old age.

This could have been the only reason she gave me the ear-box. But going along the road I resolved that I would hold out in the apprenticeship however hard it might be and later establish a bakery, so that my parents could live with me in their old age, although I was then, in their eyes, the worst of all their children.
n. This is not affection or generosity but the wish to even up— the desire for response and recognition expressed in a daydream.[33]

Still later in his life he is said to be under the influence of a desire for recognition when he plans to save money and establish his own bakery.

No, I must work, put money together and establish my own

32. *Ibid.,* p. 1924.   33. *Ibid.,* pp. 1945–1946.

bakery. Then I can say boldly that I have (a secure existence) and even a better one than a teacher.

n. This is probably the moment when the idea of having a bakery of his own, which remains Wladek's dream and keeps him from complete pauperization, is established as a definite practical aim, while formerly it was rather an indefinite expectation of something to come in an undetermined future. The desire for recognition is the main basis of this aim; even comfort and security are secondary. The attitude was established by the humiliations of his wanderings and the crisis is constituted by the comparison of his own situation with that of Stach, which makes him understand the strong position given the individual by conformity with social regulation.[34]

To talk about such situations as these in terms of a desire for recognition is certainly one way to do it. One feels constantly, however, the lack of a firm footing for such wishes in the organism and also that the situations in question are not very penetratingly dissected. If we knew how a desire for recognition was elaborated out of yet simpler organic attributes, we might be able to use it in more complicated situations with security.

It is not any easier to manage the "desire for response" which we meet so constantly in the footnotes to the document. It is recognizable as a wish for a more intimate reaction than in the case of the desire for recognition, and response in this sense seems to come from the (parental) family and later intimates. The best illustration of this desire can be found in the material relating to Wladek's love life. His relation to women is identified not only by sexual but by social desires.

The desire for response is particularly clear in his relations with women. His search for the company of women seems motivated not only by sexual but by social desires. He is usually surer of the response of women than of men, probably because, not be-

34. *Ibid.*, p. 2078.

ing a permanent member of any community, he has no powerful emotional interests in common with the men he meets (except his brothers), whereas the sexual instinct gives a strong emotional background on which sympathetic responses can develop. And his behavior toward women is typical. He never dares reject any open or half open advance from a girl, even if he is not interested in her and if he has another love affair going on, and he never dares to break a relation openly.[35]

He is, in fact, so at the mercy of his need for response that he never dares to reject an advance from a girl or to break a relationship with her openly and provoke a crisis. The authors appear to say that sexual behavior in adults is not motivated in any simple sense by a sexual instinct but that this instinct is also already vigorously conditioned. In so far as the wish for response has a sexual element in it, either of a direct or sublimated kind, we can see that it must have a history; to be sure, the authors do not tell us how crude sexual wishes are elaborated into socialized wishes, such as a "need for response," but they do seem to assume that such a process takes place. The wish for response, therefore, always contains a dynamic element which is convincing, even though the analysis of it is not complete. It is difficult for Wladek to say anything that will displease anybody because of his dependence on favorable response.

Once Miss Helena told Stasia that I had called her a whelp (silly child; rather offensive) and said that I would marry her only if Mr. L. gave me a full 1,000 roubles of dowry. Mr. and Mrs. L. got very angry and began to reproach me with this when I came to them. From word to word we quarreled a little, for they loved their daughter deeply and did not want anyone to offend her.

n. His desire for response gets him into difficulties by leading him to say everything that will please anybody at a given moment.[36]

35. *Ibid.*, pp. 2231–2232.   36. *Ibid.*, p. 2176.

Again he feels strongly rebuffed when he is no longer included in the family group of a baker for whom he worked.

Then Mr. K. laughed ironically, saying: "How is that? Did I
not bring you my sister? It is not my fault if you are a gaper."
—"Well, how could I guess that it was destined for me, this gift
in the person of Miss Helena?"—"It is a pity," said Mr. K.,
"perhaps I should have brought her to the bakery or to your
room?" . . . Nevertheless, Mr. K. did not improve at all, but
became more and more brutal toward me and manifested his
superiority, while it was not so formerly. So I resolved to change
my place.
n. He had been treated as a member of the family, while now he
   is treated as a mere workman, and this is probably what he
   means when he says that Mr. K. "manifested his superiority."
   The change has meant much for him, in view of his strong desire for social response.[37]

In view of this rebuff and a strong desire for social response,
it is said to be intelligible that he resolved to quit his job. The
theoretical solution provided by the authors does not seem
satisfactory in this case, but it is difficult to examine the
matter more carefully because Wladek has set down the material and does not have to answer any questions other than
those he chose to answer when he first wrote it. This must be
viewed as a methodological weakness. Wladek says he is unable to swear and this fact is interpreted as being due to his
strong desire for social response which leads him to avoid
behavior that would bring criticism from others.

Moreover I was not bold and not foul-mouthed. As to swearing,
I was almost unable to express it.
n. His strong desire for social response leads him to avoid anything which might provoke an unfavorable reaction.[38]

Again we note that Wladek's kindness has its source in the

37. *Ibid.,* pp. 2091–2092.   38. *Ibid.,* p. 2092.

"wish to avoid trouble" and we assume that this is a kind of sub-wish which stands in parallel to the wish for response.

He had passed a hard school of life and knew how to persuade and to excuse others. In a word, he was a man seldom found, and our characters were completely alike, with perhaps the one exception that he was less developed, which did not hinder him nevertheless from being good, polite and indulgent.

n. In spite of the naive conceit of the comparison, there is an external similarity of behavior in the two men. But we know sufficiently that Wladek's kindness has its source in the wish to avoid trouble, to provoke only response that will be pleasant to him.[39]

The wish for response would then seem to be defined, not as a wish for just any response, but as the wish for pleasant, positive, and loving response. If so, it should be so stated; it might come down to a wish to be loved, which would be somewhat more manageable in ordinary speech and experience. We must confess that we have not had any better success with the wish for response than we had with the wish for recognition from the standpoint of tracing them to their somatic sources. Indeed, these wishes seem to be referred to group life, rather than to the organism, and to be brutally posited rather than genetically derived.

In the case of the desires for new experience and stability or security we will have better luck in finding their organic sources. We have noted and note again that they seem to be derived from the instinctual behavior of fear and curiosity.

To represent these two permanent tendencies as they become parts of character in the course of the social development of a personality we shall use the terms *"desire for new experience"* and *"desire for stability."*[40]

39. *Ibid.,* p. 2213.   40. *Ibid.,* p. 1859.

Elementary curiosity is apparently elaborated as a desire for new experience, and fear has as its correlate a desire for stability. We find at least one implication that the desire for new experience is accompanied by buoyancy and the desire for stability by depressive tendencies.

And we find in his temperament neither any exceptional buoyancy which would push him to search continually for new experiences in any one line nor any exceptional depression that would lead to a too great stability. The relative proportion in which these two desires manifest themselves alternatively in his life seems to be quite average. . . .[41]

Wladek is said not to be characterized by either tendency to excess. This seems a very interesting lead, but we are left with this bald notion. Beyond this theoretical statement we do not have anything to go on as to how fear is related to a desire for security. It seems probable enough, but we could hope for a more energetic and detailed analysis which would reveal how such a tendency as fear is attached to acts and objects in complex social situations.

At a number of points in the narrative we find Wladek responding to a desire for new experience, for example, the point in his adolescence when he insists on leaving home to become a baker's apprentice, despite his mother's wish that he remain.

When I had finished the confession and my clothes were ready and nothing remained but going to the apprenticeship, suddenly my mother changed her mind. She no longer wanted me to go to learn to be a baker, but to remain at home for some time and learn the butcher's trade from my father. When I grew stronger I could go to town and learn how to make a greater variety of products, for my father only knew how to make sausages, pudding-sausages and *podgardlanki*, though in winter we killed a hog almost every week. Mother really wanted me to take my

41. *Ibid.*, p. 2227.

father's place at home in the future. But I did not want even to listen to this and I continually asked for an apprenticeship.
n. Desire for new experience.[42]

It would seem from the material given that the situation is a complicated one and that a more careful analysis of the behavior in question would be warranted. But we are asked to understand it via the emergence of a desire for new experience in the writer. The same desire is invoked to explain why he left a certain job.

The next day my week ended, so I began to prepare for the journey. Up to the present nobody believed that I would really leave, but when they saw that I was getting ready they began to dissuade me. I would not listen to anybody, although really I regretted to leave, but I did not want to beg Mr. K.'s pardon, for I was more than sure that in a few days the same thing would repeat itself, while Mr. K. was too proud to beg me to remain with him.
n. His unwillingness to stay after he has thought of leaving is characteristic (cf. p. 2007, note, and 2027). In view of the awakened desire for new experience actual conditions appear as undesirable, even independently of their objective value.[43]

His employer had been very kind to him, taken him into the family and offered Wladek his sister in marriage; Wladek did not understand his employer's offer, or pretended not to, and the employer was insulted and angry with him. He abused Wladek and Wladek decided to leave. In such a case it may be that a wish for new experience was operative, but it would seem again that Wladek's whole situation had been redefined in a disagreeable manner and that we might as well postulate a wish to avoid "bad experience." In no case that we have been able to find in the life of Wladek can the wish for new experience be isolated from a very complicated con-

42. *Ibid.,* pp. 1943–1944.   43. *Ibid.,* p. 2093.

text in which it is almost impossible to tell from the material what was actually operative in leading him to change his situation. It is very difficult to feel our way back to the biological component in this case or to see how "curiosity" can be serviceable as a basis for the concept of the wish for new experience.

In the case of the sexual life of Wladek the wish for new experience is frequently invoked. Wladek's first reported sexual experience with another person came during adolescence with an older girl in the neighborhood. Finally he says he tired of this girl and desired to seduce her younger sister.

This lasted for more than two years, until I went to apprenticeship, but toward the end of this time I grew tired of that older sister and desired Kazia.* But I could in no way seduce the latter.

* *n.* This and the episode with his sister show how spontaneous is the desire for new experience in the sexual line. The limitation of sexual intercourse to one person demands a social organization of the whole relation, either in the form of a socially sanctioned bond (marriage), or in the form of a system of common habits gradually formed (cohabitation) or in the form of a concentration of ideas and emotions not exclusively sexual around the other personality (romantic love). That is to say, monogamous regulation of the sexual impulse must come from other sources than the sexual impulse itself.[44]

We judge that a wish for new objects is characteristic of the unsocialized sexual impulse, according to Thomas and Znaniecki; here, however, we face the unusual reversal that the sex impulse itself is treated as a special case of the desire for new experience. We can only say that the analysis of the concrete behavior seems inadequate, without implying either that anyone else could do it better with the material available. There are times when he is unable to exhibit his sexuality even

44. *Ibid.,* p. 1936.

when the object is new to him, and in one such case he states that he does not know why himself.

> I went to her as usual twice or three times a week. Mr. Stanislaw was not at home in the evenings, so we were alone and sat on his bed and even lay upon it, for I did with Helcia whatever I wanted, and it was difficult to hold out. But I did not begin to foolish although I was sure that Helcia would not defend herself at all. I don't know myself why I would not do it.[45]

Evidently the wish for new experience is at this point blocked by some other wish or barrier. We must note in passing that while the document reveals a good deal of sexual behavior on Wladek's part, there is very little in the way of theory to manage this behavior nor are his relationships either to women or to men very carefully analyzed in concrete terms. We see Wladek as a person moved occasionally throughout his narrative by one or other of the fundamental wishes, but the use of these concepts leaves many strange and unexplained acts which do not fit into the scheme of analysis by wishes, for example, Wladek's concern and fear when he was asking the hand of a certain girl in marriage.

> I wanted to profit of this, arose from my chair, kissed Mrs. P.'s hand, shook hands with Mr. P., and began to explain my request. My legs shook as if upon springs, sweat broke out upon my brow. Mrs. P. noticed it and told me to sit down and not to be so moved. I was glad of this permission, for really I was ashamed to stand any more, my legs trembled so.
>
> n. He is sure of being accepted and he does not care (except for social opinion) whether he is accepted or not. So his emotion is due to the social importance traditionally associated with the act of proposal.[46]

His emotion in this case seems hardly to be explained by stat-

45. *Ibid.*, p. 2215.   46. *Ibid.*, p. 2178.

ing it was "due to the social importance traditionally associated with the act of proposal." Certainly Wladek himself must have felt the emotions in question, and if he did they must somehow be related to his social and emotional life. There seems no way of explaining such a fact under the scheme which has been provided us by Thomas and Znaniecki. We cannot regard it as unimportant either that Wladek is the seduced rather than the seducer in most of his sexual relations. This was certainly true of the three women who played the largest roles in his life. Such a striking fact ought somehow to be reconciled with the doctrines of the wishes. That it is not done seems to indicate that perhaps the wishes as stated do not enable us to deal adequately with some of Wladek's most important characteristics. If it is true that the wishes lack a solid footing in the organic life of the individual, as we believe, and also that the account of the elaboration of primary impulses into social attitudes is sketchy, then we should expect the system to prove inadequate at just such points as these. We cannot say that the method of social reworking of biological impulse is here profoundly treated.

Criterion V. The continuous related character of experience from childhood through adulthood must be stressed.

Even after our frustrating experience in the last section we need not say that Thomas and Znaniecki do not understand the aim of effort in the life history field. They do, and are able to state it quite specifically. They say, for example, that "the ultimate question is not what temperaments and characters there are but what are the ways in which a definite character is developed out of a definite temperament."

It must be remembered in particular that the fundamental problems of the synthesis of human personalities are not problems of a personal *status* but problems of personal *becoming*, that the ultimate question is not what temperaments and characters there are but what are the ways in which a definite character is developed out of a definite temperament, not what life-organizations exist but by what means a certain life-organization is developed.[47]

This is a very satisfactory statement and we judge that if the authors have not realized their aim it was because they could not, and not because they had an incorrect conception of the goal. Theoretically, also, they stress the genetic element in the growth of the individual and put emphasis on the continuity of the life history. They urge that by so doing we diminish the danger of misinterpreting actions which is always present when we consider an isolated act.

An attitude as manifested in an isolated act is always subject to misinterpretation, but this danger diminishes in the very measure of our ability to connect this act with past acts of the same individual.[48]

At a number of points during the autobiography they call our attention to continuities in behavior and attitude. We shall examine some of these.

But before we do this we must note one thunderingly important fact. Wladek begins the detailed discussion of his life when he was exactly six years old.

I begin my description with the first day that I went to school. I was exactly six years old when my father took me by the hand and led me to the school, a few yards distant from our house. When the teacher learned what brought us to him he gave me a book and my examination began.[49]

The authors do not appear to be disturbed by this fact nor do they indicate that they would wish to know more in detail what had transpired previously. This is certainly a defect in their curiosity and a marked limitation to their ability to show the continuous character of Wladek's attitudes. In point of fact, we see him emerging out of the veil of obscurity

47. *Ibid.*, p. 1843.   48. *Ibid.*, p. 1833.
49. *Ibid.*, p. 1918.

which hangs over the first six years of his life a rather well-formed little Wladek, with at least the structure of the chronic attitudes which later distinguish him. Presumably, therefore, we would have to go behind the beginning of the record to learn just the things we would want to know, namely, "not what life-organizations exist but by what means a certain life-organization is developed." By the time of six years the elementary temperamental attitudes are already organized into his character and are firmly overlaid with social directives and definitions. From the scientific standpoint, the fact that Wladek cannot report anything before his sixth year does not excuse us from assuming that many important things, perhaps even the most important, may have happened to him before that time, events which serve to generate the character pattern which we actually observe in his later life. It may be that the desires postulated in section IV would become subject to much more useful definition if they could be followed into the period of their actual genesis. We must confess, therefore, that we cannot accept the six-year period as the beginning of a continuous and connected life-history document.

We have already observed the dependence of Wladek upon social recognition and response. This dependence seems to be accompanied by a type of vanity which makes him remember every trifling gratification of this kind.

n. Wladek always mentions every trifling satisfaction of vanity experienced through the appreciation of his superiors. He makes no mention of his relations to other children in school, and nowhere shows a marked tendency to gain recognition through excellence among his equals. In a six-year-old boy the general demand for recognition could have taken either direction, depending on the environment. In an American boy it would have taken a direction opposite to that shown by Wladek.[50]

50. *Ibid.*, p. 1919.

He seems especially prone to getting his recognition by pleasing superiors directly rather than by competing with his age mates and getting satisfaction from them. This is a well-formed character pattern which apparently protrudes, fully organized, at the beginning of the life history. Another of his early recollections is that of deceiving his father in order to gratify his interest in pigeons and to avoid oppressive sessions of family prayer.

I disliked this Sunday prayer very much because I could not go outdoors, look at the pigeons nor chase them awhile with the other boys. So I used a trick. When I saw through the windows that the pigeons were flying, I asked father for permission to go to the privy. When father gave me permission I went straight to the pigeons, and more than once the prayer was over by the time I got back. I always buttoned my trousers while entering the room and father said: "Well, you have been rather long at the privy." And he said nothing more.

n. This typifies very well the effects of the endeavor to develop new attitudes by external authority appealing to fear and based on physical sanction. The wish opposed by authority produces at first deceit, as a practical solution of the situation. . . . Possibly Wladek learns not to lie to his father, but he preserves the method of deceit during the whole of his life in all its social relations.[51]

This method of deceit he preserves "during the whole of his life in all its social relations." This is certainly a valuable insight and does have the continuous character which our criterion requires, but, as we have noted, the attitude is first seen after the age of six years and its genesis is, to say the least, in doubt. This type of behavior may also have some relation to the "teacher's pet" attitude which he also exhibited.

His childhood relations with the family of the teacher D.— even more cordial than those with his own relatives—are based

51. *Ibid.,* p. 1921.

on the same desire for response. There are in this relation no considerations of family pride, economic success, etc., which frequently cause his own family to assume unfavorable attitudes toward him. As a small boy he is the favorite of the teacher, a little later, of the priest. During the period of his apprenticeship he won the favor, if not of his masters, then of their wives and daughters. For the same reason he succeeds in winning the favor of his superiors in Germany and in the army. He thus shows a particular adaptability in securing response from his superiors. . . . But the contrary is not true; we never see him taking sides with his equals against his superiors, except for a short time in the army, against one man whose superiority he does not recognize. There is nothing of the spirit of class-solidarity in him.[52]

We find him repeatedly playing for response and it is indeed continuously manifested from late childhood on through his life. Since this is such an important designating attitude for our subject, we should be particularly grateful if the conditions of its development were adequately outlined. The authors, however, seem to show no concern, in a scientific sense, about describing the specific genesis of this attitude. We might say that they are convinced of the continuity of the life history,—minus the first six years.

In the case of Wladek we find very little behavior which can be designated under a desire for security and hence this desire is not very thoroughly discussed in relation to the material. It would seem that just this wish is one which would show a profound background in the childhood experience of the person and which would therefore have an important genetic feature. The authors seem to have a notion that a life may be described in terms of a successive dominance of the different wishes.

As the reader knows already, I corresponded with Kazia, so I resolved to call on her in passing through Warsaw and if it

52. *Ibid.*, pp. 2230–2231.

proved possible to propose at once. Stach and our parents
agreed with this.

n. Another manifestation of maturity. He has never loved Kazia
and never recorded anything but indifference toward her; she
has no dowry and he really needs money to pay his parents.
But she now appears as a proper mate because married life
with her would bring no surprises, would be foreseen and determined and thus in accordance with the settled system of
attitudes which Wladek has recently acquired. This security,
which formerly would have been an undesirable element as
against the youthful expectation of new experience, becomes
now a sufficient asset to cause him to neglect the sentimental
aspect.[53]

It is commented that Wladek's late-appearing wish to marry
is a reaction of the desire for security which would have
seemed undesirable "as against the youthful expectation of
new experience." At another point we observe a different description of Wladek's growth; in this case it is a gradual
evolution from Bohemianism to Philistinism.

It will make us realize also that the greatest defect of our entire
civilization has been precisely the existence of a culturally passive mass, that every non-creative personality is an educational
failure. It will show the sources of such failures and thus open
the way for a more successful social education in the future. . . .

The author of our autobiographical record, whose life is an
alternation of periods during which he drifts into Bohemianism
with periods of Philistinization, and shows a gradual increase of
Philistine tendencies in the total curve of its evolution, exhibits
thus both of these social failures and is typical not only for the
study of each of them separately, but also for that of their combination, since many Bohemians sooner or later begin to tend
toward Philistinism and there are hardly any Philistines who
never showed Bohemian tendencies.[54]

53. *Ibid.*, pp. 2198–2199.   54. *Ibid.*, p. 1908.

This seems to be a rephrasing of the already mentioned tendency to successive dominance, first of the wish for new experience exhibited in Bohemian tendencies, and latterly of the desire for security as shown by the consolidation into Philistinism.

These concepts acknowledge after a fashion the continuity and integration of the life-history material, although, to be sure, the early genetic emphasis is missing. The attempt, however, has been useful in that it strives to emphasize character types and attitudes which are relatively consistent and which refer both to the person and to his social adjustment.

Criterion VI. The "social situation" must be carefully and continuously specified as a factor.

The phrase "definition of the situation" is so specifically identified with the name of W. I. Thomas, it must be clear that we have to thank him for aid in defining the criterion itself. This being the case, his use of the concept may be expected to be above reproach. We may note that in using this concept he has stressed the element in it which was particularly valuable to professional students of culture, namely the psychological aspect which points to what we have called the inner, as opposed to the outer, "definition of the situation." Following Thomas we have stressed the fact that "the situation" is defined in two ways, first privately, personally, and uniquely by the subject, and secondly officially and abstractly by observers who see it from the average cultural standpoint. Thomas and Znaniecki make this point clearly in connection with the life history of Wladek.

His influence upon the environment may be scarcely noticeable socially, may have little importance for others, but it is important for himself, since, as we have said, the world in which he lives is not the world as society or the scientific observer sees it but as he sees it himself.[55]

55. *Ibid.,* p. 1858.

They say "that the environment . . . to which he adapts himself is *his* world, not the objective world of science."

We must put ourselves in the position of the subject who tries to find his way in this world, and we must remember, first of all, that the environment by which he is influenced and to which he adapts himself, is *his* world, not the objective world of science— is nature and society as he sees them, not as the scientist sees them.[56]

We would rather stress as the other view of "the situation" the objective world as given naïvely to members of the culture instead of the objective world of science. This point of view is magnificently illustrated by the background of Polish culture, as Thomas and Znaniecki exhibit it in their study; this culture itself is Wladek's "situation." His group is represented as a transition group which has broken away from the older primary group organization and which has not yet been able to reconstruct a stable culture.

But the abnormal political conditions have hampered the application of the new methods, so that at the beginning of the present war only a certain part of the lower classes had been rationally reorganized on the new basis; a large part still preserves, as we have seen in the first two volumes, the old primary group organization, while the rest has already broken with the old forms of social life without being able to construct any new personal life-organization. Wladek—for reasons which his life-record will show—belongs to the latter group.[57]

For this reason Wladek was never socially "placed" in the older Polish class system.

No definite social place can be assigned to the Wiszniewskis in the old class-system; in the new class-system they certainly belong to the intermediary class between the unskilled workmen

56. *Ibid.*, pp. 1846–1847.   57. *Ibid.*, pp. 1910–1911.

and the lower-middle class. A few members of the family succeed in getting into the lower-middle class.[58]

His contacts, therefore, were limited to the stimulations gained from his "intermediary class between the unskilled workmen and the lower-middle class." This is, in a massive sense, a definition of the social situation for Wladek, a definition indeed whose sweep of vision is wider than that of his particular class group. It accounts for a vast number of more specific "situations" which were presented to him in the course of his career.

In the course of his life as a journeyman baker he "defines" the situation with his sweetheart, Dora, in such a way that he decides to leave her. Some of the factors in defining the situation are listed as "by his innate tendency to change, by the tradition that a journeyman should wander. . . ."

But when I remembered that I should be obliged to leave her I felt a terrible regret, for should I never find another such in the world? What was Kazia or Antosia in comparison with her? It is true that they also permitted me to kiss them, but not with such ardor and not with such fire in their eyes as Dora. But it was certain that I must leave her. I could not work always for such a small salary, and then I was young, I wanted to know the world.

n. Wladek's definition of the situation here is assisted by his innate tendency to change, by the tradition that a journeyman should wander, by his reading and the stories of Mr. Leon, and perhaps even the relation to Dora has helped to develop expectations of interesting things in the future.[59]

It would appear from this that the private definition of the situation is for Thomas always a conscious one; at least our authors give no hint of the possibility that a situation may have unconscious reactions as major defining factors. He seems again not to regard the situation as adequately defined

58. *Ibid.*, p. 1909.   59. *Ibid.*, p. 1998.

unless it is clearly and consciously formulated. As an alternative view it seems quite possible that meanings are brought to any new situation which automatically define it, to which only later is added in some cases the perspicuous conscious definition. We find repeated reference to absence of reflection on Wladek's part, a reflection which seems to be necessary to an adequate definition of the situation in the view of Thomas and Znaniecki. We should rather urge that "the situation" may be significantly and accurately defined and reacted to without conscious reflection at all, although reflection may define the situation better and make it more manageable. We must confess that in practice it is hard to find a situation of Wladek's which seems to be adequately and clearly outlined from the psychological side. The authors realize that there is a private definition of the situation but they are not altogether skillful in giving a convincing account of any such given version of any concrete situation. To be fully adequate the fact of private definition of a situation would have to be more relentlessly described than they seem able to do.

Criterion VII. The life-history material itself must be organized and conceptualized.

The authors have tried after their own fashion to make sense out of the life of their subject and to put us in a position to view it as a unit event. Both by footnotes and theoretical discussions they have organized the material. It is true that many questions have arisen about the adequacy of their system and much of Wladek's action remains unintelligible when seen from the angle of their interpretations. Their concept system seems to be guided by *a priori* reference to group life rather than to have grown out of the linear study of Wladek himself. Still we must affirm the fact of their striving to give a systematic view of the material.

THERE are a few other comments on this work which need to

be made. The narrative of Wladek's life seems to go pretty much its own way with only occasional interjections and interpretations by the authors in terms of their four wishes. In most cases these interpretations seem to be affixed, like tabs in a manuscript, rather than to come organically out of the material. Such an interpretive device as is used by Thomas and Znaniecki implies that the author is able to give in his autobiography all the necessary material to enable them to give a correct theory of his life. If it should prove that Wladek did not or could not do this, their interpretations would be subject to serious question and the whole doctrine of the desires would be put in doubt. It is certainly a limitation of the autobiography that you have to take it as given and cannot ask questions of it. For example, from the cultural side there is the strong probability that Wladek is so set up by his Polish culture that he will not offer to our analysts of his autobiography all of the material that they need for their task. A man, as achieved by his culture, may be the kind of a subject who cannot spontaneously reveal the influence of his culture on him by writing. This possibility should certainly be considered. If we were to agree that a man is such a creature, it would throw serious doubt on the naïve written autobiography as a source for social science knowledge of the life of a person in culture.

We have noted also throughout the manuscript that the authors do not, as it were, consider the material of Wladek's life on conceptual hands and knees; they take it rather in a general sense and do not take the trouble to argue very closely back and forth in constructing a theory of his life. We should rather ask of them a tighter knit and closer reasoned theory which would pinion the material more closely into a set of concepts that fit. The "fit" of their scheme of desires to the material does not seem to be very tight. Even with the material available one feels that the whole document

could be more closely figured and estimated and that more
might be derived from it in a theoretical sense.

We have not had time to notice a number of important
ideas for social science which the authors bring forward; our
scheme of criteria, of course, has not permitted a total assess-
ment of their work. They stress, at least in theory, that the
development of the individual "is always a struggle between
the individual and society," in which struggle "society" attempts to subject the individual to its purposes while the
individual struggles for self-expression.

There is, of course, no pre-existing harmony whatever between
the individual and the social factors of personal evolution, and
the fundamental tendencies of the individual are always in some
disaccordance with the fundamental tendencies of social control.
Personal evolution is always a struggle between the individual
and society—a struggle for self-expression on the part of the
individual, for his subjection on the part of society—and it is in
the total course of this struggle that the personality—not as a
static "essence" but as a dynamic, continually evolving set of
activities—manifests and constructs itself.[60]

They have also outlined a scheme of types including three
main items: the Bohemian, the Philistine, and the creative individual. This scheme is oriented around the ability of the
individual to emancipate himself from the strict grasp of the
culture and to produce independent new cultural values. A
"spontaneous constructive power of individuals," manifested
against traditional values, is postulated.

We must realize that social education in the past, viewed from
the standpoint of the human personality, has always been a
failure and that whatever social progress and whatever personal
development has ever been achieved was due to the spontaneous
constructive power of individuals who succeeded, not thanks to
social help but in spite of social hindrances. The best that society

60. *Ibid.,* pp. 1861–1862.

has ever done for its members was to put at their disposal materials for creative development by preserving values produced by the past.[61]

The preëxisting group is seen as putting the materials at the disposal of the individual and on these materials the constructive power of the individual is exercised. Those of high independence and creative capacity are the "creative men."

61. *Ibid.,* p. 1906.

CHAPTER VII

THE CRITERIA APPLIED: *THE JACK-ROLLER**

THE writer of the autobiography was a twenty-two-year-old boy at the time of the completion of the document. He was a young man from a social area in Chicago where family and neighborhood life was markedly unstable and where criminal patterns of activity had emerged. His own major delinquency was jack-rolling, that is, robbing drunken men, sometimes with and sometimes without violence. Stanley wrote out the story of his life at the behest of Mr. Shaw. The document is said "to illustrate the value of the 'own story' in the study and treatment of the delinquent child."

The author's contact with Stanley has extended over a period of six years, the initial contact having been made when Stanley was sixteen years of age. During this period it has been possible to make a rather intensive study of his behavior and social background and to carry out a somewhat intensive program of social treatment. The case is published to illustrate the value of the "own story" in the study and treatment of the delinquent child.[1]

In the case of "own story" material the experience of the writer is presented as he himself sees it without alteration by filtering through the bias or conceptual scheme of any observer. As we frequently are reminded, the boy's *attitudes* toward the persons and events of his life are shown. Whether

* Shaw, Clifford R., *The Jack-Roller,* Chicago, The University of Chicago Press, 1930. All of the extracts in this chapter are taken from this book with the consent of the publisher. The permission thus granted is warmly appreciated.

1. *Ibid.,* p. 1.

or not Stanley presents an objectively correct account of his life is not the point; what is important is that he shows how he actually feels and felt. No alterations have been made in the story by Mr. Shaw apart from a few corrections in punctuation.

> *n.* This is the first chapter of Stanley's "own story" of his experiences in truancy and delinquency. Aside from a number of corrections in punctuation, the story is presented precisely as it was written by the boy. He is also entirely responsible for the organization of the material into chapters, and suggested all of the chapter headings with the exception of that of chapter X. The sincerity of the story cannot be questioned.[2]

The document seems internally coherent and consistent, and we can agree with the author that "the sincerity of the story cannot be questioned." The technique of writing the autobiography is easily defined. In a first interview Mr. Shaw secured a list of Stanley's "behavior difficulties, delinquencies, and commitments"; these were arranged in chronological order and the boy was asked to give a "detailed description of each event, the situation in which it occurred, and his personal reactions to the experience."

Our first interview with Stanley occurred when he was sixteen years and eight months of age. Through that interview we secured a list of his behavior difficulties, delinquencies, and commitments. These were arranged in chronological order and returned to him to be used as a guide in writing his "own story." He was instructed to give a detailed description of each event, the situation in which it occurred, and his personal reactions to the experience. His first document was a brief account of his experiences up to that time.

Our study of this case was interrupted by the boy's commitment to the Chicago House of Correction. At the end of this

2. *Ibid.,* p. 47.

commitment the study of the case was continued. On resuming
the study, our first interest was to secure a more complete written document. We pointed out to him that his first story was an
excellent summary of his life, but lacked detailed descriptive
material. In response to our suggestion that he write a more detailed story, the original document was increased to its present
length, which is approximately two hundred and fifty type-
written pages. All of the suggestions and illustrations used to
indicate the sort of material desired were drawn from his own
experiences.[3]

No suggestions were made about the document which did not
come directly out of the boy's own experience and we may
accept it as relatively free from interference and influence by
the sociological clinician. The point could still be raised, of
course, that the document is not "unbiased," for the student
of culture may argue that Stanley could not give us a complete and useful account of his life, if he would, and for exactly the reason that inhibitions established by his culture
would constantly operate as a block to many types of relevant material. The author does not consider this possibility
as a limitation to the "own story" document. Actually, it may
be demanding too much of Stanley to suppose that he could
write an account of his life which would be of service to the
sociologist in a scientific sense. Nevertheless we are glad to be
assured that we have only to deal with Stanley's cultural bias
on this point and that we do not have to face in addition a
selection on the part of the social investigator. It is quite possible, of course, that we should be grateful for more interference on the part of Mr. Shaw rather than less, if it would
have added to the intelligibility and power of the document in
making Stanley's life clear to us; the virtue of non-interfer-
ence is at best a negative one because we certainly have no
warrant that the "right type" of interference would not have
enabled Stanley to do a much better job of presenting him-

3. *Ibid.,* p. 23.

self. Certainly the life history of Stanley is an enigmatic document with many situations inadequately defined and with many interrogations that beg for further light from the writer.

Criterion I. The subject must be viewed as a specimen in a cultural series.

The intent of this criterion is admirably met by this study; that is to be expected since the criterion itself derives from the work and thought of ethnologists and sociologists and especially from that of W. I. Thomas and E. W. Burgess. The latter refers indeed to the point specifically when he says, "The individual person is more intrinsically a specimen of any group of which he is a member than is a plant or animal of its biological species."

The individual person is more intrinsically a specimen of any group of which he is a member than is a plant or animal of its biological species. The plant or animal is a specimen of botanical or zoological species, because through heredity there is transmitted to it a uniform morphological and physiological pattern. The human being as a member of a social group is a specimen of it, not primarily, if at all, because of his physique and temperament but by reason of his participation in its purposes and activities. Through communication and interaction the person acquires the language, tradition, standards, and practices of his group. Therefore, the relation of the person to his group is organic and hence representative upon a cultural rather than upon a biological level.[4]

We are stressing here, of course, that the person is a specimen of a continuous tradition as well as a specimen of a statically conceived group, but this is merely a corollary of the point made by Burgess. To be sure, in Stanley's case he is presented less as a specimen of an historical tradition than as a result of a breakdown of the Polish culture and of a

4. *Ibid.*, p. 186.

reorganization in terms of delinquent patterns. We see Stanley released from an historically continuous family background and at the mercy of a series of different social patterns in his area. These patterns are convincingly delineated in the autobiography and discussion of it.

His career is a series of acts in response to changing social situations; the discrimination of his stepmother against him in favor of her children; the freedom and release of exploration in a disorganized immigrant area; the patterns of stealing presented by the neighborhood tradition; the lures of West Madison Street; the repression of treatment in the correctional and reformatory institution; the fellowship and code of an oppressed group and the education in crime freely offered him by his associates in these institutions; the thrill of adventures in crime; the easy money quickly obtained and spent; the dulness and monotony of the chances to reform offered him. These are factors common to the actual experiences of thousands of youthful bandits and gangsters.[5]

The overwhelming power of the delinquent situation is clearly presented and the writer of the autobiography is seen by himself, as well as his social analysts, as a "function" of the collective life into which he chanced to come. Indeed, it strikes the discriminating reader of the document that it is less a life history in the sense of an account of the socialization of a person than it is an inside view of the gangland culture. We shall attempt to elaborate this view later. The authors are certainly aware of the value of the present document, for the study of the "traditions, customs, and moral standards of neighborhoods, institutions . . ." Since every statement of a cultural fact must initiate in observation of some person's behavior, we may say that even an ethnographic account of a culture is a series of autobiographic fragments; in the case of Stanley we have an exceptionally complete comment on his

5. *Ibid.*, pp. 189–190.

group life, or at least some portions of it. What distinguishes the life history proper from such an autobiographic illumination of the social group is the specific stress on how the personality is formed by cultural pressure directed against the biological life of the person. In the case of Stanley this discussion tends to be muted and neglected, while the illumination thrown on group interaction is stressed.

A second aspect of the problem of delinquency which may be studied by means of the "own story" is the social and cultural world in which the delinquent lives. It is undoubtedly true that the delinquent behavior of the child cannot be understood and explained apart from the cultural and social context in which it occurred. By means of personal documents it is possible to study not only the traditions, customs, and moral standards of neighborhoods, institutions, families, gangs, and play groups, but the manner in which these cultural factors become incorporated into the behavior trends of the child.[6]

The power of the preëxisting culture in predicting the course that an organism coming into it will take is dramatically shown in the life of Stanley. It is one of the triumphs of sociological research to have established this point in relation to delinquent behavior. We learn that Stanley was born into a disorganized community situation where the *mores* of his family and community group, as traditionally transmitted in Poland, could not be maintained; the result is the freeing of the boy from traditional controls and making him accessible to delinquent patterns.

In the light of the disorganized community situation back of the yards, the persistence of a high rate of delinquency is not at all surprising. With the marked changes in the composition of population, diffusion of divergent cultural standards, and the rapid disorganization of the alien culture, the continuity of community traditions and cultural institutions is broken. Thus

6. *Ibid.*, p. 7.

the effectiveness of the community in the control and education of the child is greatly diminished.[7]

He was inducted at seven years of age into a delinquent gang and began his anti-social career under the guidance and example of this group.

According to official records, Stanley's first contacts with delinquents occurred when he was about seven years of age. At that time he became a member of a gang of older delinquent boys, among whom was his older stepbrother. This gang had a long tradition of petty stealing, burglary, and sex practices. Many of the members had records in the Juvenile Court and a few were already on parole from correctional institutions. It was while in the company of members of this group that Stanley's first experiences in pilfering, stealing from railroads and markets, and sex experiences occurred.

This gang is more or less typical of the numerous delinquent groups which develop in the delinquency areas of the city. It consisted of about twelve members, who ranged in age from six to seventeen years. The major activities and moral code were essentially delinquent in character. It is from such groups that professional criminals are largely recruited.[8]

We learn also that "this gang is more or less typical of the numerous delinquent groups which develop in the delinquency areas of the city" and that from such groups "professional criminals are largely recruited." Stanley grew up in such a gang and became such a criminal, although he was never able to achieve high status in the underworld. A series of delinquency areas are defined, in two of which Stanley lived at different periods in his life. In area A, where he spent his childhood, and in area B, where he spent a good part of his adolescence, the delinquency rates are markedly higher than where he later settled down as a result of the treatment program.

7. *Ibid.*, p. 37.　　　　　　　　8. *Ibid.*, p. 44.

The rate of delinquency among the young men between seventeen and twenty-one years of age for the period 1924 to 1926 was only 3.6 per cent as compared to 28.0 per cent in area A, and 26.5 per cent in the area west of the Loop. Of the total number of boys from ten to seventeen years, only 1.7 per cent were dealt with by the juvenile police probation officers as alleged delinquents in 1926; while in area A, the rate was 17.6 per cent, and in the area west of the Loop 22.0 per cent.[9]

Delinquency is here viewed, of course, merely as a function of the disorganization of family life and traditional control characteristic of the immigrant groups which live in these areas. Area B, the rooming-house district, seems to be characterized by opportunities for pleasure-seeking not accessible in other and better organized districts of the city, as well as by tolerance toward and encouragement of criminal means of making a livelihood.

Map II, which shows the home addresses of 7,541 adult male offenders, indicates a marked concentration of cases in this rooming house district. The freedom and anonymity of the situation offer an environment in which the adult offender may live in relative obscurity and with a minimum of interference from the police. Although most of the criminals living in the district commit their crimes in the more well-to-do sections of the city, cases of "jack-rolling" and homosexual practice are especially common in, or adjacent to, the rooming-house district.[10]

Stanley's resistance against this scene, once living in it, is low and he accepts one of its criminal forms, that of jack-rolling, as his career.

Not the least revealing aspects of his autobiography are his contacts with other criminals in correctional institutions and their indoctrination of him into the criminal code and culture. This is true of his first incarceration in the Deten-

9. *Ibid.,* p. 39.   10. *Ibid.,* p. 38.

tion Home where he meets and admires an older criminal and learns much about the technique of theft and self-protection.

> During the times I was in the home I met crooks of every creed and color. They were there for every crime, running away from home, bumming from school, taking automobiles, stealing from parents, shoplifting, breaking into houses and stores, petty stealing, and sex perversions. It was a novelty to learn that there were so many crimes and ways of stealing that I had never heard about. I was green at first, and the boys pitied and petted me, but I was well on the way to Crookdom at the end of my stay in that place.

> *n.* Our case histories indicate rather clearly that the social contacts established in institutional situations are a medium through which delinquent codes and techniques are transmitted from one boy to another. This social process is well illustrated by Stanley's experiences in the Detention Home and the institutions to which he was subsequently committed.[11]

It is equally true of his high school course in crime at Pontiac where "his wishes and ambitions become organized in terms of the values of the adult criminal group," in this case again by contact with an admired older criminal of greater experience.

> He indelibly impressed two things upon my mind.* First, never to trust anybody with your affairs in crime. You never know when a partner will rat you if he gets into a close pinch and finds it an advantage to "sell his soul" to the police. Billy would ask me questions about my rap and my past experiences, but he would not talk much about himself.

> * *n.* Stanley's contact with Billy illustrates the manner in which the code of the adult criminal world is transmitted to the young delinquent. Through such contacts the youthful offender not only becomes identified with the criminal world,

11. *Ibid.,* p. 58.

but his wishes and ambitions become organized in terms of the values of the adult criminal group.[12]

In Stanley's still later term in the House of Correction he experiences again the scorn which mature criminals have for the small thief and learns to share the ambition of the criminal group to "pull a big deal or none at all."

That evening as I sat on the floor of my cell I got acquainted with Halfpint,* my cell buddy. . . . "Kid, you're in here for a year for jack-rolling. This ought to teach you a lesson. Leave me tell you, the next time you pull anything off, pick out a racket where there's dough, so if you get caught it's worth doing time for, and if you get away, you're all set for the rest of your life. Now compare us here. We both got the same rap, one year in this hell-hole, but I pulled a ten-thousand-dollar deal, and you got less than a hundred dollars. Don't you get me? Besides, get into a respectable racket, so you can dress well and mingle in society. A jack-roller hain't got any chances, anywhere.

* *n.* Stanley's contact with Halfpint is another excellent example of the manner in which the young delinquent assimilates the social values and philosophy of life of the experienced adult criminal. Through such contacts the young delinquent not only acquires new knowledge concerning criminal technique but acquires the code of the adult criminal group.[13]

For some reason, we cannot help noting, the highest and most dangerous standards of criminal practice did not take on with Stanley since he never rose higher in the criminal hierarchy than jack-rolling; if he had really been thoroughly accessible to the gangland culture, he had certainly some opportunity to go after big money before he was twenty. We can only assume that this limitation of accessibility to the highest values of the criminal world was due to personality difficulties of his own, not adequately specified in his autobiography.

12. *Ibid.,* p. 105.   13. *Ibid.,* pp. 152–153.

The idea of the person as a facet of group life is, however, made stunningly clear in this document. Stanley's life is at every point achieved in social interaction with the culture groups accessible to him.

Criterion II. The organic motors of action ascribed must be socially relevant.

At this point the method of work of the writer in finding evidence in the documents and discussions with regard to the criteria will be explained. It is the practice to go through the document and label in the margin of the book any citations which seem to bear on any one of the criteria. This has been done with respect to *The Jack-Roller*. It is interesting to find that no citations have appeared which seem to bear on criterion II, that is, on what the authors begin with in a biological sense about Stanley. We can say that they do not appear to posit anything from the biological side, so far as our reading of the document is revealing. Stanley simply appears at the age of four or five years and is taken for granted from then on. Attention is called to the various groups in which he participated and to their influence on him, but no systematic statement is made with regard to what these groups had to work on in the case of Stanley. It is, of course, indubitable that Stanley was "there" from his birth on and that he must have brought forward some tendencies which, in interaction with group life, resulted in the individual whom we see fairly clearly in his late childhood, but the interactive processes in these years are not revealed. We assume, of course, that if pushed the authors would have statements to make; the fact is, however, that they do not make them in connection with the life of Stanley. This can only be viewed as a serious omission since it is, after all, Stanley's life that we wish to understand, so that it does not help to make these statements in some other document. What we want to know here is what role the biological tendencies played in the elaboration of his character organization and

we cannot remit our insistence that the role of the biological
factors be specified. For example, would a starvation experience "behind the curtain," that is, before four years, play a
role in his hostility toward his real mother and secondarily
toward his stepmother? This cannot be a question of light
importance since he attributes his flight from home into
gangland patterns to a constant strife with his stepmother.
We cannot, of course, answer but we can say that in the lack
of specific information on such a point the character organization of Stanley, once emerged, is inadequately defined. It
would seem that some of the factors in his development that
we want to know most are denied us by this account. The
biological life of Stanley and its early conditioning remain
in a theoretical vacuum. An unhappy feature of the discussion is that the authors show no discomfort on this point and
make no apologies for their failure to illuminate Stanley's
life in this respect. The value of their whole document is remarkably impugned if they can have such an easy theoretical
conscience about a point of such great possible importance.
After all, we would hardly accept in the field of physics scientists who arbitrarily define as their province the last thou-
sand feet that a body falls; we would still have to ask where
the body was in the first place and how it began to fall at all.

*Criterion III. The peculiar role of the family group in
transmitting the culture must be recognized.*

We might expect that the authors of this document would
show the power of the family group in the life of Stanley
with special nicety. This is the case, subject to the important
reservation that the family is visible in its effects on Stanley
only after he was four or five years of age. One possible inference is that the sociologist can afford to neglect events
preceding this time in a total account of the emergence of
such a personality as Stanley. However this may be, concepts
of the utmost value are stressed by Shaw and Burgess. We
learn, for example, to see a family conflict as incident to a

conflict between a cultural group and its environment, in this case the Polish neighborhood, back of the yards, in Chicago.

In the present Polish neighborhood back of the yards, with a population in 1920 of 52.1 per cent foreign-born, there is a definite break between the foreign-born parents and their native-born children. In many of the families the relation between the child and parent assumes the character of an emotional conflict, which definitely complicates the problem of parental control and greatly interferes with the incorporation of the child into the social milieu of his parents.[14]

It is stressed that the culture conflict assumes the form of an emotional conflict between the older and younger generations in the family and that family control of the child is thereby diminished. We see that Stanley came into a family in which "disorganization, emotional tensions, and marked confusion of moral standards were outstanding features."

The family situation in which Stanley lived during his early childhood presents a rather complicated picture of human relationships. The situation was one in which family disorganization, emotional tensions, and marked confusion of moral standards were outstanding features. The significance of these conditions is probably reflected in the ineffectiveness of the family in the discipline and control of its members.[15]

Under these circumstances we might expect, and do find, that Stanley's life will exhibit a similar disorganization from the point of view of traditional control and the values of the wider society. We learn that Stanley's mother was the second wife of his father and that she died when he was four years of age.

His first wife, whom he married in Poland, bore him five children. She died in Chicago fifteen years after their marriage. Soon

14. *Ibid.,* p. 35.   15. *Ibid.,* p. 40.

after her death the father married the young woman who became Stanley's mother. She, too, was born in Poland of Polish peasant parentage, and had emigrated to the United States with her family when she was a small child. Stanley was her second child, a brother being older and a sister younger. When Stanley was four years old, his mother died of tuberculosis. Unfortunately, it is nowhere recorded whether she and the father were compatible; nor do we have any description of her personality. A few months after her death his father married a widow who had seven children from two previous marriages. She, too, had been born in Poland of peasant ancestry.[16]

About this period between zero and four years we know, as we have said, nothing about Stanley's career, and the authors comment that we also know nothing about the mother's personality or her compatibility with the father. Stanley was himself a second child, with a brother three years older and a sister two years younger than he. We cannot gain any clear picture of the character of either sibling from Stanley's autobiography. The picture becomes clearer after the father's third marriage which took place when Stanley was five years old. Two situations emerge of considerable relevance to his character and career. One was that the father was said to be "a heavy drinker and abusive."

After the father's third marriage intense emotional conflicts developed within the family group. The stepmother complained repeatedly that the father was a heavy drinker and abusive. When Stanley was seven years old, she had the father arrested on a charge of excessive drinking and cruelty. He was arraigned in the Court of Domestic Relations and placed on adult probation. In addition to the difficulties between the father and stepmother, conflicts developed between the different sets of children. The stepmother favored her own children and discriminated against Stanley and his brother and sister.[17]

16. *Ibid.*, pp. 40–41.   17. *Ibid.*, pp. 41–42.

The implication is that he was abusive to the mother since Stanley does not charge him with hostile behavior against himself. In a record of Healy's which is fortunately preserved the same judgment is made about the family and it is added that the "boy (is) poorly nourished and neglected."

In his study of Stanley's early behavior difficulties that Healy attached considerable importance to the family situation is suggested in the following extracts from his record (report made at the time Stanley was seven years and ten months of age):

The home conditions in this case are very bad. Father heavy drinker. Boy poorly nourished and neglected. Dislikes stepmother. Says she beats him and sends him out to steal. Boy very unhappy at home. Wants to live in Detention Home. Should be placed in congenial foster home. Not likely to be any improvement if he remains in his own home.[18]

A second factor in the family situation was Stanley's intense resentment of his stepmother and his belief that she preferred her own children to him and his brother and sister, and that she maltreated her stepchildren. His hostility was so great for her that he says, "My fear and hatred made me avoid her and resent her caresses."

The stepmother also made us (brother, sister, and myself) do all the hard work in the house. And then she would beat us if we complained. That is what embittered me against her and her children. I developed a hatred against her that still lasts; a hatred that was so burning that when she would look into my eyes she would read it there, and in that way she knew my feeling. The Lord knows I tried to love her, but my nature could not stand her caresses in one of those sympathetic moods which she seldom had. Occasionally she would seem to feel sorry for her abuses and cruelty, and would ask me to kiss her; but my feelings protested. My fear and hatred made me avoid her and resent her caresses. Then she would get angry and beat me.

18. *Ibid.,* p. 43.

n. Family situations of this kind are not at all uncommon in the cases of truant and delinquent children. It is probable that such situations not only play an important part in the formation of delinquent behavior trends, but greatly influence the development of attitudes and personality. Presumably Stanley's attitudes of persecution and suspicion originated in the antagonistic family relationship described in this paragraph. Among the more important factors in the situation is the stepmother's attitude of partiality toward her own children and her discrimination against Stanley and his brother and sister.[19]

The actual situation would seem to have been that the stepmother was not uniformly mean to him but that he was unable to accept mitigating tenderness from her. Just why this was the case is certainly one of the most important, though unexplained, aspects of his personality.

The authors are concretely aware of the importance of this family situation for Stanley's career and in particular for his delinquent behavior.

It was assumed, also, that certain elements in the family situation were clearly related to the onset of the delinquent career. For instance, it is probable that the intense antagonisms which developed after the father's marriage to the stepmother, not only led to a breakdown of a parental control, but were largely responsible for Stanley's repeated truancy from home. Perhaps the persistence of this family conflict situation largely explains Stanley's failure to make an adjustment in his own home at the time of his parole from the various correctional institutions to which he was committed. Another important element in the family situation was the fact that the stepmother not only sanctioned but actually participated in Stanley's early stealing activities. This is especially significant as an indication of the attitudes and moral standards of the family group.[20]

19. *Ibid.,* p. 50.   20. *Ibid.,* p. 165.

His antagonism toward his stepmother and his discomfort at home led him to run away frequently and made it impossible for her to win his allegiance to socially approved behavior patterns. If this element acted as a push, the lure of the street life acted as a pull which made it impossible for some time thereafter for Stanley to accept a home life in a normal home situation. The authors attribute a great importance to "a sense of injustice" which they take to be a key trait in Stanley's character and refer it to the unfairness of the stepmother in treating him and his brother and sister.

The early rise and persistence of *a sense of injustice* may be taken as the key trait of which the others are natural outcomes. A situation in which a sense of injustice arises is one in which the stepmother discriminates against him as a stepson in favor of her own children. Stanley and his brother and sister refused to accept this situation and persisted in running away. Stanley, in his struggle with his stepmother, is sustained by the feeling of his own worth and her unfairness.[21]

It confirms our feeling of the importance and reality of this family conflict to know that the brother and sister, as well as Stanley, also persisted in running away, though Stanley seems to have laid a special stress on her hostility and shows the more dramatic delinquent career. The disorganization of Stanley's home is concretely symbolized by the fact that the stepmother herself condones Stanley's petty stealing and apparently acted as a receiver of his stolen property; in some instances she specifically urged him to steal.

Another important aspect of the family situation was the fact that the stepmother condoned Stanley's petty stealing. There is considerable evidence to indicate that she not only received stolen property, but actually encouraged him to steal from markets and freight cars.[22]

21. *Ibid.*, p. 191.   22. *Ibid.*, p. 43.

It is interesting to note that this was one suggestion from his stepmother to which he was not immunized by virtue of his hatred for her, perhaps because it accorded so well with the gang patterns to which he was subjected outside the home. The more importance we attribute to Stanley's hostility to his stepmother in motivating his delinquent life at its origin, the more this hostile attitude seems worthy of special study and consideration. We have to be content, however, with what Stanley can give us on this point and it seems to be true that in an overhead sense his family directly set the pattern of his delinquent career. It is only on the point of description of the specific manner in which this was done that we wish for more concrete evidence. We may say that the authors accept our criterion, with reservations stated above, in a very useful sense.

Criterion IV. The specific method of elaboration of organic materials into social behavior must be shown.

We should expect an unsatisfactory state of affairs in regard to this criterion on the basis of our experience with criterion II. We found there that the authors do not give us a stable biological point of reference from which we could expect the "attitudes" of Stanley to develop. Failing this, we are bound to be more or less at sea, and we are; we have abundant illustrations of attitudes and personality sets given us by the authors, but very little indication of how the personality was germinated from the impulse life of the subject.

We should indeed expect a greater definiteness on this point in practice because the theoretical statement of the point leaves nothing to be desired. We find that "the point to be grasped is that the formation of the personality pattern is a natural product of forces in the constitution of the individual and in his childhood situation."

Stanley, no more than anyone else, is neither to be praised nor blamed for his personality traits. They were formed for him before he gained conscious control of his destiny. The point to be grasped is that the formation of the personality pattern is a natural product of forces in the constitution of the individual and in his childhood situation. Once this conception of behavior is clearly understood, we will learn to accept people as they are and work with, rather than against, the basic set of their personality.[23]

If one had read this, but no other statement in the volume, one would expect that the constitutional factors would be clearly delineated and that their interaction with the childhood situation would be shown specifically in the case of Stanley. That this is not done is evidenced by the fact that we must accept Stanley as "given" at the age of five or six years. It is true, as stated, that "the cultural patterns . . . define his wishes and attitudes and so control, almost in a deterministic fashion, his behavior."

In penetrating beneath the external behavior of the delinquent boy it reveals the intimate interplay between his impulses and the effective stimuli of the environment. It shows how the cultural patterns, of his home, of his associates in the neighborhood, of the delinquent and criminal groups outside and especially inside correctional and penal institutions, define his wishes and attitudes and so control, almost in a deterministic fashion, his behavior. His account also discloses how certain changes in his social environment, by affording contact in an intimate and sympathetic way with the cultural patterns of normal society, redefine his impulses and direct his conduct into fields of socially approved behavior.[24]

To be able to say this with such authenticity and vigor as Shaw and Burgess do is a real gain and a very important contribution to social science; what is missing is a really clear discussion of how the culture patterns hook on to the

23. *Ibid.*, p. 193.   24. *Ibid.*, p. 197.

organic man. It is this statement which is required by our criterion.

Let us examine a few of the attitudes and personality characteristics of Stanley which are identified by the authors. It is shown that Stanley has an "egocentric" personality and we are grateful for this designation, but it is not shown just what an egocentric personality means in terms of elaboration of the impulse life.

Because of his egocentric personality, it was thought necessary to select a family in which the relationships were sympathetic and informal. It was considered extremely important, not only to avoid formal methods of control, but to guard against any behavior which might be construed by him as personal discrimination on the ground of his inferior social status and delinquent record.[25]

It is just this account which we need, but instead we are asked to posit the egocentric personality and take it as a datum. We consider that our authors may be fairly held accountable for such a statement; it seems quite impossible, granted their point of view, that they would dodge behind the idea that such a personality is given at birth. If they did not, they would then have to account for its development.

In a footnote we find reference made to a "self-justificatory attitude" on the part of Stanley and this attitude is certainly amply illustrated in his autobiography.

n. This introductory paragraph is typical of Stanley's self-justificatory attitude toward his own problems and situations. In this paragraph and throughout the entire document, he makes a rather definite attempt to place the responsibility for his misconduct upon fate, circumstances, and other persons, particularly his stepmother. Regardless of the justifiability of this attitude, it reflects a fundamental aspect of his personality.[26]

25. *Ibid.*, p. 166.   26. *Ibid.*, p. 47.

The authors remark that "regardless of the justifiability of this attitude, it reflects a fundamental aspect of his personality." This is true, but we wish to know how he comes by an attitude which seems to characterize him as distinguished from other persons. It may be a justification of the life-history document to say that we see the attitudes of the person through it, but it is certainly not a complete justification. The authors point out in many instances that to exhibit an attitude is important whether or not the attitude is objectively justified in the eyes of others.

The absolute truth about these or other points cannot be secured by the life-history and probably cannot be obtained by any other known method. But in human affairs it is not the absolute truth about an event that concerns us but the way in which persons react to that event. So in the case of Stanley, it is his reactions to the events of his experience that interest us, because they give us the materials by which we can interpret his attitudes and values, his conduct and his personality.[27]

This is true, but it does not settle anything. Unless the life-history document reveals not only that an attitude exists but also how it was formed, we cannot be content with its validity. The important problem is, as W. I. Thomas has pointed out, the problem of generation of attitudes. On this score we must remark that the authors seem quite indulgent with themselves and do not present their theoretical queries with sufficient earnestness. It may be better to get a naïve autobiography than not to get any autobiography at all; but if the naïve autobiography does not answer all of our legitimate questions, then we must admit it and continue the research or give up the problem. We are glad indeed to have the autobiography show us the autobiographer's view of the world and to have his subjective views of the objective situation.

Thus I roamed and begged and stole food until four days later,

27. *Ibid.,* p. 189.

when I was arrested. The policeman took me to the station, and the desk sergeant ordered some bread and milk put before me. I thought that, compared with the place I called home, the jail seemed more like a haven of rest. I told them about my stepmother and my stepbrother, but they said, "You will have to go back home." My adventurous spirit sank to zero. They called my father, who came to take me back home. As we got near home, I was growing nervous because I knew I was due a beating as soon as my father went to work. My stepmother smiled when we got home, but when my father left she took a stick, and I got the beating of my life. After she got through, she said, "Run away again, I don't care; I don't want you around here, you'll lead all my boys to be criminals."

n. In a recent conversation with Stanley (December, 1929), he made the following significant statement with regard to his stepmother: "I don't believe that I exaggerated the faults of my stepmother, but if I did I certainly didn't exaggerate my feelings toward her." This statement illustrates one of the primary assumptions of this volume, namely, that in the study and treatment of the delinquent child it is essential to deal with his personal attitudes, his definition of the situation, although these may be exaggerations or even misinterpretations of the objective situation. Even if it were true that Stanley's interpretations of the family situation were somewhat exaggerated, it cannot be doubted that he acted "as if" these interpretations were true.[28]

But if the subject seems to have very "queer" private definitions of a situation we cannot hold back the question as to how he comes by them. We note, for instance, that other of Stanley's attitudes are given as those of "persecution, suspicion, resistance to discipline and authority, self-justification . . . self-pity, fatalism, and . . . placing the blame on other persons."

In the third place, the case-study revealed certain aspects of

28. *Ibid.,* p. 55.

Stanley's personality which greatly complicated his adjustment to other persons. Among the more outstanding of these aspects of personality were his attitudes of persecution, suspicion, resistance to discipline and authority, self-justification, and a definite tendency to excuse his misconduct by means of self-pity, fatalism, and by placing the blame on other persons.[29]

Some of these attitudes seem related in a more or less general way to his supposed persecution by his stepmother; but suppose we do not interpret them thus, and the authors say that we may be dubious about this point. We should then have to confess that Stanley's document leaves some of the most important situations and personality characteristics unaccounted for.

The conclusion seems irresistible that the response of our authors to this criterion indicates a soft spot in their work. They are quite clear about the need for a systematic account of the development of the attitudes of the individual from a biological substratum, but they do not give a pointed and concrete statement in the case of Stanley. We find, on the other hand, many attitudes appearing which are not referable to his social experience as it is defined by his autobiography.

Criterion V. The continuous related character of experience from childhood through adulthood must be stressed.

As will subsequently be shown, the authors accept this criterion very completely in theory and, with some limitations, also in fact. We will begin our discussion with the limitations of their acceptance. Stanley begins his life history by mentioning the death of his mother when he was four years old and the remarriage of his father when he was five.

As far back as I can remember, my life was filled with sorrow and misery. The cause was my stepmother, who nagged me, beat me, insulted me, and drove me out of my own home. My mother

29. *Ibid.*, p. 165.

died when I was four years old, so I never knew a real mother's affection. My father remarried when I was five years of age.[30]

We do not begin to see him in a social situation until his stepmother is already on the scene. From this point on he gives us a very definite picture of the social situation in which his stepmother plays an outstanding role. Oddly enough, his father does not appear in any real sense in this report by Stanley on his early life. One wonders why, since contributory evidence seems to show that the father was a hard drinking man and apparently a disorganizing factor in the home. We cannot blame Stanley, of course, for being unable to give us a full report of this period nor for failing to recollect the events which preceded the remarriage of his father; we may well ask, however, why the authors do not stress this inability on his part as a defect in the record. Aside from Stanley's own reports there is very little information to be had on the first four years of his life at home and we cannot make any assumptions about it except that his father was already drinking at that time and that Stanley's early in-family experience could hardly have been without influence from his father. We might say, therefore, as a not unfair summary, that the authors accept the necessity of giving a continuous account of the life of the person minus, in the case of Stanley, the first four or five years. If they were to take specific account of the possibility that some of Stanley's most important character patterns were set in the first five years, they might have come out with a different evaluation of the material and one which would have made much more forceful the cultural point which they represent; but they might have had also to raise many damaging doubts about the scientific value of the "own story."

In view of this limitation it is surprising to find that the hypothesis is accepted "that the main outlines of the per-

30. *Ibid.,* p. 47.

sonality pattern are fixed in the early years of the child's social experience."

The study of life-history documents has led the writer to accept, at least tentatively, the hypothesis that the main outlines of the personality pattern are fixed in the early years of the child's social experience and are subject to only minor modifications in youth and manhood.[31]

We should want to ask how early may the years be, and if the study does not begin with the child's birth, at what point may one begin and still survey the main attitude-forming situations. We see, therefore, that the theoretical statement is certainly adequate; its application in the case of Stanley leaves about five years to be desired. Equally gratifying is the view that "any specific act of the individual becomes comprehensible only in the light of its relation to the sequence of past experiences in the life of the individual."

There can be little doubt that behavior trends, and perhaps the total personality as well, are greatly influenced by the situation pressures and experiences which occur in the life of the individual. Therefore, any specific act of the individual becomes comprehensible only in the light of its relation to the sequence of past experiences in the life of the individual.[32]

If we apply this statement to any one of the instances where Stanley transfers blame from himself to persons and situations in the milieu, we can follow the act back to the very first words of his autobiography which deal with his earliest reported experience. We find that he is doing it already there and we judge that this tendency has a history that is not reported by him. The discrepancy between statement and practice becomes clear in such a case. Still more specific is the statement that "the personality pattern, according to our

31. *Ibid.,* p. 191.　　　　　　　　32. *Ibid.,* p. 13.

tentative hypothesis, is formed in infancy and early childhood."

The personality pattern, according to our tentative hypothesis, is formed in infancy and early childhood through a conjunction of constitutional and experiential factors and persists with some modification and elaboration as a relatively constant factor through later childhood, youth, and maturity. It is determined, it should be noted, in the interaction between persons, but not by imitation.[33]

Such a statement leaves us somewhat aghast that the authors have not clearly called attention to their inability to discover via the autobiography of Stanley just how his personality was formed. We should expect them in all candor to lay heavy stress on this fact and to state that they knew that essential trends must have been laid down before the record begins but that they were unable to reach this area in his life with their instrument, the naïve autobiography. As matters stand, persons who do not read the text carefully will hardly notice that they do not treat the actual personality-forming situation which they posit in theory did exist. Burgess and Shaw make an invaluable distinction between the "social type" of a person and his personality pattern, and what they have done becomes much more intelligible in terms of this distinction.

The transformation of Stanley from a criminal to a law-abiding citizen was a change in social type; his personality pattern remained the same. All similar conversions as from sinner to saint, radical to conservative, Democrat to Republican, dry to wet, or vice versa, are changes in social type, not in personality patterns. Our hypothesis is that personality patterns, since they are fixed in infancy and in early childhood, are likewise susceptible to reconditioning only in this same period. The conditioning of

33. *Ibid.,* p. 193.

social types takes place in later experiences and may accordingly be reconditioned in youth and maturity.[34]

They explain that "the transformation of Stanley from a criminal to a law-abiding citizen was a change in social type; his personality pattern remained the same." We have seen that they believed the personality pattern to have been set in Stanley's case in infancy and early childhood and although we cannot locate the defining factors, we can observe the continuity of this pattern through his life. The social type, on the other hand, changes with the social group in which the person participates. We infer that in the case of Stanley, for example, he may be an egocentric person in a conventional social group as well as in his life as a criminal; his social type would change when he moves into the business group while his personality pattern would remain the same. The real contribution of this study seems to be to indicate how the social type changes and to show how Stanley, as a social type, is conditioned. The authors state that "the conditioning of social types takes place in later experiences and may accordingly be reconditioned in youth and maturity." They seem to infer that the personality pattern cannot be reconditioned, certainly a dubious inference.

If we agree to begin the life history of Stanley where he begins it himself, the continuity of behavior is certainly clearly shown. We find him a delinquent during his late childhood and continuously on through his adolescence until he came into the hands of Mr. Shaw.

As indicated in the foregoing official record of arrests and commitments, Stanley was habitually truant from school. He entered public school at the age of six years. Despite his frequent truancies, he was graduated at the age of thirteen and a half, while in the St. Charles School for Boys.[35]

34. *Ibid.*, p. 194.   35. *Ibid.*, pp. 31–32.

This continuity of delinquent behavior corresponds perfectly to the continuity of a delinquent milieu.

On arriving in Chicago, my escort, one of the officers of the "School," instructed me to be in bed by nine o'clock, and to keep out of bad company. It was useless to explain that to me, for I had heard it so many times that I knew it by heart and always expected it on such occasions. I left him at the Aurora and Elgin station and strolled out to State and Congress streets.

n. At the time of Stanley's parole, Mr. Cone was the only St. Charles parole officer in the Chicago district and was responsible for the supervision of more than three hundred delinquent boys. At present there are two officers, each of whom has more than two hundred cases. With this large number of cases, the officer's contact with the boy is obviously extremely infrequent and superficial. In the absence of adequate follow-up work, any beneficial influences resulting from the boy's institutional experience are necessarily lost as he returns to the neighborhood situation in which his delinquent experiences occurred.[36]

The perspicuous delineation of this external situation and the full evaluation of its effect on the life of this delinquent boy alone makes of this autobiography a valuable contribution. We might note in passing that Stanley's tendency to shift the blame to his environment is one which the professional sociologist is particularly predisposed to share. Evidence on just this point is likely to be welcome and convincing to the professional student of culture.

Some evidence is given also as to the continuity of the attitude structure in the case of Stanley and a good example is the hypercritical attitude toward his stepmother. We are told that this attitude "develops into unsparing criticism of the institutions of which he is an inmate and of persons whom he dislikes."

36. *Ibid.,* p. 79.

Toward his stepmother he continues to be *hypercritical* in attitude; this develops into unsparing criticism of the institutions of which he is an inmate and of persons whom he dislikes. It follows that in his unequal struggle against Fate (to use his own term) he tends to take the position of being *always right*. In this document he is disposed never to take blame, but to blame others or Fate.[37]

This seems a very important point and it shows the weight which the authors attach to the continuity of the attitude structure. It seems to stress also the importance of understanding the true origins of this attitude, origins which are not accessible to us through this record. The idea of the transfer of "attitudes" from family members to other persons and institutions is a very important one in social science, since it links family influences to the wider structure of the society. It seems that in Stanley's case this hypercritical attitude was transferred in a generalized way to oppressive persons and institutions.

It would seem that the authors are inclined to accept the personality as given and to attempt to find a group situation into which the personality will fit. Technically stated, they attempt to change the social type in a direction approved by the wider culture and to adjust the personality pattern to this new type. We see that Mr. Shaw has, with great ingenuity, intuited that Stanley's personality would receive a socially acceptable form of expression through activity as a salesman.

(Two and a half years after release from House of Correction.) "With my success in selling came a feeling of confidence in my ability to get along in the business world.* Sometimes I feel despondent; having a criminal record is a heavy hardship to carry through life. There is always the danger of it becoming known.

37. *Ibid.,* pp. 191–192.

n. Stanley has already demonstrated considerable ability in salesmanship. This seems to be one situation in which his personality traits are definite assets. He is able not only to dominate the situation and assume a superior rôle, but in this field he is permitted to work more or less independently of other persons.[38]

In practice this change proves to be a success.

From the foregoing it must be clear that Shaw and Burgess count very definitely with the continuity of the life of a person and that they are disposed to view it as a single event for purposes of scientific study. Their full acceptance of the point is modified by the necessity of dealing with Stanley's life in a limited sense, that is, without data on the first years of life. There seems little doubt that the continuity point could be strengthened rather than weakened if they were to take fully into account the growth of the personality pattern.

Criterion VI. The "social situation" must be carefully and continuously specified as a factor.

Many citations already made from *The Jack-Roller* have established how well these authors distinguish between the situation as it seems to Stanley and the average or cultural view of it. We will cite a few more only to clinch the point. Speaking as these authors do primarily for sociologists who are accustomed to thinking of the culture as defining the situation for any individual, they have stressed consistently the subjective and private definition of the situation. We find them, for example, checking up on the objective facts of Stanley's life, so far as checkable, and contrasting these facts with his own "often widely different interpretations of these facts."

The net result was the substantiation of the objective facts as given by Stanley, but quite often widely different interpretations of these facts. Stanley, in telling the truth as it appears to him,

38. *Ibid.*, pp. 181–182.

unwittingly reveals what we want most to know, namely his personality reactions and his own interpretation of his experiences.[39]

His interpretations, we have learned, show us his private and affectively toned versions of the "standardized" definitions of the situation. Indeed they make a great point of the use of the "own story" just because it shows the variant definitions of the situation by the individual.

The boy's "own story" is of primary importance as a device for ascertaining the personal attitudes, feelings, and interests of the child; in other words, it shows how he conceives his rôle in relation to other persons and the interpretations which he makes of the situations in which he lives. It is in the personal document that the child reveals his feelings of inferiority and superiority, his fears and worries, his ideals and philosophy of life, his antagonisms and mental conflicts, his prejudices and rationalizations.[40]

If the individual defines a situation in a way differing from others, this difference must be accounted for by reference to the development in him of differing attitudes. We have noted the lack of a thorough genetic account in respect of Stanley's most important "attitudes." Although the "own story" is limited in this way, it certainly does give a useful picture, especially if compared with an abstracted statistical definition of a delinquent in terms of number and types of crime.

In regard to the cultural definition of the situation we find the authors equally explicit, indeed it is in this field that they are most effective. Stanley is careful to specify the nature of the delinquent group into which he was inducted as a small boy and in which delinquency came to seem to him a "normal" mode of life.

39. *Ibid.*, p. 188.   40. *Ibid.*, pp. 3–4.

So I grew old enough to go out on the street. The life in the streets and alleys became fascinating and enticing. I had two close companions that I looked up to with childish admiration and awe. One was William, my stepbrother. The other one was Tony, a dear friend of my stepbrother, William. They were close friends, four years older than me and well versed in the art of stealing.

n. As indicated in Healy's case-study, Stanley's initial stealing and sex experience occurred while he was in the company of William and Tony. It may be assumed that Stanley's initial experience in delinquency was an aspect of the play activity of his gang and neighborhood.[41]

The behavior patterns of conventional society which seem normal to us were simply not accessible to Stanley. The authors believe that such types of social situation frequently generate delinquent careers; it could still be inquired whether "stealing" was not tabooed as between family members, and if so, whether its amoral significance was not recognized. In the same way that he first became a delinquent Stanley became later a criminal by participation in centers of transmission of criminal behavior patterns (i.e., penal institutions). He tells us dramatically of how he came to a full conception of his criminal role while in Pontiac Reformatory.

As I sat on my bunk thinking, a great wave of feeling shook me, which I shall always remember, because of the great impression it made on me. There, for the first time in my life, I realized that I was a criminal. Before, I had been just a mischievous lad, a poor city waif, a petty thief, a habitual runaway; but now, as I sat in my cell of stone and iron, dressed in a gray uniform, with my head shaved, small skull cap, like all the other hardened criminals around me, some strange feeling came over me. Never before had I realized that I was a criminal.* I really became one as I sat there and brooded.

41. *Ibid.*, p. 50.

* *n.* This is a vivid illustration of the type of situation in which the delinquent's conception of his rôle changes from that of a juvenile offender to that of an adult criminal.[42]

We might add, as a matter of inference from the life history, that Stanley never apparently had the personality capacity to become fully assimilated into one of the higher and more dangerous criminal careers. His personality pattern seems to have limited him to theft via the jack-rolling technique. It was certainly not for lack of experience with criminals that he did not become a burglar or bank robber, nor was it because of his youth. Apparently, therefore, there is a limit to the defining power of the criminal group for Stanley, this limitation being his own personality pattern and possible lack of courage.

The power of the group is no less adequately shown when Stanley is re-aligning himself with the forces of conventional society. We see him struggling between the definitions of a desirable life offered by a new home and his older action patterns and relationships in the delinquency area.

I finally told Mrs. Smith about being dismissed from the telegraph company. Of course she was surprised, and so was I when she calmly and kindly inquired about my leaving the job. I related the details to her, and she pointed out my weaknesses and the way to prevent its happening again. I then told her of my new job, and that it paid me more money, and she was glad and cautioned me about falling again. I worked at this job for two months and during those two months I spent my time foolishly, hanging around at my sister's home, and then spending the evening gambling with the guys in the neighborhood.

n. It is clear, from these statements, that Stanley's group relationships in the stock yard district continued to exercise considerable control over his behavior for a long period of time after he was placed in the home of Mrs. Smith. The influence of these earlier relationships did not begin to diminish until

42. *Ibid.,* p. 103.

other interests and relationships were established in his new situation.[43]

This struggle is one of the most convincing evidences of the power of group definition. Stanley's conception of himself changes still more when he begins to work with a scientific group and in this group meets a girl who represents its standards and behavior expectations.

I looked back at my foolishness and compared the fun I was having now. It was different. It filled me with new life. It made me feel like somebody, instead of going home late at night tired after dissipating my time gambling. I now wanted to get new clothes and look well and appear well in the eyes of the people I was meeting. I began to see how negligently I dressed. I wanted to look neat and business-like, like the doctors and the internes. More so, I fell in love with one of the girls at the hospital. She swept me off my feet the first time I saw her, and I began to dream dreams of future happiness. Dreams I had not dreamed before. So I began to take note of my personal appearance. I wanted to look well in the eyes of the girl of my dreams. . . .

In the morning going to work I would board the elevated train which brought me to work. Sitting in the car, I would try to imitate some big business men, by scanning the morning paper hurriedly but importantly and putting on an air of reserved dignity. I felt like I was somebody and I wanted to act like one.

n. This is one of the many incidents indicative of the influence of the new situation in bringing about a change in Stanley's conception of himself.[44]

Stanley, with a "gangland self" would hardly be acceptable to her and he must revise his older conception of himself to conform to this new situation and develop the attitudes appropriate to it. It is quite astonishing to see how completely this transformation in social type has taken place and how thoroughly Stanley's allegiance to conventional social

43. *Ibid.*, pp. 174–175.   44. *Ibid.*, p. 178.

groups is affirmed. We are told that Stanley's reformation has lasted for at least five years before the publication of the document.

More than five years have elapsed since Stanley was released from the House of Correction. During this period there has not been a recurrence of any delinquent behavior. Furthermore, he has developed interests and a philosophy of life which are in keeping with the standards of conventional society. While it is impossible to analyze all the factors which have been instrumental in producing these modifications in his interests and conduct, it may be assumed that they were due, in large part, to changes in group relationships. In other words, his present behavior trends, interests, and philosophy of life have developed as a product of his participation in the life of conventional social groups.[45]

Mr. Shaw has himself been a bridge figure, aiding the boy to re-orient and revise his attitudes from the *mores* of gangland to those of the wider society. Although Shaw does not stress the role which he personally has played in this transformation, it cannot have been other than a potent one and must have cost much time and effort and other qualities which are not so easily purchased.

We can give our authors a clean bill of health in respect of this criterion.

Criterion VII. The life-history material itself must be organized and conceptualized.

The foregoing material illustrates that the authors do attempt to work up the material on Stanley's life in conceptual form, although we note that the case and description of the community is presented by Shaw and the discussion and analysis of the case by Burgess; the latter presumably presented the conceptual orientation with which the research was begun and carried on. We see in use such concepts as "de-

45. *Ibid.*, p. 183.

linquency areas," "disorganized group and family life," "social type," and "personality pattern," and a definite attempt is made to grasp the whole material of the autobiography and make conceptual sense of it.

The terms used to indicate the current cultural situation are quite specific and apropos, and this fact leaves us with the suspicion that the document can be best used to illuminate the current cultural situation rather than the life of Stanley in a systematic sense. This point has not escaped the authors who say, "To many readers . . . its far-reaching significance will inhere in the illumination it throws on the causation, under conditions of modern city life, of criminal careers . . ."

To many readers the chief value of this document will not consist in its contribution to an understanding of the personality of Stanley and other delinquents or of the methods of treatment of similar cases. To them its far-reaching significance will inhere in the illumination it throws on the causation, under conditions of modern city life, of criminal careers and upon the social psychology of the new type of criminal youth.[46]

This is certainly the truth, though an under-statement of it. To the professional student of the life history this is its single systematic contribution. Stanley's genesis, as a personality, remains obscure. This point is somewhat blurred by the argument that the "own story" gives us insight into the personality structure as it exists at the time of writing the autobiography.

n. The story should be read with a view to getting insight into the boy's attitudes, typical reactions, and the social and moral world in which he lived. From this standpoint, as previously indicated, rationalizations, prejudices, exaggerations are quite as valuable as objective description.[47]

46. *Ibid.*, p. 196.   47. *Ibid.*, p. 47.

This is true, but our knowledge of what Stanley is does not help us to understand how he became what he is. It is on this point that the authors have failed us on an essential responsibility. In welcoming their concept of social type as an indispensable one we cannot relax our insistence that they account also for the personality pattern.

In reference to the growth of the personality pattern the authors make much of the fact that an autobiography of this type is not biased by the concepts of a reporter; the "own story" comes clean of influence from the outside.

The life-record itself is the delinquent's own account of his experiences, written as an autobiography, as a diary, or presented in the course of a series of interviews. The unique feature of such documents is that they are recorded in the first person, in the boy's own words, and not translated into the language of the person investigating the case.[48]

There is good reason to doubt that Stanley's autobiography is as clean of influence from Mr. Shaw as this statement would imply. For example, there arises the suspicion that Stanley's constant transference of blame to the environment was not unwelcome to a man who approached Stanley's life with a vivid concept of the culture area. We may well believe that both Stanley and Shaw played into each other's hands on this point. Such a bias, quite legitimate of course, might lead the authors to be indifferent to material in Stanley's life which would not serve to support the delinquency area hypothesis of the origination of criminal patterns. For example, one might argue that "delinquency areas" do not cause delinquent behavior but merely release it; this would imply a very different conception of culture and personality from that which Shaw and Burgess use, and would certainly alter significantly the treatment of their materials. It might lead them, for instance, not to be suspicious about the small

48. *Ibid.*, p. 1.

role that Stanley allots to his father in his life; why should this seem unusual if the stepmother plays so neatly, as she does, the role of deflecting Stanley into criminal practices and releasing him from family controls.

It would certainly seem that too much of a burden is put on Stanley when it is assumed that his "own story" will give a sufficient and adequate account of the genesis of his personality. It would seem rather that a systematic use of the cultural hypothesis would intimate that he would *not* be able to tell his own story with sufficient clarity to be useful to social scientists. Stanley really appears here as a fragment of a group, a group which has in turn been posited from the behavior of such people as Stanley and his family.

In the face of the weakness of the "own story" as a device for defining the life of the individual, it is no wonder that the authors come to the conclusion that "it is probable that in the absence of such additional case material any interpretation of the life-history is somewhat questionable."

As a safeguard against erroneous interpretations of such material, it is extremely desirable to develop the "own story" as an integral part of the total case history. Thus each case study should include, along with the life-history document, the usual family history, the medical, psychiatric, and psychological findings, the official record of arrest, offenses, and commitments, the description of the play-group relationships, and any other verifiable material which may throw light upon the personality and actual experiences of the delinquent in question. In the light of such supplementary material, it is possible to evaluate and interpret more accurately the personal document. It is probable that in the absence of such additional case material any interpretation of the life-history is somewhat questionable.[49]

The additional material mentioned included the family history, the medical, psychiatric, and psychological findings,

49. *Ibid.*, p. 2.

etc. We agree as to the high desirability of gathering such materials but we feel also that the authors have really deserted the most essential problem, that of the study of the life of the person as a unit event. It does not argue against the use of complementary materials to urge that the study of Stanley's life, as he himself could report it, is very inadequately achieved by the "own story." So far as we can see the additional records here accessible have not played any great role either in the interpretation of the case or in the treatment program; what seems to ring the bell is the life history of the subject, defective as it is, and the light that this history throws on the social milieu.

It would detract not one whit from the power of the social type analysis presented by the authors if the study of the personality pattern were complete and convincing. It seems plain that a sociological study of the personality cannot come out with satisfactory answers if only the social type is delineated. The social type accounts for the reactions of the subject only in general and never in specific, and leaves us at sea with regard to many essential points, such as, for example, why Stanley never progressed to the upper hierarchy of criminal activity. This point cannot be viewed as unimportant from the standpoint of social analysis and can only be reached by a more searching analysis of the personality pattern.

CHAPTER VIII

THE CRITERIA APPLIED: *EXPERIMENT IN AUTOBIOGRAPHY**

I T is not quite in the line of our preceding discussions to take the work of a lone autobiographer and subject his product to our critical machine. We observe, for instance, that Mr. Wells has not attempted to set a pattern of interpretation of life-history materials which he expects others to follow, but rather he is setting down his life for the value of the exercise to himself, as he says, and presumably also for the sympathetic response which it may induce from others. This is a very different task from that of regarding his life as a specimen of the way in which people grow up in our society. The material would be more nearly suited to our uses if someone else had taken the document after Mr. Wells finished it and provided a set of critical and integrative footnotes.

We have taken his autobiography for review, nevertheless, as a sample document from the field of autobiography and are passing it experimentally before our criteria. Since the life history may come forward both in the form of biography and autobiography, the question would otherwise remain open as to what the result of our research would be in the case of an autobiography. We have therefore taken Mr. Wells' "own story" and thrown the spotlight on it at various points.

We must note that Mr. Wells is not innocent of the objective of giving a "truthful self-portrait of a very definite individual."

* Wells, H. G., *Experiment in Autobiography,* New York, The Macmillan Company, 1934. All of the extracts in this chapter are taken from this book with the consent of the author. The permission thus granted is warmly appreciated.

In my effort to combine the truthful self-portrait of a very definite individual with an adequate reflection of the mental influences of type and period and to keep my outlines firm and clear, I have deliberately put many vivid memories and lively interludes aside, ignored a swarm of interesting personalities I have encountered, cut out great secondary systems of sympathy and said nothing whatever about all sorts of bright, beautiful and pleasant things that have whirled about me entertainingly for a time and then flown off at a tangent.[1]

In a sense such a task makes him responsible from our standpoint and brings his autobiography within the range of our evaluation. He notes also the other possible function of an autobiography which he phrases as an "adequate reflection of the mental influences of type and period," or as we have phrased it, an inside view of the society. In point of sheer space devoted to these two tasks, Mr. Wells gives much more to the second, that is, to the milieu analysis, than to the first. There is a third element that is very well marked and of course quite inseparable from an autobiography of Mr. Wells, and that is a kind of propaganda of his views on world planning.

Among other people who were excited by *Anticipations* was myself. I became my own first disciple. Perhaps at the outset of this series I was inspired chiefly by the idea of producing some timely interesting articles. But before I was half way through the series I realized that this sort of thing could not remain simply journalistic. If I was not doing something widely and profoundly important I was at least sketching out something widely and profoundly important. I was carrying on the curves instead of the tangents of history. I was indicating, even if I was not to some extent providing, new data of quite primary importance for rationalized social political and economic effort. I was writing the human prospectus.[2]

1. Wells, H. G., *Experiment in Autobiography*, New York, The Macmillan Company, 1934, pp. 703–704.
2. *Ibid.*, p. 552.

His many imaginative flights into the future are well known to all civilized readers of English and he has undoubtedly played a great role in suggesting the possibility of social foresight and planning in our society. His attention is therefore swinging between his body as an accumulative series of experiences in a social milieu, his world as he passed through it and the future as he attempts to anticipate it. The second and third of these tasks are possible and valuable in an autobiography but to us of less value than the primary task of defining the growth and maturation of the individual; and it is on this problem of growth and maturation in a social milieu that our criteria tend to be revealing. We are not cranky with Mr. Wells on this point; a man can write in his autobiography what he chooses and say as much or as little about himself as he likes. We contend only that he cannot hold out the autobiography as a valuable account of his growth unless his document assays well when examined carefully in the light of our criteria. The conclusion is unavoidable, too, that a man's intimate autobiography is related to his social type; his social type is not simply imposed on his personality pattern but grows out of it with a kind of necessity. However industrious and clear the analysis of the overt social world of Mr. Wells might be, it would still fail to account for Mr. Wells unless the survey be pushed into the details of his acculturation. We must know, that is, not only that he was a member of a lower-middle-class English family structure, but also in just what ways this structure so impinged on him as to produce the indubitable person that he became. English middle-class structure was "there" for millions of persons who did not become Mr. Wells. We feel justified in holding him to his self-set task of a "truthful self-portrait" and in trying to examine with the aid of our criteria how far he has succeeded in this task.

Criterion I. The subject must be viewed as a specimen in a cultural series.

Mr. Wells realizes very clearly in a practical sense that his life is to be viewed as an item in cultural transmission and re-organization between 1860 and 1935. He sees himself clearly as fashioned by the processes of social change operative before and during his life time. The educational system of his time he recognizes as growing out of the economic and status organization of the period.

In my opening chapters I have tried to put my personal origins into the frame of human history and show how the phases and forces of the education that shaped me, Tommy Morley's Academy, old-fashioned apprenticeship, the newly revived Grammar School at Midhurst, the multiplying colleges at South Kensington, were related to the great change in human conditions that gathered force throughout the seventeenth, eighteenth and nineteenth centuries. World forces were at work tending to disperse the aristocratic estate system in Europe, to abolish small traders, to make work in the retail trades less independent and satisfactory, to promote industrial co-ordination, increase productivity, necessitate new and better informed classes, evoke a new type of education and make it universal, break down political boundaries everywhere and bring all men into one planetary community. The story of my father and mother and all my family is just the story of so many individual particles in the great mass of humanity that was driving before the sweep of these as yet imperfectly apprehended powers of synthesis.[3]

He speaks indeed of his father and mother as "so many individual particles in the great mass of humanity that was driving before the sweep of these as yet imperfectly apprehended powers of synthesis." He is quite aware that he did not invent many of the leading ideas which characterized him, but rather shared them with other persons of his time and class; he specifies some of these as religious scepticism, socialism and sexual rationalism.

3. *Ibid.,* p. 196.

So, before I was eighteen, the broad lines of my adult ideas about human life had appeared—however crudely. I was following a road along which at variable paces a large section of the intelligentsia of my generation was moving in England, towards religious scepticism, socialism and sexual rationalism. I had no idea of that general drift about me. I seemed to be thinking for myself independently, but now I realize that multitudes of minds were moving in precisely the same direction. Like forces acting upon like organizations give like results. I suppose when a flight of starlings circles in the air, each single bird feels it is moving on its own initiative.[4]

These ideas were peculiarly accessible to a young Englishman on the march from a lower to an upper class position in English society and they may indeed identify the fact of his social advance. His father, he believes, had only rarely, if at all, glimpsed the possibility of such a vertical rise in status and had accepted his lower middle class status as a matter of enduring fact.

I wish I knew more than I do of my father's dreams and wishes during those early years before he married. In his working everyday world he, like my mother, was still very much in the tradition of the eighteenth century when the nobility and gentry ruled everything under God and the King, when common men knew nothing of the possibility of new wealth, and when either Patronage or a Legacy was the only conceivable way for them out of humdrum and rigid limitation from the cradle to the grave. That system was crumbling away; strange new things were undermining it, but to my mother certainly it seemed an eternal system only to be ended at the Last Trump, and I think it was solely in rare moments of illumination and transparency that my father glimpsed its instability.[5]

By way of defining the culture out of which he came Wells tries to project himself imaginatively into the minds of both

4. *Ibid.,* pp. 147–148.   5. *Ibid.,* p. 36.

of his parents before his birth and to see the world as they saw it; this is, of course, an admirable device for specifying the cultural set into which he came and gives a good practical notion of the culture. As a lady's maid his mother also accepted the English class society and its expectations of her with unfailing confidence in its permanence and rightness.

But that is anticipating. For the present I am trying to restore my mother's mental picture of the world, as she saw it awaiting her, thirty years and more before I was born or thought of. It was a world much more like Jane Austen's than Fanny Burney's, but at a lower social level. . . . In the lower sky and the real link between my mother and the god-head, was the Dear Queen, ruling by right divine, and beneath this again, the nobility and gentry, who employed, patronised, directed and commanded the rest of mankind. On every Sunday in the year, one went to church and refreshed one's sense of this hierarchy between the communion table and the Free Seats.[6]

We will gain throughout his document a good concrete notion of the world of his parents in terms of the status hierarchy and its attendant economic privileges and benefits. Wells himself got settled in this world and seemed very likely to have to accept it as a personal frame of operation. He had, however, the good fortune to glimpse a method of escape from his ordained position and the energy and talent to exploit it; his "escape" is, as he knows, no less a function of the times than the fixed devotion of his parents to the older system. They too had opportunities for such escape in the form of emigration; they did not accept this possibility although it lured them as an alternative to the difficulties of their roles as shopkeepers, perhaps because, as Wells thinks, they had not developed the initiative to enter on a new course of action; they had perhaps accepted their world too thoroughly.

Perhaps it was as well that he did not attempt pioneering in

6. *Ibid.*, pp. 28–29.

new lands with my mother. She had been trained as a lady's maid and not as a housewife and I do not think she had the mental flexibility to rise to new occasions. She was that sort of woman who is an incorrigibly bad cook. By nature and upbringing alike she belonged to that middle-class of dependents who occupied situations, performed strictly defined duties, gave or failed to give satisfaction and had no ideas at all outside that dependence. People of that quality "saved up for a rainy day" but they were without the slightest trace of primary productive or acquisitive ability.[7]

As an example of the shifting cultural scene which affected Wells we have a quite explicit description of the schools he attended, of the growth in types of school and of the relation of an expanding educational system to the needs of an industrial society. He, of course, attended a middle-class private school and shows himself to be proud of it and its ideals.

The more ancient middle-class schools, whatever their faults, were saturated with the spirit of individual self-reliance and individual dignity, with an idea, however pretentious, of standards "a little above the common," with a feeling (however vulgarized, debased and under-nourished) of *Noblesse oblige*. Certain things we could not do and certain things were expected of us because of our class. Most of the bickering of Morley's Bull Dogs was done against odds, and on the whole we held our own. I think it was a very lucky thing for me personally that I acquired this much class feeling. . . . My thought, as I shall trace its development in this history, has run very close to communist lines, but my conception of a scientifically organized class-less society is essentially of an expanded middle-class which has incorporated both the aristocrat and plutocrat above and the peasant, proletarian and pauper below.[8]

As a young man he identified himself definitely with the views and aspirations of his class and appears indeed never to have changed this view. As a lower-middle-class person does and

7. *Ibid.*, pp. 38–39. 8. *Ibid.*, pp. 68–69.

should, he retains a sense of the value of those classes in the hierarchy above his own and thinks less well of those classes below that from which he came. His picture of the ideal world is still "not in the form of a democracy of insurgent proletarians, but as a world of universal gentlefolk."

Their culture, like the culture of the ancient world, rested on a toiling class. Nobody bothered very much about that, but it has been far more through the curiosity and enterprise and free deliberate thinking of these independent gentlemen than through any other influences, that modern machinery and economic organization have developed so as to abolish at last the harsh necessity for any toiling class whatever. It is the country house that has opened the way to human equality, not in the form of a democracy of insurgent proletarians, but as a world of universal gentlefolk no longer in need of a servile substratum.[9]

It seems as if he has simply transposed his status outlook as a child and generalized it for the world as a whole. It may also be that it is this strong identification with the English class structure which makes him acceptable to so many English readers despite his participation in various idea systems that are opposed to the existing culture. We can only be grateful for the candor with which he sets these matters before us. To return to the school, he is quite aware that the school that he attended had a very limited but definite cultural objective, that is, "the production of good clerks"; this again corresponds with his class position and the outlook of his family as to his possible future.

The production of good clerks (with special certificates for bookkeeping) was certainly one of the objectives of Mr. Thomas Morley's life. The safety, comfort and dignity of Mr. and Mrs. Thomas Morley and Miss Morley were no doubt a constant preoccupation. But also there was interest in wider and more fundamental things.[10]

9. *Ibid.*, p. 105.   10. *Ibid.*, p. 65.

Although in a somewhat argumentative and controversial sense, he also realizes the structured character of the religious organization into which he came. Against this feature of English middle class culture he seems to be in revolt, but in the very fact of his revolt he defines its impact on him.

And from this starting apprehension, my realization that all religious buildings are in reality kinetic, spread out more and more widely to all the other visible things of human life. They were all, I began to see dimly, ideas,—ideas clothed and armed with substance. It was as impossible just to say that there was no hell and no divine Trinity and no atonement, and then leave these things alone, as to declare myself republican or claim a right to an equal education with everyone else, without moving towards a clash with Windsor and Eton. These things existed and there was no denying it. If I denied the ideas they substantiated then I proposed to push them off my earth; no less.[11]

This revolt is also, of course, not an individual matter but is a cultural current of great power in the modern world, as has since been widely demonstrated. It would seem that he has accepted from his English background the ideal of the gentleman but not that of the cleric. But again he does not fail to specify the religious institutions as cultural facts with which he was presented.

What might seem to weaken the clarity of Wells' view of cultural organization for the professional student is his vivid sense of the defects of our existing society and an effort to re-orient our society in directions more to his liking. The cool vision and affectless handling of cultural facts characteristic of the ethnologist is lacking in him; he defines the culture surrounding him as a means of pitting himself against it or of giving it his approval. This evaluational attitude has been deliberately, possibly unwisely, excluded from the techniques of the social scientist; in fact it is a large part of the training

11. *Ibid.,* p. 131.

of the student of the social sciences to shatter this attachment to given culture forms and to blight the tendency to advocate any specific social organization. We must conclude that Mr. Wells does have an efficient sense of the culture in which he matured and that his autobiography is exceptionally vivid and realistic on this score. He does not describe it as the professional student of culture might; for example, instead of talking about similar culture patterns or traditions he is likely to speak about similar brains.

There is a necessary parallelism in the matured convictions of all intelligent people, because brains are made to much the same pattern and inevitably follow similar lines of development. Words, colourings and symbols can change very widely but not the essential forms of the psychological process.[12]

On Mr. Wells' reification of the "brain" we will comment more in detail in the next section, but terminological matters aside, he gives us an unusually powerful sense of the cultural set into which he came and does it so explicitly that we are able to make inferences about his acting self which he does not happen to point out.

Criterion II. The organic motors of action ascribed must be socially relevant.

Mr. Wells presents one of the most interesting attempts to state socially relevant biological factors. Probably as a result of his training in biology the concept of the brain has come to have great meaning for him; his "brain" is one of the fundamentals to which he constantly refers in explaining his development and his character as an adult. He believes, for example, that his "relative readiness to grasp form and relation" has a direct parallel in the structure of his brain given at birth and he is almost able to make visible to us, as the neuro-anatomist cannot, relevant considerations as to its cells, fibres, and blood vessels.

12. *Ibid.,* pp. 705–706.

And I believe that its defects are mainly innate. It was not a good brain to begin with, although certain physical defects of mine and bad early training, may have increased faults that might have been corrected by an observant teacher. . . . I know practically nothing of brain structure and physiology, but it seems probable to me that this relative readiness to grasp form and relation, indicates that the general shape and arrangment of my brain is better than the quality of its cells, fibres and blood-vessels. I have a quick sense of form and proportion; I have a brain good for outlines. Most of my story will carry out that suggestion.[13]

He does not claim to have had an unusually good brain to begin with. The power of this conception for him is shown by his constant reference to it and his constant linking of adult performance with a specific picture of his brain. His vision of a scientific world order is explained as established "in the grey matter of my brain."

So far I have been telling of my life in London entirely from the student's end, for that, during these crucial years, was the vitally important end. A vision was being established, in the grey matter of my brain, of the world in which I was to live for all the remainder of my years. Every week-day we students converged from our diversified homes and lodgings upon the schools in Exhibition Road to learn what the gigantic dim beginnings of the new scientific world-order, which had evoked those schools, had, gropingly and confusedly enough, to tell us.[14]

This brain is for Mr. Wells quite a tangible article and one from which one can argue directly to the behavior which he exhibits when mature. He contrasts himself and Arnold Bennett as differing in that Bennett had a "loose *sweeping* brain," while Wells' was described as "narrow, centralized, economical and exacting."

13. *Ibid.*, pp. 14–15.   14. *Ibid.*, p. 217.

I will venture here to throw out a wild suggestion to the brain specialist. The artistic type relative to the systematizing type may have a more vigorous innervation of the cortex, rather more volume in the arteries, a richer or more easily oxygenated blood supply. But the difference between the meticulous brain and the loose *sweeping* brain may be due not to any cortical difference at all, but to some more central ganglionic difference. Somewhere sorting and critical operations are in progress, concepts and associations are called up and passed upon, links are made or rejected, and I doubt if these are cortical operations. The discussion of mind working is still in the stage of metaphor, and so I have to put it that this "bureau" of co-ordination and censorship, is roomy, generous and easy going in the Bennett type, and narrow, centralized, economical and exacting in my own. I believe that, corresponding to these mental differences, there was a real difference in our cerebral anatomy.[15]

It is plain that Mr. Wells attributes much to brain structure which others describe as "personality," "character," "complexes," and "attitude structure." He tries, in other words, to translate socialized character formations directly into terms of brain structure. He realizes that he is using a metaphor, but it is a metaphor to which he sticks with remarkable tenacity. As an explanatory principle the brain carries a heavy load in his autobiography. For example, he details a situation where he forgot the name of a young woman, discounts any possibility of a psychological explanation and attributes it to a "second-rate brain fabric."

The psychological explanation of such forgetfulness is a disinclination to remember. But what conflict of hostilities, frustrations, restrained desires and so forth, is here? None at all. It is merely that the links are feeble and the printing of the impressions bad. It is a case of second-rate brain fabric. And rather overgrown and pressed upon at that. If my mental paths are not frequently traversed and refreshed they are obstructed.[16]

15. *Ibid.*, pp. 537–538.　　　　16. *Ibid.*, p. 17.

The brain, however, is not Mr. Wells' only resource when seeking an organic platform on which to build up the record of his personality growth. He also indicates egoistic and sexual systems as fundamental points of reference and believes that discussions of both systems should appear in every autobiography.

Nevertheless the sexual complexes constitute the only other great and continuing system. I suspect the sexual system should be at least the second theme, when it is not the first, in every autobiography, honestly and fully told. It seizes upon the essential egoism for long periods, it insists upon a prominent rôle in the dramatization of the *persona* and it will not be denied.[17]

The egoistic self-defining tendencies are not more specifically defined than to state their names; in the case of the sexual impulse, however, he believes that it was awakened in him between his seventh and eighth years and that it was stimulated by outside factors, in this case the idealized pictures of women which are used in popular magazines to represent various nations.

At any rate I am convinced that my own sexual life began in a naive direct admiration for the lovely bodies, as they seemed, of those political divinities of Tenniel's in *Punch*, and that my first inklings of desire were roused by them and by the plaster casts of Greek statuary that adorned the Crystal Palace. I do not think there was any subconscious contribution from preceding events to that response; my mind was inherently ready for it. My mother had instilled in me the impropriety of not wearing clothes, so that my first attraction toward Venus was shame-faced and furtive, but the dear woman never suspected the stimulating influence of Britannia, Erin, Columbia and the rest of them upon my awakening susceptibilities.[18]

He is not able to report any earlier sexual excitations, al-

17. *Ibid.*, p. 348.   18. *Ibid.*, p. 56.

though it is worth noticing that in some way or other the sexual impulse was already condemned when he noticed its awakening and he did not approach the pictures in question with the naïveté one would expect of an innocent impulse on its first appearance. He believes that "sex life" begins with adolescence and adds his belief that it ought to really begin in fact as well as in organic potentiality.

I was working out the collateral problems with an ingenuous completeness, and I did not mean to relinquish that enquiry. I had come to the conclusion that sex-life began with adolescence, which after all was only discovering what "adolescence" means, and that when it began—it ought to begin. I thought it preposterous that any young people should be distressed by unexplained desires, thwarted by arbitrary prohibitions and blunder into sexual experiences, blindfold.[19]

Here he is plainly rehearsing a cultural point, since it is one of our cherished beliefs that the sexual impulse emerges at adolescence; Mr. Wells' own experience seems to contradict this idea and perhaps he has fallen into the error of identifying sexual life with the capacity for reproduction. After all, as we have indicated, it is a respectable error since this view of adolescence is one of our most vigorous cultural beliefs. Again with respect to adolescence he argues directly from endocrinological changes and a better dietary to such personality characteristics as "challenge to authority, the release of initiative, the access of courage," which, he believes, attend physiological maturation.

Puberty is certainly a change in much more than the sexual life. The challenge to authority, the release of initiative, the access of courage are at least equally important. But added to this normal invigoration was the escape from the meagre feeding and depressingly shabby and unlit conditions of Atlas House. There I had a great advantage over my two brothers and I think a quite

19. *Ibid.*, pp. 398–399.

unusual push forward. I was living in those crucial years under healthier conditions; I was undergoing stimulating changes of environment, and, what is no small matter, eating a more varied and better dietary.[20]

This attribution of social effects to postulated biological factors is quite characteristic of his thought; we find him saying, "Like most undernourished growing boys I was cowardly."

Like most undernourished growing boys I was cowardly and I found the last stretch from Clewer to the inn terrifyingly dark and lonely. It was black on the moonless nights and eerie by moonlight and often it was misty from the river. My imagination peopled the dark fields on either hand with crouching and pursuing foes.[21]

What we wish to stress here is that undernourishment is conceived to be a factor directly related to such a psychological event as fear of the dark.

We have found in this section that Mr. Wells gives us a rather miscellaneous group of biological events which are viewed as being related to social events. Not all of his categories are comparable; for example, he puts the "brain" in parallel with the sexual system as basic to behavior. We see, at any rate, on what initial structures he attempts to base his life and in section IV we will be able to give a more effective discussion of how these initial factors are organized into social experience.

Criterion III. The peculiar role of the family group in transmitting the culture must be recognized.

In the preceding discussion Wells has already given us a good deal of material on his family; although the picture of his family is strengthened and specified in more detail in what is to follow, it does not reveal any clear sense of the immediate impact of the family on the growing Wells, es-

20. *Ibid.,* p. 111.   21. *Ibid.,* p. 95.

pecially in the earliest years. His parents seem to him, and they seem to us from what he says, rather as impersonal surrogates of a class structure than as the concrete persons who managed and formed his "brain." He is aware in a vague sense of this relation to the family, but to be satisfactory from our angle his awareness would have to be made much more concrete and systematic than it is.

I suppose every biography, if fully told, would reveal this early predominance of home affections and the successive weakening out and subordination of one strand of sympathy after another, as new ones replaced them. It is clear that up to my thirtieth year there was still a very powerful web of feeling between me and the scattered remains of my home group. I was at least half way through life before my emotional release from that original matrix was completed. That, I think, must be the normal way of the individual life.[22]

Wells gives us some sense of his social lineage by pointing out that his ancestors also came of the upper-servant, tenant-farmer class and notes the cultural fact that family given names tended to repeat themselves.

The lack of originality at the Christenings is appalling. The aunts and uncles were all as far as I can ascertain, of the upper-servants, tenant-farmer class, except that one set of my father's first cousins at Penshurst, bearing the surname of Duke, had developed an industry for the making of cricket bats and balls, and were rather more prosperous than the others.[23]

His own family had the expected lack of "educative atmosphere" characteristic of the nineteenth century middle class home; to this influence Wells relates "a certain timidity of utterance and a disposition to mumble and avoid doubtful or difficult words and phrases."

22. *Ibid.,* p. 312.   23. *Ibid.,* p. 34.

The atmosphere of my home and early upbringing was not a highly educative atmosphere; words were used inexactly, and mispronounced, and so a certain timidity of utterance and a disposition to mumble and avoid doubtful or difficult words and phrases, may have worked back into my mental texture.[24]

We might really say that what Wells does is to give sketchy, imaginative biographies of his parents in lieu of showing them as concrete individuals bearing on his life. He tries through his account to show us his parents before they had met and married. He knows that his father was a gardener and cricketer and attempts to give us some sense of his career.

I do not know what employment my father found after he left Redleaf, which he did when his employer died, before he came to Up Park and met my mother. I think there was some sort of job as gardener or under-gardener at Crewe. In these days he was evidently restless and uneasy about his outlook upon life. Unrest was in the air. He talked of emigrating to America or Australia.[25]

He feels that his father's failure at gardening was due to his intractable temperament, which refused to accept "service," rather than incapacity for gardening.

I do not know why my father was unsuccessful as a gardener, but I suspect a certain intractability of temper rather than incapacity. He did not like to be told things and made to do things. He was impatient. Before he married, I gather from an old letter from a friend that has chanced to be preserved, he was talking of going to the gold diggings in Australia, and again after he left the cottage at Shuckburgh he was looking round for some way out of the galling subordinations and uncertainties of "service."[26]

24. *Ibid.*, p. 14.   25. *Ibid.*, p. 35.
26. *Ibid.*, p. 38.

Wells' father is, taken by and large, a vague figure who never actually comes to life and Wells' attempts to feel his way into his father's premarital experience are not very convincing. Much the same is true of the picture of the father in the family. We should be particularly grateful for more detailed information on the father as he actually seemed to Wells because such information would permit us to see the cultural model of man which was actually presented to him for identification or resistance.

The case is somewhat different with the mother who is much better sketched, in part no doubt because she left a diary which enabled a better definition of her personality. It would be very interesting to know in detail why a disproportionate amount of space seems to be given to descriptions of the mother; it may be that since she was more in contact with the growing child, he remembers her personality more clearly and it may also be due to other factors which the autobiography fails to define. We know, at any rate, that the mother was trained as a lady's maid and that she met the father while he was a gardener on the same estate.

She had left the Fordes because her mother was distressed by the death of her sister Elizabeth and wanted Sarah to be in England nearer to her. And at Up Park she met an eligible bachelor gardener who was destined to end her career as a lady's maid, and in the course of time to be my father. He wasn't there to begin with; he came in 1851. "He seems *peculiar*," says the diary, and offers no further comment. Probably she encountered him first in the Servants' Hall, where there was a weekly dance by candlelight to the music of concertina and fiddle.[27]

It seems probable that his mother's Protestant piety was actually transmitted to her, as Wells says, by her own mother along with other of her characteristics; one of these was her poor cookery.

27. *Ibid.*, pp. 30–31.

A natural tendency to Protestant piety already established by her ailing mother, was greatly enhanced. She was given various edifying books to read, but she was warned against worldly novels, the errors and wiles of Rome, French cooking and the insidious treachery of men, she was also prepared for confirmation and confirmed, she took the sacrament of Holy Communion, and so fortified and finished she returned to her home (1836).[28]

Wells, who does not make his mother very real as a person, presents her as maintaining to the end of her life her faith in the class system and her religious practices.

Without reverie life would surely be unendurable to the greater multitude of human beings. After all opium is merely a stimulant for reverie. And reverie, I am sure, made the substance of her rare leisure. Religion and love, except for her instinctive pride in her boys, had receded imperceptibly from her life and left her dreaming. Once she had dreamt of reciprocated love and a sedulously attentive God, but there was indeed no more reassurance for her except in dreamland.[29]

The record of her efforts to indoctrinate him with these beliefs is given and it may be noted that he strenuously opposed both religion and the class system in later life, though still clinging to the role of the gentleman, as a preferred expression for every human being. He believes that her religious emotions became formalized under the shocks of life and assigns her various gratifications in revery and fantasy in lieu of her lost spiritual consolations. During most of Wells' childhood his father was a storekeeper and we learn that they were poor and lived under rather unsatisfactory and unhygienic home conditions.

The impression of the parents given by the autobiography presents them in a desiccated and unreal manner, as though the genuine affects appropriate to them in childhood were stripped away when the adult man came to the task of re-

28. *Ibid.*, p. 27.   29. *Ibid.*, p. 52.

membering back on how it was. This gives the parents a
peculiar impression of being figurines and supports the conclusion that his parents are better described as class members
than as real persons facing him in childhood.

*Criterion IV. The specific method of elaboration of or-
ganic materials into social behavior must be shown.*

With a statement of the biological substratum of his life
so imperfect and confusing, we will hardly expect Wells to
give a very logical and capable account of the modification
of his instinctual life under social pressure. If it should be
protested that one could hardly expect him to give this account, we admit the justness of this contention; but we
should add that this autobiography cannot, then, give us the
knowledge, desired by the social scientist, of the actual
growth in culture of the author.

Mr. Wells would, I suppose, regard the development of
what we speak of as "social attitudes" as a modification of
the brain structure which he envisions so clearly. We have
already pointed out in discussing the brain as he conceives
it that he tends to find a correspondence between this brain
and various of his social capacities, such as the gift of organizing already referred to. In a loose manner of speech we
might say that the "brain" plays the same role in his thinking as the instinct does in that of other social scientists. In
this section it will be possible to point out rather the need for
the kind of an account which our criterion demands than
illustrations of how the criterion is met. The maturation of
the sex impulse will serve as a useful example. We have already observed that Wells was, as it were, seduced into sexual
fantasies by the Homeric women who represent nationality
stereotypes in the popular magazines. Taking him at his
word in this respect, we see this fact as an excitation of the
sex impulse under social pressure. We learn that he heard of
sexual matters from the boys in the private school to which
he first went.

Now that I had arrived at knickerbockers and the reading of books, I was sent to a little private school in the High Street, Bromley, for boys between seven and fifteen, and from my school-mates I speedily learnt in the grossest way, imparted with guffaws and gestures, "the facts of sex," and all those rude words that express them, from which my mother had hitherto shielded me. . . .

The clash of these gross revelations about the apparatus of sex with my secret admiration for the bodily beauty of women, and with this personal conceit of mine, determined to a large extent my mental and perhaps my physical development. It imposed a reserve upon me that checked a native outspokenness. . . . Personally I recoiled, even more than I cared to show, from mere phallicism. I did not so much begin masturbation as have it happen to me as a natural outcome of my drowsy clasping of my goddesses. I had so to speak a one-sided love affair with the bedding.[30]

He perceived this information as distasteful as compared with his private fantasy realm of sexual objects and believed that these revelations "imposed a reserve . . . that checked a native outspokenness." If true, this is the kind of elaboration of an impulse into a social attitude for which we are proselyting in this section. Indeed, he believes that his contact with these early sources of information had satisfied his sexual curiosity when he was nine or ten years old and that it was stronger then than at twelve or thirteen.

I recall no marked sexual or personal elements in my early reveries. Until my adolescence, sex fancies came to me only in that dim phase between waking and sleeping. I gave myself gladly and willingly to my warfare, but I was shy of sex; I resisted any urge I may have had towards personal romancing and sensuous fantasies.

My sexual trend was, I think, less marked or more under control when I was twelve and thirteen, than it was when I was nine

30. *Ibid.,* pp. 57–58.

or ten. My primary curiosities had been satisfied and strong physical urgencies were still unawakened.[31]

He does note, however, various sadistic fantasies relating to warfare which intervened at the point where sex fantasies are usual, but he makes no connection between the two. Only later when he is an apprentice in a draper's shop do we meet further clues to his sexual development.

Once, I suppose, that one had penetrated these complicated defences and got to the live body inside, one could think of individualized physical love, but at that I never arrived at Southsea or Midhurst. Mother Nature did what she could to egg me on, and stripped a girl apprentice I thought rather pretty and the costume lady who was my official Sister, in my dreams, but the old harridan accompanied this display with so many odd and unnecessary exaggerations and accessory circumstances, that it made me rather more shy and unreal and decorous than ever when I encountered her victims in my waking life.[32]

We find that he "stripped a girl apprentice" in his dreams, a fact cited here because it illustrates again the elaboration of an impulse by the dream mechanism. In an excellent discussion of jealousy which he relates to the sexual impulse he indicates jealous motivation as a check to the free-moving sexual behavior which he had early fantasied as a desirable possibility for men and women, and he notes very cleverly that "parents, onlookers, society could be jealous."

Gradually as my disputes and controversies went on, my attention was forced back, almost in spite of myself, towards these profounder elements in the human make-up which stand in the way of a cheerful healthy sexual go-as-you-please for mankind. I was obliged to look jealousy in the face. All this tangle of restriction, restraint, opposition and anger, could be explained as so much expansion, complication and organization of jealousy.

31. *Ibid.*, p. 76.   32. *Ibid.*, p. 145.

Jealousy may not be a reasonable thing, but it lies at least as close to the springs of human action as sexual desire. Jealousy was not merely a trouble between competitive lovers. Parents, onlookers, society could be jealous.[33]

We must comment that his own experience of jealousy and his insight into the way jealous feelings can be actualized in group behavior can only have arisen in experiences of this type in his own life. Not, we hasten to add, that Mr. Wells is distinguished by an especially jealous character, so far as his reports about himself show the matter.

We do note, for example, some other attitudes of Wells about whose genesis we have legitimate questions. We find him in the course of his career rebellious against the ideas of God, King, and Owner, and against the social systems in which they fit.

Chief of these was the conception of a society in which economic individualism was overruled entirely in the common interest. This was my first encounter with the Communist idea. I had accepted property as in the very nature of things, just as my mother had accepted the Monarchy and the Church. I had been so occupied with my mental rebellion against the ideas of God and King, that hitherto I had not resented the way in which the Owner barred my way here, forbade me to use this or enjoy that.[34]

This may well be explained in part by the fact that this rebellious tradition was accessible to him as his intellectual life matured; the fact that in his broken cultural field he took advantage of it we must attribute exclusively to Mr. Wells and his character as formed in his life career. Here it would be virtually mandatory to have an account of his relationships with authoritarian persons extending back to his earliest childhood and specifying over what issues his conflicts with such persons arose. This issue is the more important in

33. *Ibid.*, p. 400.   34. *Ibid.*, p. 141.

view of Wells' disinclination to give credit to persons who happen to symbolize leadership in our culture.

(Probably I am unjust to Comte and grudge to acknowledge a sort of priority he had in sketching the modern outlook. But for him, as for Marx, I have a real personal dislike, a genuine reluctance to concede him any sort of leadership. It is I think part of an inherent dislike of leadership and a still profounder objection to the subsequent deification of leaders. Leaders I feel should guide as far as they can—and then vanish. Their ashes should not choke the fire they have lit.)[35]

We are impressed by his honesty in confessing this inherent dislike of leadership though we may well doubt that it is inherent or that it is unrelated to his specific social development. Every unanswered question of this type must be mercilessly exposed as a riddle in order to show clearly in what respects the autobiography is incomplete. Mr. Wells himself can be pardoned for passing over such matters as irrelevant to his purpose in writing his autobiography, but the social scientist who reads it and tries to evaluate it as a contribution to the study of individual life cannot be indifferent to such riddles.

Criterion V. The continuous related character of experience from childhood through adulthood must be stressed.

If a life history is going to be continuous, it would have to account, by definition, for the whole life of the person, would show the interaction between the organic life and acculturated persons, and would note the constancy of certain emotional sets once established throughout the whole life. It is just in the description of this earliest period of life, in which many important strands of character are determined, that our autobiographers usually fail us, and Wells is no exception. The line of the life history seems to emerge rather late, around six, seven or eight years, and by this time certain

35. *Ibid.,* p. 562.

emotional sets are established. These "sets" we are then asked to accept as the basis of the life and are expected to work with them from then on. If we take this "from then on" platform we shall find many evidences of the interconnection and coherence of Wells' experience, though we shall also find that many important trends disappear, unaccounted for, behind the veil of his memory.

True to type, in this as in other places, we find Wells talking about how his "brain" came into existence and began to register impressions and acquire reflexes.

This brain of mine came into existence and began to acquire reflexes and register impressions in a needy shabby home in a little town called Bromley in Kent, which has since become a suburb of London. My consciousness of myself grew by such imperceptible degrees, and for a time each successive impression incorporated what had preceded it so completely, that I have no recollection of any beginning at all. I have a miscellany of early memories, but they are not arranged in any time order.[36]

What is happening, as he sees it, is a kind of growth and organization of the physical brain. In the early years he gives us a few recollections which he realizes are not arranged in time order and also many scattered impressions of his physical milieu. None of these, however, seem to bear very much on the formation of his character, at least as they are recited in the autobiography, and he remains a scientific mystery until he is well past the stage of primary character formation. Such crucial attitudes as those toward authority and toward women come forward already established at the point where he begins to remember and record his life in the first person.

If we put these very weighty considerations to one side we will find him, nevertheless, indicating certain experiences which define one or another type of attitude. His mother, we

36. *Ibid.,* p. 21.

learn, attempted to impress him with an admiration for the Queen, an admiration which he could not share; her continued efforts to indoctrinate him with this class concept "deepened my hostility and wove a stout, ineradicable thread of republicanism into my resentful nature."

For my own part, such is the obduracy of the young male, I heard too much of the dear Queen altogether; I conceived a jealous hatred for the abundant clothing, the magnificent housing and all the freedoms of her children and still more intensely of my contemporaries, her grandchildren. Why was my mother so concerned about them? Was not my handicap heavy enough without having to worship them at my own mother's behest? This was a fixation that has lasted all through my life. Various, desperate and fatiguing expeditions to crowded street corners and points of vantage at Windsor, at Chislehurst near Bromley (where the Empress Eugénie was living in exile) from which we might see the dear Queen pass;—"She's coming. Oh, she's coming. If only I could see! Take off your hat Bertie dear,"—deepened my hostility and wove a stout, ineradicable thread of republicanism into my resentful nature.[37]

The "republicanism" is certainly a marked feature of Mr. Wells' character and social attitudes. Although we will hardly believe that it was set in this way alone we can take this instance as a symbol of the more intricate scheme of experiences in which it was actually germinated.

The author attributes a tremendous importance to an accident which he suffered sometime between his seventh and eighth birthdays. He had broken a leg and "learned" to read in an effective sense, that is, became enthusiastic about the kind of world which reading opened up to him.

My leg was broken for me when I was between seven and eight. Probably I am alive today and writing this autobiography instead of being a worn-out, dismissed and already dead shop

37. *Ibid.,* p. 28.

assistant, because my leg was broken. . . . I had just taken to reading. I had just discovered the art of leaving my body to sit impassive in a crumpled up attitude in a chair or sofa, while I wandered over the hills and far away in novel company and new scenes.[38]

This again is seen as having a marked and obvious effect on his later life and as preparing the way for his adolescent rebellion against the draper's trade and his creative flight into school teaching. A quaint example of the continuity point is the bad start which he received in the study of the French language.

But most of the other stuff I got was bad. Old Tommy taught French out of a crammer's textbook, and, in spite of the fact that he had on several occasions visited Boulogne, he was quite unable to talk in the elusive tongue; so I learnt hardly anything about it except its conjugations and long lists of "exceptions," so useful in written examinations and so unimportant in ordinary life. He crippled my French for life. He made me vowel-shy in every language.[39]

The teaching he acquired was so eccentric that it "crippled my French for life." Whether we are to take this observation seriously or not, it is certainly an example that is paralleled by many types of experience in the individual life.

It is a matter of fact that as a novelist he owes much to his early naïve experience. He indicates in many places that characters and idea systems represented in his books are related to his earlier life. In *Tono Bungay,* for example, aunt and uncle Ponderevo are derived from persons whom he actually knew in his short experience as an apothecary's apprentice.

I spent only about a month amidst the neat gilt-inscribed drawers and bottles of Mr. Cowap at Midhurst, rolled a few score

38. *Ibid.,* pp. 53–54.   39. *Ibid.,* p. 66.

antibilious and rhubarb pills, broke a dozen soda-water siphons during a friendly broom fight with the errand boy, learnt to sell patent medicines, dusted the coloured water bottles, the bust of Hahnemann (indicating homœopathic remedies) and the white horse (veterinary preparations), and I do not think I need here devote very much space to him and his amusing cheerful wife, seeing that I have already drawn largely upon this shop, and my experiences in it, in describing aunt and uncle Ponderevo in *Tono Bungay*.[40]

We have posed the problem of Wells' resistance to certain authoritarian institutions, economic, religious, and social, in the preceding section. Some light is cast on one aspect of this trait when we hear about his uncle Williams, who also displayed a great contempt for "religion and the clergy" and a general skeptical attitude toward established matters. Wells indicates that he found his uncle Williams "bracing" and adopted to a considerable degree his point of view.

My Uncle Williams was a man of derisive conversation with a great contempt for religion and the clergy. His table talk was unrestrained. He talked to me frankly and as if I were an adult; I had never in all my life before had that sort of talk with any grown-up person. It braced me up. He could talk very entertainingly about the church and its faith and about the West Indies and the world as he had seen it. He gave me a new angle from which to regard the universe; I had not hitherto considered that it might be an essentially absurd affair, good only to laugh at. That seemed in many ways a releasing method of approach. It was a fresh, bright way of counter-attacking the dull imperatives of life about me, and taking the implacable quality out of them. . . . He (Wells himself) certainly owes a great deal more to this second start in life than to the first. A facetious scepticism which later on became his favourite pose may owe a great deal to Uncle Williams.[41]

40. *Ibid.*, p. 107.   41. *Ibid.*, pp. 98–99.

What probably happened was that Wells was able to express his sense of criticism about persons and institutions by identifying with his uncle. At any rate, this critical attitude has remained a permanent and very stimulating characteristic and one which has been of the greatest social value to him and to others. One does not need the needle and thread of interpretation to see how it runs through his life. A trivial but interesting example of the continuity and interconnection of experience is the "war games" which he played as a continuation of his adolescent war fantasies. These games recall the "peculiar quality and pleasure" of those earlier fantasies and were apparently a considerable source of gratification to him as an adult man.

For many years my adult life was haunted by the fading memories of those early war fantasies. Up to 1914, I found a lively interest in playing a war game, with toy soldiers and guns, that recalled the peculiar quality and pleasure of those early reveries. It was quite an amusing model warfare and I have given its primary rules in a small book "for boys and girls of all ages" *Little Wars* [42]

If we were able to make out on what this adolescent pleasure was based, we should indeed have a very interesting connected account of this strand in his personal development.

In summary we may say that Wells strives (naturally without meaning to, from our standpoint) to connect and unify his experience; he seems to feel in some blind way responsible for making a cohesive account of his life even though he does not try to represent it as rising to a fore-ordained climax or as an unconditional success. A life that is a failure can have just as well the element of continuous pattern. The omission of the early situations which serve to define his character necessarily limits the completeness with

42. *Ibid.*, pp. 75–76.

which he can accept our criterion of continuity and integration.

*Criterion VI. The "social situation" must be carefully and
continuously specified as a factor.*

There is no doubt but that Wells could, as a person, see the
difference between private and official versions of any given
situation, and that if he had taken the trouble he could have
distinguished many such "situations" in his own life. His
autobiography offers many opportunities for making the observation required by this criterion. In point of his actual
practice Wells does not utilize this idea systematically; we
have already noted that he is not trying to contribute to a
science of the life history, but presumably to satisfy himself
by viewing his own life and writing out his experience for the
appreciation of others.

The fact that Wells does not do it does not mean that it
would not be useful if he had. He could obtain a much clearer
grasp on his own psychic life if he were to distinguish carefully between the formal, cultural versions of his situation
and his own private attitudes toward them. It may also be
that his failure is due in part to his use of the "brain" concept. Instead of thinking of man as a socially organized
craving mechanism, he thinks of a set of brain patterns. This
manner of thinking tends to rob the story of his life to some
degree of a dynamic sense and to undervalue the picture of a
character structure in constant contact with successive social
situations. A man with cravings can be understood in an
actual situation but it is hard to bring a set of brain traces
in touch with a concrete social milieu. It would seem that
Mr. Wells is undercutting the social level of observation at
this point and consequently finds difficulty in keeping himself firmly in contact with his milieu.

In order to make the distinction demanded by this criterion the sense of an accumulated psychic life in terms of
which new situations are defined must be firmly preserved. In

discussing criterion V we found that Wells' appreciation of this point is partial and unclear. He would therefore have had to take special pains to meet criterion VI with adequacy, if he had attempted to do it.

Criterion VII. The life-history material itself must be organized and conceptualized.

We have already repeatedly allowed for the fact that Wells is not trying to invent a social psychology. His technical analysis of his autobiography seems to be composed of such scraps of various psychological systems as a very intelligent layman would pick up and be able to utilize in studying himself. We do find him constantly attempting to make sense of his life and to give some capsule interpretations of it. Such a term as "a good brain for outlines" is an attempt to systematize, using, of course, a biological metaphor for the purpose. We find him also distinguishing between the "persona" and the personality, the latter being a description of what the person "really is," and the former an outline of what he would like to be and achieve. We find that his definition of his "persona," that is, his mission of propagandizing and planning a world state, is clear enough; it is his personality which is not clearly indicated by a conceptual system.

We have noticed that he acknowledges at some point or other every one of our criteria except the sixth, but the impression of the whole is blurred and we do not have a manageable conception of his personality at the end. From the standpoint of a scientific study of the life history this is a great defect. After all, it is the task of the scientist to "say it right," or "to say it better," and to classify and make communicable on some kind of principle the events which he sets himself to study.

It would be folly to be impatient with Mr. Wells on this score. He has not set himself this objective and he has not, with all his gifts, negligently succeeded in accomplishing it.

The conceptual analysis of his life is faulty and inadequate to organize and define the events reported.

A FEW more critical comments need to be made which do not fit very well into the discussion of the criteria. We may say in general that Mr. Wells seems unable to separate out a physical event, like a broken leg, from the psychic impressions which such an event makes on the person who suffers it. Therefore, he uses specific physical traumas and diseases too much as explanatory principles; his life indeed seems to turn on such events.

I have already explained how I became one of the intelligentsia and was saved from a limited life behind a draper's counter by two broken legs, my own first, and then my father's. I have now to tell how I was guided to mental emancipation and real prosperity by a smashed kidney, a ruptured pulmonary blood vessel, an unsuccessful marriage and an uncontrollable love affair.[43]

We can hardly grant that "life begins with a broken leg" at eight years. We must insist that the broken leg happened to a Wells who already had lived a vigorous life, that this event came into a context and that Wells "took" the broken leg as he did, by turning to reading, because he was already a personality cued to making such an adjustment. Broken legs in real life are not uncommon in any culture or generation, but Mr. Wells' are. What is missing is the intra-psychic history which would adequately define his own injury, the meaning of his father's injury for him, and elaborate them both into an adequate picture. Wells does not distinguish adequately between the event as commonly defined and resulting in certain overt sociological changes and the event as defined in terms of the serried events of the intimate psychic life. A real sense of the latter is what we want and miss.

43. *Ibid.*, p. 237.

To those familiar with the intimate history of the individual it would be of some advantage to know whether or not Mr. Wells was a youngest child. One infers this from the document, since no others younger are mentioned; but one would like to do more than infer it. It may indeed be a fact whose further elaboration would aid us greatly in understanding the rest of Wells' autobiography. We have already noted that a pall of smoke hangs over his early experience in his own family.

The fact that Wells was trained as a biologist under Huxley is of no small importance for his autobiography. The reality of the brain concept for him is no doubt related to this experience. It should be stressed, however, that the brain is not a motor of action but rather a tool which stands between the organic impulsions and their actualization in a social milieu. We have already discovered that the impulse life is not adequately discussed from the theoretical standpoint. To use a biological metaphor it would seem that Mr. Wells' psychology includes figures of speech from brain anatomy but that he does not count with endocrinology. It is very questionable, however, whether mechanistic biological terms will be suitable for labeling events in an autobiographical account.

In stressing the sociological forces which lay around him during his life we lose the sense in the autobiography of the projectile nature of the psychic life which operates selectively on its milieu. We understand to some degree why Mr. Wells was successively a draper's apprentice, a biology teacher, a Fabian, and a writer, but we do *not* understand why he was Mr. Wells. So, in a sense, our view of all of the sociological influences is made less clear.

We have already noted the important role which Mr. Wells assigns to the sexual impulse. It may even be that he exaggerates its importance, at least in the sense of failing to stress other aspects of the impulse life which would put the sexual life in its proper frame of reference. It is, however, just in the description of his sexual experiences that there are many unsolved riddles. It is not at all so clear as Mr. Wells seems to feel why he fell in love with and married his cousin (his first marriage).

It was practically inevitable that all this suppressed and accumulating imaginative and physical craving in me should concentrate upon the one human being who was conceivable as an actual lover; my cousin Isabel. She and I had from the outset a subtle sense of kindred that kept us in spite of differences, marriage and divorce, friendly and confident of one another to the end of her days, but I think that from the beginning we should have been brother and sister to each other, if need, proximity and isolation had not forced upon us the rôle of lovers, very innocent lovers.[44]

He seems to feel that the matter is explained by his own inhibitions in this sphere and by their physical proximity. We would have to note that in the case of many other persons physical proximity of this type and close blood relationship seem to inhibit erotic feeling rather than to make its expression inevitable. Again we do not see why (in terms of his autobiography) he divorced his first wife, or why he experienced a "storm of irrational organic jealousy" when he heard of her remarriage.

After that I set myself to forget my imaginations about her, by releasing my imaginations for other people. But in that I was unsuccessful for a long time. Five or six years afterwards she married; I do not know the exact date because for more than a year she kept this from me. And then came a still more illuminating incident. When at last I heard of it, I was overwhelmed by a storm of irrational organic jealousy. It took the form of a deliberate effacement of her. I destroyed all her photographs and letters and every souvenir I possessed of her; I would not

44. *Ibid.*, p. 231.

have her mentioned to me if I could avoid it; I ceased all communications. The portraits I have reproduced here I have had to borrow. That bitterness again is quite incompatible with the plausible and conventional theory that she was nothing more to me than an illiterate young woman whom I "dropped" because she was unequal to a rôle in a literary world. I burnt her photographs. That was a symbolization.[45]

After this news he destroyed everything he had that might remind him of her and says, "That was a symbolization." Certainly, but of what? His second marriage was to one of his students and this also turned out to be rather thin from the erotic standpoint. Why, one may ask, does he make two marriages neither of which is expressive and supportive of his life in a sexual sense. He confesses that he does not himself apprehend this situation perfectly.

I realize how difficult an autobiography that is not an apology for a life but a research into its nature, can become, as I deal with this business of my divorce. I have already emphasized the widening contrast between the mental range of myself and my cousin. I have shown a disposition to simplify out the issue between myself and Catherine Robbins and Isabel to an issue between how shall I put it?—wide-scope lives and narrow-scope lives. That makes a fairly acceptable story of it, with only one fault, that it is untrue. It is all the more untrue because like a bad portrait there is superficial truth in it. The reality was far more complicated. Much more was entangled in the story. I confess that I feel that there are elements in it that I myself apprehend only very imperfectly. Let me take up this fresh chapter, as though I were a portrait painter taking a fresh canvas and beginning over again.[46]

This unusual candor of an autobiographer increases our respect for Mr. Wells since it is very difficult to mention a situation of such importance in one's psychic life which one does

45. *Ibid.*, pp. 359–360.   46. *Ibid.*, pp. 348–349.

not understand. But that does not help matters much; we can only agree that we also do not understand some of the most important events in his life and that they remain outside the purview of scientific discussion.

Wells' thinking about current society is at many points quite unrealistic, and although this is outside of our critical bailiwick we cannot withhold one observation and a very important one. He knows that he has resisted the trends and currents of his times at many points, especially with regard to the *mores* governing sexual and economic matters. He believes that his immunity to punishment lies in the fact that his generation is moving in the same direction, if less explicitly and articulately than he.

We advanced thinkers owe our present immunity, such as it is, very largely to the fact that even those of our generation who are formally quite against us, have nevertheless been moving, if less rapidly and explicitly, in the same direction as ourselves. In their hearts they do not believe we are essentially wrong; but they think we go too far,—dangerously and presumptuously too far.[47]

This seems a true but inadequate comment. The fact of the matter would appear to be, judging from his life history, that since Mr. Wells is in business for himself, is an independent economic competitor and has a very wide and broken field in which to compete, he is immune to punishment, at least in the form of withdrawal of economic support. If he were a University professor, tight in the grip of an institution which moves with the slower currents of our time, he would find the inarticulate public quite unable to help him. It is the fact that he competes independently and stands outside of our most conservative institutions that guarantees an immunity from reprisal by the group he offends.

No sensitive reader of English prose can be immune to

47. *Ibid.*, p. 705.

Mr. Wells' capacity to bring forward a flashing phrase and to turn a vigorous and expressive sentence. He believes, for example, that by the time of his birth his mother's religious faith had lessened in intensity and had become formalized and says, "She wanted me to believe in order to stanch that dark undertow of doubt."

Our Lord was dumb, even in dreams he came not, and her subconsciousness apprehended all the dreadful implications of that silence. But she fought down that devastating discovery. She went on repeating the old phrases of belief—all the more urgently perhaps. She wanted me to believe in order to stanch that dark undertow of doubt.[48]

Such glowing sentences give pleasure quite apart from the scientific evaluation of the document.

We made it clear at the outset that we were examining Mr. Wells' autobiography from a very critical standpoint and that he had not written it with the idea of passing such tests as we have proposed. We do not, therefore, regard it as a defect of what he has done that his document is not an addition to our scientific view of the life history. His work must be classified primarily as artistic and pleasure-giving, secondarily as a reflection of his "times," and thirdly, and insignificantly, as a workmanlike account of an individual experience in culture.

48. *Ibid.,* p. 45.

CHAPTER IX

A REFERENCE TO *CRASHING THUNDER**
AND JUNG'S PSYCHOLOGY

WHEN this research was projected in the mind of the author, it was planned to include an analysis of *Crashing Thunder*. My memories of the book at that time were somewhat hazy but indicated that here might be something of value for our ends. A re-reading of the book has been a source of pleasure and illumination, but not in the direction expected. This autobiography should be taken as an inside view of the Winnebago culture rather than as a careful analysis of a human life. Professor Radin gives us an introductory chapter in which he comments on the unusual realism and non-suggestible character of its author; he notes with proper amazement the manner in which Crashing Thunder is able to distinguish the reactions expected of him by his culture and the actuality of his somatic experience. These features of the document are unmistakable and valuable. The author does not, however, give a severe chronology of his life, especially the earliest reaches of it, and the editor does not attempt to discern from the document the slow elaboration of the instinctual life by the impact of the culture. In saying this we mean merely to stress that, as a whole, there is very little attempt at analysis and synthesis of the material or at systematic formulation of the growth of a life. The editor's comments, while revealing and sympathetic, are few and are characterized by a literary and impressionistic admiration rather than by a laborious theoretical construction of Crashing Thunder's life experience. The footnote comments in the document are designed mainly to

---

* Radin, Paul (edited by), *Crashing Thunder,* New York and London, D. Appleton and Company, 1926.

paint cultural backgrounds without which a particular autobiographical point would be unintelligible.

The great value of this autobiography is to give an intimate view of present-day Winnebago social life and to indicate that the individual is often not able to accept emotionally the definition of himself provided by his culture. This
point should be of greatest interest to the formal student of
culture patterns because it indicates a dichotomy between the
"phrasing" which the culture gives to certain activities and
the actual response of certain individuals. An excellent example of this is the behavior of Crashing Thunder when he is
in prison and is told that his wife has gone to live with
another man. Actually Crashing Thunder loses his appetite
and indulges in a series of sadistic fantasies about how he will
mistreat his wife when he gets out, such as "I thought I
would disfigure her, cut off her nose, then take her to the
wilderness, give her a sound beating, and leave her there."
This is not his official response to the event, however; he follows the phrasing of the culture in such matters and says, "I
am glad to hear about this report that my wife has married
again. When I get out of prison I will pay the one who has
married her, for he is taking care of her until my release."[1]
Under ordinary circumstances presumably the investigator
would receive only the formal statement of the matter and
would have no way of pushing beyond this to the subject's
actual response. It is a dangerous possibility that much of
our ethnological material is derived from such formal statements and that a great many of the grotesque contrasts
which are shown between the behavior of persons in other cultures and our own are made only because the formalistic
statement is accepted. This contention of Professor Radin is
one which puts a very important issue up to his colleagues
who content themselves with discovering the official pattern
of action proposed by a culture.

1. *Ibid.,* p. 167. Quoted by permission of D. Appleton and Company.

Professor Radin has therefore indicated a very important use of the autobiographical document. It is not, however, the one on which we are here centering our attention. Crashing Thunder is unable to give us a systematic account of his life, or at least does not do it in this document, and the editor makes only the skimpiest of inferences from the material. Our conclusion, therefore, is that it is not reasonable to subject this document to elaborate analysis from the standpoint of our system of criteria. The life-history document as a searchlight thrown on cultural forms revealing the manner in which they are drenched with individual affect is quite another undertaking and must be judged by separate criteria set up for the purpose.

One wonders what might happen to our conventional ethnographical view if Professor Radin's point was taken seriously and a large number of autobiographies of primitive persons were collected. It could not fail to result in a great enrichment of our view of other cultures and might strip our present researches of some of their stilted and abstracted character.

WHY NO CRITIQUE OF A JUNGIAN DOCUMENT

After an exploration as thorough as time has permitted I have been able to find no serviceable example of a life history gathered and interpreted from the standpoint of Jung's psychology. I have therefore not risked attempting to apply my criteria to his general views. This would be decidedly unfair both to him and to the other authors treated, since I have considered their psychologies as apposite to our ends only as they are exhibited in a concrete piece of work to which anyone may refer. Various reasons suggest themselves as to why a life history interpreted on Jungian principles is so difficult to find. The most plausible is that no Jungian has happened to take the trouble to do it. Another possibility is that the use of the hypothesis of the racial unconscious diminishes the importance of the actual career of the person to such a degree, for the Jungian, that the investigation of his specific growth in culture is not appealing. The individual life would appear at best as an appendix to a stream of phylogenetically determined images and attitudes. A third possibility is that the use of the type hypothesis, the types being fixed structures of a sort, tends to take the emphasis off the linear sequence of the life experience. Whichever of these suppositions is the correct one, or whatever combination of them describes the matter adequately, no document has revealed itself which is suited to our type of analysis.[2]

We may note in passing that the student of culture finds at the root of the Jungian system an hypothesis, that of the racial unconscious, which tends to take the stress off the existing culture as the essential dilemma presented to the organism. Such an emphasis makes the formal study of cultures a much more difficult matter since the life of the individual has a pole not only in the current social inheritance but also in the past social inheritance as precipitated in the germ plasm and biologically transmitted from parent to child.

2. Dr. Leonard W. Doob has thoughtfully suggested that the Miller phantasies and poems used in C. G. Jung's *Psychology of the Unconscious* (New York, Moffat, Yard and Company, 1916) might do service as a life history. A re-examination of this vigorous book does not support the hope. There is no attempt to present Miss Miller's life; her materials are used rather as starting points for a development of Jung's libido theory in reference to mythological and literary materials.

CHAPTER X

FOR TEACHERS AND STUDENTS: HOW
TO USE THE CRITERIA

IT is hoped that these criteria will prove useful to teachers and students in the social science field and that they will give a tangible point of attack on problems of the life history. Since the life history is emerging as an ever more important tool to the social researcher, we will apparently need an increasing number of students who are familiar with its use. The object in this chapter is to provide some help to instructors and students who want practice in the evaluation of life-history materials.

An additional gain from the standpoint of the author would be the value of having the criteria proved out by other researchers. The only way that this can be done is by using them on specific life-history materials. Through such use there will be the possibility of amending and consolidating them into a structure useful for our field. Critical communications on this point are particularly acceptable from students familiar with the actual technique.

It is possible that the use of the criteria can become a facet of training in courses in social psychology, clinical psychology, sociology, and psychiatry as well as for those special students in history and literature who are concerned with the biography and autobiography. The effort in constructing the criteria has been to meet a need which exists wherever the life history is used in any of its forms. In some cases this need is already appreciated and in others it remains as a latent awareness. The following suggestions for the use of the criteria are based on the author's own experience in writing the foregoing chapters on life histories. The suggestions will be made in didactic form as though the reader were about to undertake immediately the task of reviewing a document from the standpoint of the seven criteria.

1. Read the discussion in chapters I and II on the criteria and the reasons for selecting them. It is important that the student or researcher get each of the criteria well in mind so that he can use it without continuous reference to the written material. Otherwise it will be necessary to go back constantly to the text. Even if this is done, however, the reader will soon master the leading idea of each criterion.

2. Select a life history on which the criteria are to be used. This may be an autobiography, biography or clinical history; even a social service case history or a psychiatric document would not be out of place; in fact, extensions to such materials might yield interesting results. For the student at the college or graduate level it might be advisable to select a document in parallel to those in the text, such as another of Freud's case histories or Adler's or a sociological or ethnological document. The result of the student's work could then be compared with the author's analysis of the system given in the text. If the criteria are to be used it is indispensable that an actual life history be studied because the full reality of the problem cannot emerge unless the attempt is made to utilize them.

3. Read the document with the criteria in mind and mark in the margin of the book in pencil the passages to be excerpted. A penciled bracket around the citation can later be erased and a slip of paper at the appropriate page will remind the student of the marked citations. In addition to the bracket the number of the criterion on which the passage bears should be indicated in pencil. For example, a I can be used when the passage is seen to illustrate or refer to criterion I. As the reading of the book progresses the student will be assembling and indicating the material which will enable him to discuss the book from the standpoint of the criteria. This method involves reflection about the life his-

tory in terms of the criteria as the book or document is read; mere impressionistic reading of the book will not enable the student to make an analysis according to the criteria. His reflection, however, will be well rewarded since he will be thinking throughout about some of the polar concepts in social science.

4. Copy the citations and sort them according to the criterion number on each one. For example, all the slips bearing the mark III will be sorted together. Then examine the citations, say, under III, and put them in sequence so that writing can begin. No plan for this sequence is indicated but should be left to the student. Do the same for the other criteria and arrange the slips in some kind of order. At this point writing out of the evaluation of the life history can begin.

5. Take the ordered citations under a given roman numeral and write a discussion of the document from the standpoint of this criterion. The document should be discussed criterion by criterion and not altogether. If no material is found under any given criterion, discuss the effect of the lack of such material on the validity of the life-history interpretation. Since the criteria are all inter-knit and inter-dependent the lack of acknowledgment of any one will be to that extent a defect in the life history. It may be more or less serious depending upon the criterion in question.

6. Give a summary view at the end of the document as a whole; this should be a point by point discussion of how the life history shapes up in view of the criteria. It will show what kind of a job the author has done in preparing the specific life-history document.

7. Remember that the document does not have to pan out and show material on every criterion; it is no proof that any document is worthless if it happens not to meet a single criterion. It may be defective at some points but very valuable in exhibiting other views. Remember also to give full credit

where it is due and to stress particularly clear ways of indicating a valuable point. These criteria are designed to guard against bias and to summarize the best views now available on what kind of document will be most serviceable in the social science field.

In the experience of the author this task could be given as a monthly report which students can perform outside of class hours or in some cases as a term paper, providing the document selected is particularly long or difficult. If a student reveals particular talent in the evaluation of life-history materials he might be encouraged to use the criteria on more than one document. A special flair for personality research could well be demonstrated by a student through the skill with which he is able to assimilate and apply material here suggested.

Specially interested classes might profit by a class discussion of the criteria before the actual analysis of a document is undertaken. New examples should be found to illustrate the use and necessity of the various criteria; in particular the sequence in which they are arranged should be noticed since it is not an accident. It should be stressed that merely learning the criteria by rote is not important; what is crucial is that the perception of the student for facts of real life experience be expanded and intensified by their use. For example, the whole matter of "drives," "instincts" and other such concepts can be discussed from the angle of social relevance, or the purely cultural aspects of any life-history document may be discussed. In the latter case one may ask the question, Suppose we had only this document, what kind of social life could be inferred from it? Intensive analysis of this type may prove more instructive and creative for the student than wider surveys of literature.

The use of the criteria in the two fields of social work and psychiatry would be particularly interesting because in both cases these specialists are actually dealing day by day with the problem of making significant statements and judgments about the individual life. Finding material is no issue in either field; the real problem is the best way to see and deal with it. If the criteria are really useful in guiding perception toward a significant view of the person, it should be the psychiatrists and social workers who are among the first to find it out in practice.

It must be remembered, of course, that the criteria do not attempt to give a specific theory of individual mental and social growth; what they do stress are the main items which will be covered by such a theory when it has at last achieved scientific agreement. The individual criteria can perhaps best be used by the psychiatrist or social worker to check up on a document and to consider whether it follows the general form of an acceptable account of a life. On matters of interpretation of specific events, of course, the criteria offer no help. For example, the psychiatrist may find the criteria useful in that the culture concept is introduced and specifically stressed as a necessity of an adequate life-history document. Social workers are inclined to use at some point or other all of the main notions expressed in the criteria, but it may be helpful in this case to have the organization and system which the interlinked criteria provide. The social worker may find here a systematic platform for the work she already does rather than any novelty of approach.

There is no reason why the teacher of sociology or psychology should hold his students to the consideration of already gathered materials. The difficulties of investigation in the field of personality and culture can be appreciated very well by the attempt to gather specific life-history material. If the student can be put in a position where it is possible for him or her to take a life history in whatever way the subject will give it, he can then review his findings from the standpoint of the criteria. This technique is particularly useful since it adds the experience of actually getting the material to that of analyzing and organizing it.

Still another possibility is to ask individual students to write autobiographies themselves, doing it in the usual narrative fashion, and then to allow them to discuss their own documents from the standpoint of the criteria. The difficulty of making clear the first cultural impacts on an individual comes out with particular force in this case.

Practice in analyzing actual life-history materials will give the student a significant concept of the organic aspect of culture, a concept which will vitalize and fructify his studies of culture patterns and institutions. It must not be overlooked that the life-history document itself can be used as source material for the analysis of culture forms; such a document as Freud's "Little Hans" can be combed for the systematically patterned activities which are referred to there. This amounts to using "Little Hans" as an informant on his Austrian culture. When full records of psychoanalytic interviewing procedures are made available, it will be useful to measure them by the criteria.[1]

1. Mr. Earl F. Zinn, now of the Worcester State Hospital, is pioneering in the task of collecting such materials.

CHAPTER XI

CULTURE, PERSONALITY AND THE LIFE HISTORY

CURRENT thought in social science has pressed on the attention of many of us the terms "culture and personality" and they have the sense of pointing a new direction of thought and effort. It will be useful to consider what they mean and to see how they are related to the problem of the adequate life history. This chapter will discuss the possible service of these terms and relate them to the material of the foregoing chapters.

In the present state of social science knowledge it is a hazardous task to attempt to say anything useful on the theme of culture and personality. For the most part the terms are used as a vague gesture in the direction of some unknown field of knowledge and the skeptical observer will consider whether they are pointing a new direction or merely concealing old scientific dilemmas. Any new term or linkage of terms must be judged by its efficiency in indicating a new problem and in suggesting a new point of scientific attack. After their own fashion the terms culture and personality perform this service; even if we designate their usage as vague and inexact, we must recognize them as a first attempt to indicate one of our most serious problems.

In our discussion we will omit reference to practical reasons for coining new terms, such as the effort to give an air of freshness to old problems and the equally banal attempt to sit astride of conduits which lead from fund-giving agencies to ambitious and impecunious scholars. Administrators in search of an ever better organization of current social life cannot long be misled by opportunistic phrase-making.

There is much more than phrase-making or mere pursuit

of advantage in the present wrestle with "culture and personality" issues. It represents a vital surge of discontent with
our present statement of cultural and psychological problems. It is in reality a muffled blow at the existing state of
knowledge in sociology and psychology. It is often more con-
venient to invent a new problem than to denounce an old
error. The use of the terms culture and personality seems to
be an effort to skid attention away from the inadequacies of
thought in present-day psychology or sociology and to pretend that it is a new field which is really not in conflict with
them and which does not represent a criticism of existing
science. We prefer organizing a new division of knowledge to
forcing on the pained consciousness of present-day sociologists and psychologists that they are not doing all that their
jobs call for. The effort to avoid this unfriendly conclusion
is one of the factors which make alternative terms and eu-
phemisms so welcome. The objection to the procedure is that
it lacks scientific candor.

The issues in question do not seem too complicated for preliminary definition. By and large those who bear the term
"psychologist" have neglected the study of the life of the
human being and devoted themselves to other types of problems. By and large the sociologists and ethnologists have abstracted somewhat fictive social structures from the visible
realities of everyday life and have become so preoccupied
with these abstracted patterns that they have lost sight completely of the culture-bearing individual. In both cases the
"proper study of man" is omitted from disciplines which
have as their professed objectives dealing with human life.
This state of affairs has produced an inevitable discontent
with our existing psychological and sociological formulations. The sociologist turns in vain to the psychologist for a
significant conception of human nature and failing to get it,
he projects his cultural pattern analysis back on the individual and tries to make out with this device. Needless to say

he fails because he omits the organic contribution to social life and he cannot say "how it feels to carry culture." This defect gives to sociological thought an abstract odor which is detectable from a considerable distance and it produces a vague discontent in those minds that are searching for a powerful grip on the character of social life.

It seems quite obvious that the problem of "culture and personality" can be phrased in another way. The real meaning of the discontent which leads to the linkage of these terms lies in the great need in the social sciences of a serviceable psychology, a psychology which comes to meet in its conceptual framework the discoveries with regard to general cultural structure which have been made in ethnology and sociology. There will be no technological unemployment among psychologists who take this need seriously because the market in social science for serviceable psychological ideas is at the present time indefinitely great. At every turn of a research problem the social scientist reaches for such a psychology, but it is not there. If, for example, he would make a study of the effects of the depression on the unemployed, he comes immediately against the question, What kind of a thing is a working man *before* he is unemployed? (in a psychological sense, of course). He ought to be able to go to his psychologist and ask and get an answer, assuming that in the peaceful pre-depression days the psychologist will have worked it out. If we do not have a theory of the growth of the individual in our culture up to the time when such an event as a depression occurs, we have no way of showing how the loss of his job will affect him.

A similar problem is revealed when we consider the data that come in from other societies. We know that ethnological researchers are both gifted and burdened with the views of our own society and that these views are deep-soaked into the vision of the observer. We know also that the researcher has been a man or woman in our own society before he acquired the ethnological mental tools and that he continues to be one after his doctoral work. What kind of bias does he bring to his work on the ground of the fact that he has been a human being in *our* culture and how shall we allow for this bias? We can give a preliminary answer to this question only when we have a social and psychological theory of individual growth in our society, a theory for which, as I have said, we reach in vain. We have no idea how drenched with selective vision our present ethnological information may be.

There is no intent to make a bad example of the ethnologist, though he provides a clear illustration; the same kind of thinking can be applied to the sociologist, psychologist, economist, psychiatrist, and others. Perhaps we have begun our search for bias in the wrong direction; instead of providing precautionary devices to correct sense perception, we should be asking first of all about the initial life experience of all who claim the right to report results in the field of social data. Nor is this a clamor for immediate perfection or a challenge to any sincere worker; it is a statement that the immediate flaming necessity for a realistic social science is a workable psychology of the individual life in culture. If we have to call it "personality and culture" in order to get it, let us then by all means do so.

It is also hard to make a case for establishing a new field of "personality" when the term psychology is so specific and widely accepted for designating the study of the mental life of the human being. To be sure, the term is burdened at the present time with a peculiar concept of its field of activity and of the methods which are likely to advance it. An easy way to visualize the differences between the plain implications of the name "psychology" and the peculiarity of its use in a university is to picture the shock of the average student who comes to a first college course in psychology. He is shown on the one hand biological and neurological facts which cannot be brought into relationship to the human mental life, and on the other hand methodologies which are fitted to deal with problems remote from the individual mental life. The usual result is to kill the interest of the student in human mental reactions. Is there, nevertheless, a Banquo's ghost of discontent which hovers over the flying statistical pencils and the clicking gadgets of the laboratories? Whether or no this is true, the mysterious life of the individual person remains as an unavoidable challenge to scientific curiosity and has the relentlessly "present" character of all genuine problems. Research procedures may dodge him for a considerable time (how long is really quite amazing), but he returns inevitably and generates uneasy feelings in those who avoided him in the first place. One of his scientific progeny is the movement to study culture and personality. It would seem trite to say that one was interested in the problems of "Sociology and Psychology" whereas we get an illusory feeling of fresh achievement from talking about "Culture and Personality"; the issue has not changed with the terms, however, and one great disservice has been done, namely, that the energies locked in the conventional sociology and psychology departments continue to pour through traditional channels and the most active problem in both fields is shoved to a "Culture and Personality" no-man's land where neither field has to face it. No doubt whatever that a psychology is needed that is acutely conscious of the fact of culture, or that a realistic sociology will be built upon a significant concept of the individual; we may be glad to see this need championed under whatever terms. But why not say it directly to the sociologists and psychologists who could then, perhaps stimulated by what at first seems a criticism, orient their activities in the direction needed. Scientists can take it, they are used to unemotional conflict.

As a matter of fact the coinage of the terms culture and personality at just this time indicates a kind of victory for the formal students of culture. Their researches and concepts have progressed to the point where they are mastering the minds of all social science students. We begin dimly to see that psychology begins wrong end to if it starts to study the individual mental life apart from its social contexts. The idea of culture is winning such control in the social science field that every problem, formerly posed without relation to this idea, has to be re-examined in the light of the new concept. It puts a new demand on the field of psychology; we must have a psychology which is not only independent and vigorous in an academic sense, but one which is oriented from the standpoint of the systematic study of culture. Any other kind of psychology will shortly be an historical curiosity.

If it is clear that the use of the terms culture and personality is a euphemistic device which permits an approach to a problem that would otherwise be more difficult to study, we can use the terms with comfort. After all, we do not object to the specific configuration of letters or syllables which are pronounced when we say culture and personality; we are only concerned that we shall not be deluded by our own terms and that we do not make another false start on one of the crucial social science problems. We are still talking about psychology when we say personality, and we are still referring to the systematic views of sociology and ethnology when we treat of culture. The essential problem, that of a psychology which is serviceable from the cultural standpoint, can just as well be discovered without using the terms at all.

If blame were to be attached to the use of the terms culture and personality we have laid ourselves wide open to it, for we have used them freely in the preceding chapters of this book. It will not have escaped any reader that the study of the "life history" is a problem in the field usually called "psychology," nor that this same life history can, even must, be seen as a cultural event. The fact of scientific importance is that neither psychology nor sociology gives a significant portrayal of the individual life and what seems to be demanded is that the life of the individual be taken as an object of study by both fields. We cannot say what such an attempt would do to the present definition of these two fields of knowledge; it might be found that the difference between them was one of emphasis, a difference so slight that it would no longer be desirable to study their object in two departments; perhaps a division of labor as yet not surmised would be discovered. The one scientifically intolerable state of affairs is the supposition that either can make much sense of its data without the other and that we are dealing with two discrete levels of useful observation. It may be we shall eventually have to go the whole way and state that there is a single social science and that what now seem like discrete fields or sciences are really shadings and points of emphasis in a unified field of scientific observation which is only distorted when we try to abstract "sciences" from it as we do at present. Just this sort of thing seems to be happening in biology today on the basis of the perception of the unified nature of the organism which is discussed by all of the biological sciences.

A good case in point is that of the ethnologist studying a primitive people. He seems to take the society as a single datum and make himself responsible for the study of it as a unit. He provides his own economics, history, linguistics and makes the best he can of the psychology of his subjects; he would testify emphatically that no portion of the culture can be parceled off for special study at least until its general outlines are established and certainly that any "psychology" of his group which did not recognize the traditional nature of human action would be worthless. Can we not bring his example back with us from the field of primitive studies and apply it at home to our own social science departments? Is it not true that we need a unification of fields and concepts rather than an ambitious proliferation of such new fields as that of "Culture and Personality"? I think so. May we not simply say that we all, ethnologist, psychologist, economist, and even in some aspects psychiatrist, are students of culture and society and let it go at that?

We should, of course, if we make this admission, immediately begin making distinctions all over again and redividing and classifying our knowledge, but very likely our new perspective would permit a much more effective grip on our object. We might, for example, pose the psychological problem in an altogether new form, say in the following way: *we want to know how a new person is added to the group*, what I have called the group-plus-one hypothesis. Every dilemma that could be tabbed as psychological would then be seen as an aspect of the acculturation of a person into group life. On the other hand such a manner of posing the psychological question would be seen at once to relate to group life and would become of interest to every student of society. The problem of instinct, drive or urge would then be a matter of asking the question, What is offered by the organism to group life and elaborated finally into the functioning adult group member? The usual definition of the "culture" would be a matter of stating what is brought to bear on the organism to form the human personality desired by the group and how this "what" actually modifies the organism.

This manner of thinking would of course have to confront most of the issues at present in dispute in both psychology and sociology but it would force a unification of viewpoint and a common attack on problems which would be fruitful; we might also imperceptibly disburden ourselves of many problems which cannot be solved as we now put them; one thinks in this connection of the difficulties which arise in connection with a theory of perception when no account is taken of the fact that a culture is itself a systematic guide to perception for its members, and can be defined as a stereotyped manner of perceiving. The idea of a kind of brute sensory perception might seem of very little interest when compared with the study of perception as a function of group experience.

Seen from this standpoint the two essential terms in cultural study would be the organic term, including bodily form, capacities and cravings, and the cultural term, that is the definition of life of the group preceding the individual; a most important manner of studying these two forces would be via their molding and blending in the course of individual growth in society, that is the impact of social life on the organic nature of man (not on personality since the individual personality is what results from this impact). The idea of a culture as "mere form" would have only marginal uses in this way of thinking since it would be seen that every acculturated act has an affect charge that is fixed inevitably to it and that to treat it as a mere pattern is a violent abstraction of limited usefulness. We might turn in our tracks and ask ourselves what is the point of endlessly abstracting and comparing formal patterns when these patterns have been divested of their significance as acts that men do and live by doing; the attention might then be centered much more on the society of living persons and the way in which that social life is a balance and interaction of the affects of its members. It is one thing to itemize and outline behavior forms in a society and quite another to give an emotionally significant account of the interaction of persons. To make the point clear one needs only to think of the difference between a schematic account of the ritual of a committee meeting and the actual interplay of forces and personalities which takes place whenever a committee sits. It is these personalities which are still mysterious and which are largely missing from present-day cultural studies. Some have referred to these types of study as the long-section and cross-section views of culture; if you refer events to the perspective of the individual life, you have one view; if you look for correspondences between events in different life careers, you have another, or the cultural view. Perhaps we will have other views still which cannot be posited until we work along with these for a while and find out their weaknesses.

Such a unified field view of sociological and psychological events as is provided by the group-plus-one hypothesis would revise our vision of many events which are now badly defined and lack a systematic frame of reference; an example is the case of the neurosis. The sociologist who hears the word neurosis would have a right to assume that the term indicates a disease in which damage to actual nervous tissue is the significant event. The remarkable discovery of Freud, however, stresses quite another view and one of much greater significance to the student of culture. The neurosis is an event which gets meaning only in a cultural frame of reference and is an example of the malfunctioning of the culture. The prohibitory and frustrating aspects of the culture scheme have been more than the neurotic can bear. He has recourse therefore to a private solution of his instinctual problems. The essential notion is either that the culture itself is unendurably strict, from the standpoint of what the organism can tolerate in the way of frustration, or that a viciously frustrating substratum of the otherwise tolerable culture has been brought in contact with the neurotic individual. Those persons are normal who find the presented culture an endurable manner of expressing their affects. This manner of viewing the problem has some advantages over that of viewing the neurosis as a private matter of the individual's contacts with other private persons. It brings the neurosis into its proper frame of reference as a deviant from a culturally established norm, on the one hand, and it points emphatically at the efficient source of the mischief, namely the culture itself.[1] We have in mind, of course, that the culture is always presented to an individual, who becomes neurotic because of

1. Freud, Sigmund, *Civilization and Its Discontents*, London, Hogarth Press, 1929, p. 45.

it, in the form of concrete persons, but we recur immediately
to the idea that the notion of culture is itself an abstraction
of the behavior of such individuals and stresses the traditional, non-biological character of the transmission of these
acts. Perhaps a bit of room should also be left for the notion
of accident and chance in accounting for the neurotic since
circumstances occur which have not been specifically planned
for by the cultural heritage; still we must remember that
these circumstances are always *interpreted* in terms of the
traditional scheme. At any rate the important line of
growth in developing the neurosis concept seems to be the
linking of it more emphatically and logically with the systematic study of social life; present psycho-pathological concepts are extremely useful ways of dealing with the fact of
neurosis but they are probably lacking in a proper frame of
reference. It is true that at the moment we have far more to
learn from the professional students of neurosis than we have
to offer them from the cultural side, but we shall not withhold
our bit for this reason. As scientists we are interested in
"saying it right," in finding the most economical ways of
thinking about enigmatic matters. It seems safer to assume
for the moment that we cannot make effective distinctions
between what different organisms bring to group life and
that we had best posit that the organic contribution to social
life is a relatively uniform one, at least when compared to the
importance of cultural stresses. This hypothesis may prove
not to be justified but there seems to be no existing evidence
on which it can be seriously attacked. If we make this assumption we can then calmly view every person as an addition to an already existing group and can study him unre-
mittingly as an exhibit of group life. We can contentedly
follow our individual wherever our study of him takes us and
not be frightened if we should trench on territory already
occupied by scientific populations. The biologists have given
us a useful example on this point; they have resolutely

pushed their mechanistic hypotheses without regard for the social nature of the individual and have profoundly advanced our knowledge by so doing. If they must yield a little bit at the fringes eventually, that will not be important as compared with the scientific value of their views.

It is important to be able to say to oneself in a slow and significant way how a culture-personality problem looks when you meet it in nature. What kind of conundrums are they that seem so bothersome as to cause all the present interest in the culture and personality field? Perhaps we can see the difference more clearly if we state first how an individual can be understood if he is viewed on the sociological level only. In this case the following sequence of operations seems to take place. In the first instance the behavior of individuals in groups is noticed and certain abstractions from it are made, as, for example, that the individuals believe that social achievement is based solely on individual merit or that it is an honorable thing to have scars sliced on the left cheek. Such a series of events is thereafter referred to as a pattern and if we wish to discover what the individual is like we can simply drop a line from the center of the pattern and it will reach an individual attitude. When lines are dropped from all the culture patterns to an organism we have the theoretical individual as he is assumed to exist by the culture in question. This procedure has a certain validity in it and it undoubtedly gives us a certain kind of idea of the individual. It is a sensible thing to say, for example, that a criminal grows up in a gang area and shares a collective life that is different from that of the wider society; since he follows the patterns of this smaller group he is automatically defined by the larger group as a criminal.

It is hard to see with equal precision just what is characteristic of the academic psychological view of the individual since the fact that the psychology of the individual is a development within collective life is so uniformly neglected.

Perhaps it is not too violent a caricature to say of the psychological view that it assumes the individual somehow to grow out of himself or just to grow. The stress is laid on the nature of the physical organism and its brute technical capacities; analogies to human action are sought in other species and it is hoped that a study of other species and of the physiological man will provide the necessary substratum for the study of the human individual. The lack of unified orientation or of a securely grasped object of research is quite striking in the psychological view. Perhaps we may say that the primary insistence of the psychologist today is that in the human being we have an organism. This can be cordially affirmed while at the same time insisting that this organism has perforce been offered up to a culture and been in an historical interaction with this culture during its whole period of physical growth.

The statement of these two views does not so far suggest a problem which might be labeled as a culture and personality problem or a sociological-psychological problem. We have already pointed out in dealing with the material of Shaw on *The Jack-Roller* that his use of the sociological hypothesis shows why the Jack-Roller became a criminal but not why he became just the kind of criminal he did. This is the kind of real situation which opens the door to a problem involving an approach from both sociological and psychological angles, with both methods preferably in the hands of a single person. Let us take the case of an optional pattern within a social group, that is, of a pattern which is present and which may or may not be selected as a possibility of expression. The pattern will be that of the monastic life and the subject an eighteen-year-old young man who is pondering whether or not he is called to this vocation. We will assume that no compulsory cultural arrangement has been made, such that he must enter the monastery. Since the pattern is not compulsory we will hardly be able to account for his choice on schematic cultural grounds; on the other hand, the psychological view will hardly be sufficient since there must be something particularly important to him about just this kind of social pattern rather than some other. The fact that there is a monastery to enter is not one which can be immediately related to the organic life of the individual but is rather a contribution from an historical past which is arbitrarily presented, at least so far as this individual is concerned. Whatever we have to do to know how and why he makes a given choice lies in the as yet unworked and unexplored territory between psychology and sociology.

For the sake of additional clarity in our illustration I will give the most reasonable view which I was able to develop by studying the case. This young man had developed an exceptional abhorrence of competition with other men for the goods and services of this world. This abhorrence was expressed by a continuous vague sense of oppression whenever he entered or thought to enter into a competitive situation. He had already largely sacrificed his normal competitive outlets, such as those in sport and in intellectual activity. In ordinary social intercourse his fear of competition was so great that he tended to accept passively any definition of a situation suggested by another man; he could not be "alone" and was in constant need of affectionate assurance that no one thought of him as a rival or protester. This state of affairs was by no means comfortable for him since he had to make the most extraordinary efforts to maintain simple life functions with effectiveness.

In the monastery he found a situation which was in many ways socially set up to meet his psychological needs. He would be relieved of oppressive and guilt-ridden competition. He would be assured of steady affection from his superiors if he conformed to the rule and otherwise carried out their wishes. He would be called upon to renounce through the vows he would take just those activities which were actually most burdensome to carry out and be relieved at one blow of the necessity of economic, sexual, and social competition.

The lingering doubt in his mind was whether he might not come later to prize what he was now so glad to give up and if he would not be driven to rebellious behavior once he had accepted monastic life. In point of fact the latter considerations did not prove important and he accepted, for a time at least, the monastic situation.

Our next step on the psychological side would be to inquire how such an intense fear of rivalry developed and how this fear was aroused by the competitive situations of ordinary social life which seem so innocent of peril to the rest of us. This question would have to be answered, though we shall not try to do it here. A knowledge of the monastic pattern would also be essential from the cultural side and might easily leaf out into historical studies of the pattern itself or into discussions of its balance and relations with other of our current group habits of the present day. In any case, we would keep our eyes fixed on the presenting issue, namely the inter-relation between the personality forces of a given human life and an institutional pattern in our society. These issues of real life seem to offer the necessary starting point, and "object of research" for a culture and personality science.

We have treated above the case where a single institution is selected from among others, on the basis of needs in a given personality. The issue can appear in still another form. In the case of patterns where there is no option, that is, where all group members must conform, personality factors will determine with what intensity the patterned experience is felt. A good case in point will be that of the outbreak of a war when the machinery of conscription gets under way; all persons who are eligible by whatever arbitrary scheme is in force will be selected without regard to "psychic fitness." Let us limit our consideration to those who are in branches of military service where the conflict with the enemy is immediate and violent and where the danger of death is a constant factor in the anticipations of the men; in this case it will be found that persons feel the military experience and allied dangers with quite different degrees of intensity and that their responses can be differentiated. The emotional tolerance of men for trench warfare, for example, differs not inconsiderably. Some wear out sooner than others and their psychic defenses against anticipated dangers are poor. Some even resort to hysterical conversion symptoms to exonerate themselves from the need of further combat. Some desert even under circumstances where a successful flight seems impossible. Others still, and the major group, apparently respond to the stimuli of war ideology and war itself with the required consistency of behavior and steady aggression. These differences in response to the war situation seem incapable of explanation on the ground of minor differences in the war pattern itself, since the role of a soldier seems among the most highly formalized and consistent that we know anything about. It must be, therefore, what is brought to the war pattern, that is, the individual personality form, that determines the response. The essential problem here would be to outline the nature of war as a social pattern, to determine for it a kind of average meaning for individuals in our culture, and then to see how persons with different careers vary in their responses to it. It was the custom in older days to account for such differences in behavior by charging them up to brute biological differences between individuals, but such an account avoids the issue rather than solves it and leaves unconsidered the effect of the childhood culture of the person on his developing character.

Illustrations showing the varying intensity with which institutional patterns are held by individuals can be made by any observing person. For example, individuals differ markedly in the comfort with which they utilize the pattern of monogamous marriage in our culture. Some individuals are able to use this pattern expressively and to maintain healthy function quite adequately within it. In other cases the formal relationships are maintained but fierce stresses are visible which are obviously dangerous to the mental health of the partners and still more so for the children. Others still find the state intolerable altogether and either do not attempt it or quickly abandon it once they do. This problem of the fit between a more or less compulsory form and the emotional capacities of those who are exposed to it is a most relevant and significant form of inquiry and would be immediately identified as a culture-personality problem. In order to solve it we should have to understand the pattern, not only in a cross-sectional institutional sense, but in the sense of the opportunities and the barriers it offers to human impulse life, as well as in terms of its function and relatedness to other social institutions. We should want to know also in the case of any individual whom we study in relation to the pattern of monogamous marriage how he or she was prepared for it through his previous experience in culture, that is, the life history of the person. It seems not beyond human ingenuity to put and solve such problems whether we call them culture-personality problems or sociology-psychology problems.

A very pretty illustration of the differing individual responses to a stereotyped social situation is given by Dr. Paul Radin in his *Crashing Thunder*.[2] The writer of the autobiography, a Winnebago Indian, was exposed, as were other Winnebago children, to the traditional situation of fasting and praying for a blessing from one of his tribal gods. The boy received all the usual instructions as to what he would experience, carried out the ritual carefully and yet did not have the experience of a vision and a blessing. He was conscious of this lack as a social deviation and claimed to his parents and to others that he had had the required blessing. He was never able, however, to stifle all his apprehension at his failure to

2. *Op. cit.*, p. 177.

respond to this pattern in the traditional manner. Many of the children apparently did have an experience of personal significance while carrying out the fasting pattern. It is important for our purposes only to note that this failure to respond in the usual manner constitutes a culture-personality problem and that we should again, in solving it, have to determine some average significance of the pattern itself and the peculiarities of the mental life of Crashing Thunder, the deviant.

These examples have been given in order to give us a little practice in what may become the kind of perception necessary to see culture and personality issues. What seems important is, in the first place, to begin at home where we have both an intuitive knowledge of the culture and a clear perception of individual differences in meeting culture forms. An equivalent clarity is much more difficult to attain in an alien culture because of the difficulty in controlling the vast apperceptive mass which the society gives to its individuals. A second step, and not an easy one, is to define our own institutional forms significantly and to see the individual career impinging on the institution. Different ways of taking the culture form will then indicate problems which will beckon to the sensitized researcher.

We are, on the whole, quite aware by now of the fact that we do have institutional forms and that these forms are socially transmitted from one generation to another, that is, they are continuously recreated through social interaction. This observation can never reach its full value until the institutional form is seen as a pattern and drape for the individual emotional life. We might be able to find indeed a description of a pattern which could be stated entirely in terms of the pressure that it exerts on individual affects. This type of statement promises to be of more scientific significance than the consideration of a cold cultural outline and scheme. In reference to the life history we are not so fortunately situated. One of the most urgent of our needs, as we have repeatedly stressed, is that for a workable psychology, that is, workable from the standpoint of systematic cultural knowledge. This psychology seems most likely to emerge from the continuous refinement of our observations on the individual life and especially from treating this life as a unit event and beginning our studies with the problems that people actually have in current life situations. If we can stimulate a number of people to cling bitterly to this problem, we shall very likely blaze one of the new and valuable paths in social science research.